THE SONG OF THE FATHER'S HEART

The Song of the Father's Heart

Phil Lawson Johnston

Terra Nova Publications

First published by Terra Nova Publications, 2004

Published in Great Britain by
Terra Nova Publications
PO Box 2400, Bradford on Avon, Wiltshire BA15 2YN

Cover design by Lion Hudson plc.

The kind support and co-operation of The Cloud Trust
in making possible the publication of this book
is warmly appreciated and acknowledged.

Phil Lawson Johnston may be contacted at
plj@glassengraver.net

ISBN 190194932X

Printed in Great Britain
by Bookmarque Ltd, Croydon

Contents

Dedication

Dedicated to Ian Luke, who gave me a model of fatherhood, and Mickey Calthorpe, a man of vision who died before his time, who inspired, encouraged and spurred me on in my faith.

This song was written with them in mind, and all those who have got there first!

HOME FOR ETERNITY

We praise You, Lord God
You've made Yourself known
To those who believe in Your name
We praise You, Lord God
Your love has been shown
You've carried our sin
And our shame
You have declared to those
Who believe
Where You are we now can be
For You have prepared
A place for us
A home for eternity
You have prepared a place for us
A home for eternity

THE SONG OF THE FATHER'S HEART

We praise You, Lord God
You have proclaimed
Your dwelling place
Will be with man
We praise You, Lord God
For ever the same
You determined before time began
That those who believe
And call on Your name
Shall open their eyes and see
That You have prepared
A place for us
Where death has no victory
You have prepared a place for us
Where death has no victory

There will be no more suffering
There'll be no more pain
You will wipe every tear
From their eyes
There will be no more sorrow
There'll be no more death
Just glorious fullness of life

We praise You, Lord God
That nothing yet seen
Can compare with the glory to come
We praise You, Lord God
What has been revealed
Is a foretaste of heaven begun
Never excluded from Your love
Living as children and free
You have prepared a place for us
A home for eternity
You have prepared a place for us
A home for eternity

Jesus, my Lord, Author of life
Friend for eternity.....

Phil Lawson Johnston Copyright ©1996 Sovereign Music UK

Foreword

Prebendary John Collins

Phil Lawson Johnston is an artist. Like Laurence Whistler, he combines the writing of poetry with glass engraving, and many of us treasure a vase or bowl that bears his signature. To be properly seen, a picture on glass needs to be lit from behind. As Whistler observed, it will then appear to be composed of light —light not so much on it, as *in* it.[1] I have often felt that there is an analogy here with Phil's musical ministry. It is not that one is particularly captivated by his voice, or by anything that he does; he would not want this. Something far more wonderful and attractive is happening —the light of Christ shines out from him.

As a musical dinosaur who rarely plays anything later than J.S. Bach, it is a great honour to be asked to write a foreword to *The Song of the Father's Heart*.

I vividly remember when Phil, accompanied by a small 'Cloud', visited the village where we were living about thirty years ago.[2] By then we were familiar with worship leaders, especially those from abroad. But this was different. Here was an Englishman, gracious, sensitive, authoritative, and a skilled guitarist, who had won the confidence of talented musicians with their violins, violas, cellos and woodwinds. Far more significant—this was clearly a prayerful group, full of faith and the Holy Spirit. Phil was not in the slightest bit interested in laying on a sacred concert. His sole aim was to bring us into the presence of Jesus. And this he did. Some years later, in London, in larger settings and with bigger 'Clouds' (summer cumuli, perhaps), Phil would sing and pray for about fifteen minutes—by which time we would all realize that the Lord was present. It was an immense privilege to speak in such an atmosphere. I was deeply grateful.

This book reveals some of the great truths he has learned from his wide experience. I warn you that you will have to do some serious digging to discover them, and that you may take many years learning to put them into practice; because this is not a matter of technique (although technique is important, and clearly young David worked hard at his harp. See I Samuel 16:17–18). Rather, the successful leading of worship embraces the whole of our Christian life and is the outward flow of our own joyful relationship with our Heavenly Father. One of Phil and Moyne's boys, Sam, grasped this at an early age. When he was seven, he went to a party where there was excellent food, Scottish reels, singing spiritual songs, and a short talk. At the end, he said, "When are we going to have another *service* like that?"

There are three matters which Phil mentions that seem to me to be particularly valuable. In the chapter entitled A Noble Theme, he encourages others to compose lyrics. I hope that they will, and that they will consider carefully what he writes. He emphasizes the importance of melody in a decade in which, influenced by secular singers, Christians may well be relying too heavily upon rhythm and a high decibel level. It is a great blessing if tunes are memorable and we can therefore sing songs as we go about our business, or at least hum them in our bath. Again, thinking of the needs of composers, this book is full of apt quotations from the Bible — a convenient quarry waiting to be worked. Worship has rightly been likened to fire, which needs fuel, the best being Scripture.

In some churches, I have to confess that worship seems to consist of a number of songs, hurriedly selected, and going nowhere. We might as well have sung 'D'ye ken John Peel?' In the chapter We Will Magnify, Phil makes it clear that his choice of songs is very different! He sees them as a *progression* 'taking people from one place to another'. The milestones along the road are the great biblical doctrines guiding us into the presence of God, expressed in the words of the different songs. I have often admired his mastery of his repertoire. There is no fidgeting with papers; rarely any introductory remark. Nothing is allowed to distract us from waiting upon God. He watches, to see what the Holy Spirit is doing —and adjusts the singing accordingly, until, almost effortlessly, the whole congregation is caught up in 'wonder, love and praise'.

A hundred years ago, Walford Davies made a useful distinction between (a) aids to worship, and (b) vehicles of worship, and he added that 'aids', such as anthems, could be sophisticated (for without them good choirs languish); whereas 'vehicles' should be simple. Phil goes one step further, pointing out that when we know that we are in the presence of God, only the simplest lyrics meet our need. Far from being banal, short sentences such as 'Lord, we love you' – the language of children and lovers – are perfectly appropriate. George Herbert discovered the same:

> Yet slight not these few words;
> If truly said, they may take part
> *Among the best in art.*
> The fineness which a hymn or Psalm afford,
> Is, when the *soul* unto the lines *accords*.

> As when the heart says (sighing to be approved)
> 'O, could I love!' And flops; God writeth, *'Loved'*.[3]

For thirty years Phil Lawson Johnston has been a pioneer, bringing great blessing to many churches. I am glad to commend this book.

---

[1] See *The Initials in the Heart* Second Edition 1966, Rupert Hart-Davies p.118.

[2] See chapter two for more about 'Cloud'.

[3] *The Poems of George Herbert*, William Pickering 1846, No. 137 'A True Hymn'.

1

Introduction

For thirty years I have been enjoying the glorious activity of 'worship'. It has been a journey of exploration, discovery and excitement, punctuated by moments of frustration and exasperation! In this book[1] I have attempted to put down on paper my ideas and experiences. I think of my contribution as the musings of a wandering minstrel; and therefore, as I usually find it easier to express what I think and feel in melody and poetry, I have illustrated many of the themes with my own songs.

Some of the chapters are scriptural essays on different aspects of worship. I have found it useful and enjoyable to study and follow certain themes through the Bible as they relate to worship, so as to increase my vision of what God is looking for. I see them as a succession of facets being cut into the rough diamond that is my understanding of worship. As each facet is polished, the colours and light of understanding are able to shine through. I follow thematic routes, studying concepts such as *In Spirit and Truth, The Fear of the Lord,* or *The Presence of God,* and work through the verses that correspond to them, to build up a picture of God and how He wants to relate to us. I often have found that I can then hold that picture in my mind as I seek to lead others in worship. Some chapters are like 'mother ships', which serve as 'launch pads' for smaller craft to

---

[1] I explain how I got started in the next chapter.

go exploring through the galaxy that is worship —for example, the chapter *The Presence of God* will provide a launch pad for *The Face of God* and *A Sense of God*. I hope these chapters may be helpful to those who are interested in following the same thought-paths I have taken. In other chapters I use the experience I have had to attempt to give some practical thoughts about leading contemporary worship music and songwriting.

Most of what I say will be based on certain assumptions: that there is only one God; He created heaven and earth; the only way to Him is through His only Son, Jesus Christ, who is equally divine; by dying on the cross He has removed all our sin and the punishment that we deserve; His Holy Spirit dwells within and empowers those who have put their trust in Him; the Bible is the true and authoritative Word of God.

Apart from my own study, I owe so much of what I have learnt to countless books and a succession of wonderful teachers and friends whose writings, tapes, sermons, and conferences on the subject of worship have shaped much of my thinking.

What is worship?

Ask anyone what they think is the meaning of worship and you will get a myriad of different replies. Some will think of cathedrals, church choirs, Sunday services, receiving the sacraments, robes and collections, others will talk about beautiful sunsets, the stars, their garden, finding the god within them, burning incense to an idol, gazing at crystals, or just being kind to others. Some will have a very fixed idea of what it means to them and to others it will be a very woolly word meaning almost anything.

Many will insist that the most important thing in life is what we do to and for others: the good deeds performed for those less fortunate than ourselves. Of course this is vital, but if one looks at what the Bible has to say, it is very clear that the first priority we have is to love God with all our heart, soul, mind and strength and to trust in His Son, Jesus. We learn from Moses (in Deuteronomy 10:12),

"And now, Israel, what does the LORD your God require of you, but to fear the LORD your God, to walk in all His ways and to love Him, to serve the LORD your God with all your heart and with all

14

your soul, and to keep the commandments of the LORD and His statutes which I command you today for your good?"

And again in Micah 6:8,

"He has shown you, O man, what is good; and what does the LORD require of you but to do justly, to love mercy, and to walk humbly with your God."

The picture of walking humbly with God speaks so strongly of friendship with respect, and we see this relationship balance appearing repeatedly throughout the Bible.

When the disciples asked Jesus what they must do to do the works that God required, He replied,

"This is the work of God, that you believe in Him whom He sent." (John 6:29b).

Without a relationship with God, whatever we do, however good or religious it may seem, is just meaningless and empty, just 'wood, hay and stubble', fit only to be burnt. And God will not recognise it.

"Not everyone who says to Me, 'Lord, Lord,' shall enter the kingdom of heaven, but he who does the will of My Father in heaven. Many will say to Me in that day, 'Lord, Lord, have we not prophesied in Your name, cast out demons in Your name, and done many wonders in Your name?' And then I will declare to them, 'I never knew you. Depart from Me, you who practice lawlessness!'" (Matthew 7:21–23).

Harsh words maybe, but we would do well to take them to heart. I consider that the relationship we have with Jesus is the bedrock of all we do, and worship is at the centre of it. Nigel Goodwin, Founder of the Arts Centre Group and director of The Genesis Arts Trust, describes worship as, "A ship full of worth; a treasure ship and a relationship, something that the creature (humankind) gives back. It is two way. The Creator having communicated with His creation most completely through His Son has given His creatures the Spirit. We who are in Christ have direct and immediate access, greater than any human technology, even the Internet, which takes three seconds! Prayer is worship and takes no time; it is both in and outside of time, not bound by it."

So what do I call, 'worship'? As far as I understand it, true worship is the surrendering of our lives to God, Father, Son and Holy Spirit, in response to all that He has done for us, showing us His love supremely though dying on the cross; allowing ourselves to be loved by Him and returning His love through obedience to His will and expressing it through what we sing, say and do.

In listening to those of us songsters who have been involved in the worldwide movement of contemporary worship music over the past few decades, we may have given the impression sometimes that we think that singing the songs is all there is to it. It is why I want to spend some time exploring worship from a wider perspective in the chapters that follow. It is not that I do not believe firmly that 'singing the songs' is a major part of what we call 'worship'; we only have to read the Psalms and Revelation to see that it is the very language of heaven, and that praise is to continue at all times:

"I will bless the LORD at all times; His praise shall continually be in my mouth" (Psalm 34:1).

But there is so much more to worship than singing.

I acknowledge that some of what we have done has been less than worthy, even to the extent of trivialising the glory of God with some of our lightweight songs. The Archbishop of York, Dr David Hope, is correct in his criticism: "Worship as entertainment; worship as distraction quite other than what it truly is or should be, namely the giving of worth to God......the Church in its worship seems to have abandoned the mysterious in favour of the banal."[2]

I agree that we should aim high and maintain a sense of awe and mystery when we worship God, but it does not necessarily mean that only the 'traditional' is worthy of God. Nor does it mean that only a formal approach to worship is the most reverent one. As Kim Swithinbank, the vicar of the Falls Church in Washington, puts it, "Many people make the mistake of confusing formality with reverence and informality with intimacy. You can have a formal service that is irreverent and an informal service that is not intimate. What you need is both reverence and intimacy."

It has always fascinated me that the one thing that should unite us, worship of our loving God, is often the greatest area of conflict within churches. What should be common ground before the throne of God becomes the battleground! I hope that painting a broad picture of all that worship means will increase our understanding of one another and help us to *seek the common good.*

---

[2] Quoted in *The Daily Telegraph,* 24th May, 2004. Reproduced by permission.

INTRODUCTION

I regard a 'time of worship', as a time of meeting with God when we minister to Him and allow ourselves to be ministered to by Him. When we respond to His love and His Word, we praise Him for what He has done and for who He is, we bring the needs of the world to Him, we adore Him and are adored by Him. This can be done in song, in prayer, in silence, in listening to His voice, and is acted upon through our fellowship with His other children, and our love and care of the needy and lost.

Most, if not all, of what I say will revolve around the central theme of a relationship with God, and my greatest hope is that you will find a hunger growing within you to deepen your knowledge of Jesus and an increasing desire to love and be loved by Him.

JESUS IS KING

Jesus is King, let all the earth be glad
He sits enthroned, He is exalted on high
Behold your God!
Behold your God!
He is surrounded with glory
He is surrounded with glory

Jesus is King, let all the earth rejoice
He moves in power, he reigns in majesty
Behold your God!
Behold your God!
He is surrounded with glory
He is surrounded with glory

As we draw near, we see His glory shine
We see the pain, yet we see triumph in His eyes
Behold our God!
Behold our God!
We are surrounded with glory
We are surrounded with glory

Extract taken from the song "Jesus is King" by Phil Lawson Johnston
Copyright ©1996 Thankyou Music*

2

REMEMBER
—MY OWN STORY SO FAR

REMEMBER

Remember the day when we discovered love
Remember the peace that flooded our hearts
Remember the joy of a passionate life
Rejecting enticing rewards for a pearl of great price

Remember the days when we would not compromise
Remember the strength of an undivided heart
Remember the love we had at the start
In an age of conflicting ideals remember the heart

Remember the song we sang every day
Remember the price we could not pay

Return to the time when we first tasted love
A banquet of joys, a feast of delights
Savour the taste, so rich and so fine
Compared to what others enjoy
Incomparable wine

I go to the place we love to meet
I delight in Your Word and presence so sweet

I turn to Your touch, gaze up at Your smiling face
I bathe in the light and look into Your eyes
I turn to the love I've had from the start
I welcome Your presence again, I open my heart
I welcome Your presence again, I open my heart

Yesterday and today, forever the same
Yesterday and today, forever the same

Phil Lawson Johnston
Copyright ©2002 IQ Music

I am hoping that you will afford me some self-indulgence as I take time to look back at my life and try to identify some of the influences that have brought me to where I am now. I do not know whether it will be of any interest to anyone else, but it has proved to be a very helpful exercise for myself. We are all made up of a complex mixture of genes and upbringing, influenced by varied experiences, and there is so much to be grateful for in my life. I admit that I come from a very privileged background, which has given me many advantages. I do not believe I need to feel guilty about that, but I am forever thankful for the start it gave me. It is, after all, what you make of what you are given that counts and although I may have squandered many opportunities, I hope that I have made good use of others. I am deeply indebted to my parents for their constant love and support and for everything that they did to create an extremely happy and stable childhood.

I was born in 1950 as the youngest of a family of four boys and one girl living in Bedfordshire. My father, Lord Luke, was a director of several companies including the 'family firm' of Bovril (invented by my great grandfather), as well as a member of numerous committees, including the International Olympic Committee. He and my mother spent a lot of time travelling, but my lasting memory of that time is predominantly of a cheerful home with an endless string of unusual dogs and country pursuits. Being the youngest by six years meant that during term time when my siblings were away at school, I spent much time on my own creating my own entertainment, making kits, playing with toy soldiers and, in summer, chasing wasps and cabbage white butterflies! My school career as a boarder, at Maidwell Hall in Northamptonshire and Eton College near Windsor, was never particularly sparkling and I emerged with few qualifications and no idea of what I wanted to do. I suppose everyone consciously or subconsciously searches for a purpose in life, and in my case it was definitely subconscious, if not subterranean! As I had spent time in Florence, Italy and a year at the Inchbald School of Design in London studying History of Art, the only possibility seemed to be some form of art occupation. However, painting was out as I had earlier failed my art A level! My pride was certainly hurt at the time, but, if I am honest, I was never really good enough to make it into a serious career.

Engraving glass
My parents had always encouraged me in art at school and, when I had left and was showing no particular sense of direction, it was my mother (as mothers are wont to do) who encouraged me and my older brother, Andy, who was in a similar situation, to look into the idea of engraving glass. I had never considered or even been particularly interested in glass before, but it seemed to be worth a try. We both investigated it and decided to give it a go. We started to teach ourselves in 1971 and we are both still scratching away! However, Andy is concentrating more on painting now.

Music
Music has also always had a significant place in my life, whether it be listening and enjoying, or expressing myself through writing songs, singing and playing the guitar. Some of my earliest memories of childhood are of a home that was constantly filled with music. There were days when the piano was in permanent use as one brother or sister would play, and as they finished, another would sit down and carry on. Some of the time I would be there with my miniature white piano trying to copy them. So, it is not surprising, I suppose,

that sooner or later music in one form or other would emerge to play an important role in what I did with my life. The guitar became my chosen instrument in my teens and still is today. I learnt the piano for many years, but I never progressed beyond playing it for a very private audience, namely myself!

Faith anniversary

In February 2002, I suddenly realised that it was thirty years to the month since a significant event which was to shape the course of my life: the moment when I finally surrendered my heart fully to Jesus. This reminder led me to write the song *Remember,* which I have quoted at the beginning of this chapter.

Journey to faith

I see my journey to active faith as a series of stepping-stones. Having been brought up in a loving and churchgoing home, regular Sunday school etc., the stories of the Bible were familiar to me, but nothing much was said, as far as I can remember, regarding a personal relationship with God. My first brush with anything evangelical, although I did not know it at the time, was when I was three or four. My father was involved with the welcoming committee for Billy Graham in the early stages of his first crusades in this country. He was speaking at Oxford and Cambridge and because our house in Bedfordshire was about halfway, he came to stay with us. I have memories of this kind but rather powerful giant towering over me! During his stay a game of hockey was organised on our lawn, with walking sticks and tennis balls, and because of his height he used an old shepherd's crook, which he proceeded to break. I am pretty sure this had no influence at all on my spiritual growth, but you never know!

At my boarding school near Northampton, aged about 13, after being prepared by a devout and prayerful head master, Oliver Wyatt, I came to be confirmed by the Bishop of Ely. I took it all very seriously at the time and one morning soon after, when I was lying in bed thinking, I had a kind of vision — in my imagination probably. I could see the cross before me, and went on to see myself being pressurised to reject my faith through some kind of torture. I remember promising God that I would never deny Him whatever happened to me. That has stayed with me ever since, even though many times I have wondered whether I would be able to keep to my promise! Although this all meant a lot to me at the time and I had the semblance of a faith, I really did not know how to nurture or sustain it.

I was a child of the fifties and a teenager of the sixties and so, grew up in the era of the Beatles, Stones and the 'permissive' push at the boundaries of conventional behaviour. The music attracted me enormously, and by the age of sixteen I was learning the guitar, and shortly after formed a rock group with friends at school. Around the same time, my parents invited me to accompany them to hear Billy Graham at Wembley Stadium. My father was on the platform and we ended up in the VIP box. I cannot remember a single thing that was said, nor even whether I understood any of it, but when the appeal came I found myself wanting to go forward with the crowds, accompanied by my mother. My decision could have been helped, I suppose, by the fact that I saw one of my favourite pin-ups of the time, Hayley Mills, going forward as well! Again, there was not much foundation to build upon and my faith wandered off again.

At Eton I had to go to chapel every day and although, in my early days there, I sang in the choir and quite enjoyed it, somehow the 'schooly', compulsory nature of it succeeded in effectively inoculating me against organised and formal religion. I am not sure I have ever really recovered from it!

Hazy days

My real 'rebellion' came after I had left school and I was attempting to improve on my rather pitiful A level results at a crammer school in Brighton. I was introduced to the world of pot and acid along with the whole package of music inspired and generated by the drug scene. My involvement lasted about two years and although there were undoubtedly pleasurable (if short-lived) experiences, with hindsight I can see how self-centred and anti-social I became. Even the so-called harmless soft drugs can change one's attitudes and perception of the world and the people around you. I remember arrogantly thinking that I knew something about life that those non-participants did not know, when in fact, I was simply blinding myself and creating an introspective little world around me.

All the while, God was a distant figure who probably existed but who was more interested in ticking a list of misdemeanours that I committed, rather than pursuing any kind of relationship with me, and so, I left Him 'behind the wall'.

I spent a rather wild three months in Florence trying to learn Italian but spending more time with English-speaking friends, sampling the local substances and occasionally busking on the Ponte Vecchio! This trip left me with a love for the beautiful city and some lasting friends, one of whom was to play a great part in God's blessing years later. About five years later, he rang me out of the blue, having heard that I had become a 'Jesus freak'. He said he was desperate to find out all about it, and I was to have the privilege of introducing him to Jesus. We have remained firm friends ever since, singing and playing, laughing and crying together on many occasions.

After my return from Italy I hit the London scene, and spent a year studying History of Art at the Inchbald School of Design. During my time there, a friend of one of my brothers, Gordon Scutt, invited me to a supper. This was to be followed by a talk at the Chelsea Town Hall. The prospect of supper was what got me there, and Gordon remembers me rather shyly hiding behind a large pot plant during the meal, but the talk had a lasting effect on me. A man called David MacInnes spoke about Jesus wanting to be our Friend, and it was as if he was speaking to me personally in the midst of about four hundred others. It was something I had never consciously heard before, that God actually wanted to know me! At the end I prayed the prayer asking Him into my life, and went away with the beginnings of an understanding of what being a Christian really meant. I joined a Bible study, which met once a week. The only problem with this was that the others were all city 'pinstripes' and I was long haired and still prone to smoking forbidden weeds! We did not have that much in common it seemed, and sadly I did not last very long there.

Conscience trouble

I carried on life much as before, but not without retaining some awareness of that prayer of commitment. Looking back, I can see that Jesus was indeed at work in my life because it was not long before my conscience began to trouble me. I had a sense that my lifestyle did not match up to God's standards, but I seemed to have no power or real inclination to change it. Increasingly, I found a conflict building up inside me until I realised that I was not enjoying being a Christian at all and something had to happen. I ran into my cousin Mickey Calthorpe at a party, we sat down and talked, and out it all poured. Amazingly, he understood perfectly what I was going through as he had been through exactly the same experience about six months before. He told me that what had made the difference for him had been the discovery of the power of the Holy Spirit. He invited me to come to a meeting he was holding at his mews house near Gloucester Road, where someone called Sandy Millar was going to speak, and I decided to go.

After the excellent talk I noticed how one person after another was going into a back room to pray and coming out full of joy. I could not really understand how they could be so joyful about being a Christian, and so I stayed around until nearly everyone had left so I could talk again with my cousin. He and a friend called Kitty sat down and started telling me about the Holy Spirit. I do not remember ever before hearing about or understanding anything to do with the Spirit, so when they suggested praying that He might come and fill me with His power so that my life might change, I could not think of any good reason not to. No drama or fireworks, but a penetrating peace entered me as the conflict and troubled thoughts of the previous years just lifted off me and I could understand with sudden clarity why Jesus died for me personally. It all began to make sense not just in a cerebral and intellectual way, but it was as if my heart came alive for the first time. I went away full of a sense of freedom and calm, knowing that something had happened deep inside. All the old clichés come to mind such as, 'my eyes were opened', 'someone turned the lights on', or, 'it was like going from black and white to colour', but looking back I think that what happened was, I finally, (to borrow classic religious phrases), repented and made Jesus my Lord.

Musical change

The first major change I noticed was with my music. I had started writing songs at school and later throughout my 'hazy' days. When I read the lyrics now they make very little sense, although sometimes the poetry is passable! In the time after my prayer of commitment at the Chelsea Town Hall I had a growing desire to write something about Jesus, but found I could not bring myself to do so out of sheer embarrassment. I managed vague references to light and truth but could not write anything too specific. During the week after I prayed to be filled with the Spirit, I wrote my first song explicitly about Jesus. What follows is one song from before and one from after that prayer, to give some idea of the change that took place.

Before:

I AM THE VAGABOND

Sitting by the path where strangers often meet
Who will know where I go from here?
I see the distant smoke and hear bravely marching feet
I see the cavalcade appear

I am the vagabond, the wanderer
I am the nomad of the sand
I am the vagabond; I do not have a home
I keep my eyes upon the land

Several strangers passing on the open road
A column bound for nowhere
I take my place and join their slowly shifting course
Soon we will disappear

I am the vagabond, the wanderer
I am the nomad of the sand
I am the vagabond; I do not have a home
I keep my eyes upon the land

Phil Lawson Johnston Copyright ©1971

After:

O, TO BE LIKE JESUS

There was a time when I was sleeping
There was a time when I was dead
I did not know just what was needed
For the life that lay ahead

26

Then came the time when I was woken
My eyes could see I was no longer deaf
I could understand just what was spoken
I began to know what being with Jesus meant

O, to be like Jesus
O, to be just as He wants me
O, to be with Jesus
And to know just how much He loves me

Phil Lawson Johnston Copyright ©1972

Devouring truth

What followed was a period of intense catching up on all that I could learn about Jesus. The Bible came alive whereas before, it had been a dry, dusty and rather impenetrable book with no real relevance to my life. I had regarded it as a list of 'dos' and, particularly, 'don'ts', rather than the place to discover how to make sense of the world and guidance on how to live an abundant life. It was as if the inventor of a new machine I had been given had arrived to explain the incomprehensible manual. I devoured every Christian book I could get my hands on and prayer became a conversation with a real person who was interested in me personally. I began to experience answered prayer too. One of my first requests was for help to give up smoking. I had wanted to do so for some time and had succeeded for the odd week or two, only to take it up again the first time I was with other smokers. I prayed that He would simply take away the desire, and one evening when I came home, I took a packet out of my pocket and was filled with a sudden disgust for them. I tore up the cigarettes, threw them away and promised (rather rashly, I suppose) that I would never smoke another. God honoured that promise in such a way that I did not suffer a single withdrawal symptom and I have never touched one since. It was entirely His power at work; all I had to do was to be willing.

Song flood

Almost everything I was learning and experiencing at this time I turned into song, and reading the lyrics now (I cannot for the life of me remember any of the tunes!) I am able, to some extent, to relive what I was thinking and going through. Here is one example:

THE LORD KNOWS — Psalm 139

The Lord knows when I'm angry
The Lord knows when I'm sad
He watches over every step I take
He knows whether I sit or stand

The Lord knows when I stop to rest
The Lord knows when I work too hard
There is no cavern deep enough
To hide from the Lord's regard

If I take the wings of the morning
And fly away to sea
Even there I could look above
And see His hand over me

You know it makes me want to worship
It makes me want to love
It makes me want to praise the Lord above
Oh that everyone could know the beloved Son
And join worship singing
Allelu, allelu, alleluia
Allelu, allelu, alleluia

The Lord knows when I'm burning
The Lord knows when I freeze
He knows which way my head is turned
He knows when I'm on my knees

The Lord knows when I wake up
The Lord knows when I sleep
He is waiting there when I stumble
To put me back on my feet

And you know it makes me want to worship
It makes me want to love
It makes me want to praise the Lord above
Oh that everyone could know the beloved Son
And join worship singing
Allelu, allelu, alleluia
Allelu, allelu, alleluia

First worship

During this period of exciting discovery, I started going to a Bible study with my cousin Mickey at his house, with a growing number of friends. There was an American there called Chuck Butler, who had been converted during the Jesus revolution that had been taking place on the beaches in California. He began to teach us the Bible and to lead us in praise and worship. We started a service at the house every Sunday night after local church services were over, so that anybody could come and praise God in an informal style. While he led I sat next to him, copying everything he did and following him on the guitar. After about six months or so he announced that he was returning to the States, and for the service to continue we needed to find a new worship leader. Everyone looked at me! And so I was thrown into the deep end and had to start swimming. I am eternally grateful to Chuck for getting me going and modelling worship leading for me.

The Kitchen

Around this time we began to feel the need of a place that we could go to on our own or with friends to eat and talk about Jesus in a relaxed and unthreatening atmosphere. Mickey got six of us together to talk about it seriously: Mindy Dewar, Annie Rice, Ann Sargent, Sarah Dulley, Mark Brooke and myself. After much prayer, fasting and practical planning we decided to create 'The Kitchen'. Mickey, who had an amazing gift of being able to create atmosphere in unpromising surroundings, designed a kitchen and eating area out of a garage that was below his house. It had a suspended platform above the kitchen area that was decked out with comfortable cushions. Great attention was given to every detail of space, colour, material, much of which was inspired by Bible passages describing the building of Solomon's temple, even to the colours of the cushions. It took several months for the work to be done, but at last it was time to open.

We had a dedication service and thereafter, continued to hold our Sunday evening gatherings there. There was not much space, but over the years we would get anything up to eighty people to a service, with every square inch covered with bodies eager to sing and pray and learn. Similar numbers came during the week for meals. Most evenings I would sit on the platform and sing worship songs while people ate. Some would join me after their meals and sing along. Many people brought friends, but there were also times when lone Christians in need of encouragement would come, and in that atmosphere, combined with the songs and being with other believers, their joy was restored. Over the years, many found faith at 'the Kitchen'.

Cloud

As I grew in confidence, I began to receive invitations to go and lead worship elsewhere, often accompanied by a few singing and playing friends. Once, during the summer, we were even asked to sing and talk about our faith at a stand run by the local church at the South of England show! I used to sing quite regularly with a friend called Ginny Cox, who had trained as an opera singer at the Royal College of Music. We were asked to sing at an event in London and, while we were sitting and planning, felt we should form a group to travel round the country encouraging people to worship. Shortly after, another friend, Sarah Dully, joined and we began the most important process of choosing a name! Having gone through a number of possibles we eventually decided to look at the passages that had given such confirmation and encouragement when planning 'the Kitchen'. I read the description of the dedication service for Solomon's temple when the ark of the covenant had been brought to its rightful place.

And the Levites who were the singers, all those of Asaph and Heman and Jeduthun, with their sons and their brethren, stood at the east end of the altar, clothed in white linen, having cymbals, stringed

*instruments and harps, and with them one hundred and twenty priests
sounding with trumpets— indeed it came to pass, when the trumpeters
and singers were as one, to make one sound to be heard in praising
and thanking the LORD, and when they lifted up their voice with the
trumpets, cymbals and instruments of music, and praised the LORD,
saying: "For He is good, For His mercy endures for ever." that the
house, the house of the LORD, was filled with a cloud, so that the
priests could not continue ministering because of the cloud; for the
glory of the LORD filled the house of God* (II Chronicles 5:12–14).

When I read it, the word, 'cloud' just leapt off the page at me and
we knew it was the name we had been looking for. We felt that a
cloud could be any size and shape and could be blown along by the
wind of the Spirit, and scripturally the cloud is a symbol of God's
presence. The context of worship and the glory of God seemed to
be exactly right for what we were setting out to do: to try, through
the process of worshipping and praising God, to create the setting
whereby it might be possible for the very presence of God to come
near and reveal Himself to us. This has been the basis for all that I
have done since, in the realm of leading worship.

You will notice I use the terms 'leading worship', or, 'worship
leader' fairly frequently, and it may be helpful at this stage to explain
what I am talking about, as I am aware that they may mean different
things to different people. What I am referring to is using songs,
hymns and music to help people draw near to God by expressing
themselves through joyful praise and more reflective adoration. The
term, 'worship', of course, means much more than just singing songs
and I will attempt to elaborate on this in later chapters.

Cloud grew in numbers, with a mixture of trained musicians and
enthusiastic amateurs (including myself). It was never a very fixed
group and fluctuated between about six and twenty-one members,
and over the fifteen years it lasted, over a hundred people passed
through. We had an active ministry of travelling to countless
churches, conferences, schools, prisons, hospitals, house groups and
fellowships. We learnt as we went along, making many embarrassing
mistakes, and yet seeing many people come alive in worship and
experience a renewed closeness to the Lord. We got involved with the
choirs for *Come Together*, the ministry musical created by Jimmy and

Carol Owens. Some of us visited Chuck Butler at Calvary Chapel in Orange County, California, and we sang at the first Greenbelt Festival at Odell, Bedfordshire, which was held on my family's farmland. In 1975 we decided as a group to join St Paul's Church, Onslow Square, London, led by Raymond Turvey.

The first album

We studied, we wrote songs, we laughed, we cried, and a year later recorded our first album, 'Free to Fly' for Musical Gospel Outreach, later to become Kingsway Music, to which Gordon Scutt kindly introduced me. We decided to record it live at St Paul's, and John Pantry produced it. It was an exciting experience, although no doubt exasperating for John because of our amateurishness, but for me it was a dream come true. I had always wanted to record, and to hold my first LP in my hands was amazing! We went on to record a total of seven albums, which sold reasonably well.

Church merger

Then, student-oriented St Paul's merged with a rather more formal society church in Knightsbridge called Holy Trinity, Brompton. Raymond used to describe the difference between the two churches this way: after the service at St.Paul's one had coffee or orange juice, whereas at Holy Trinity, one had sweet or dry sherry! We helped start an informal evening service at which we led the praise for the next twelve years, wonderfully encouraged by the different vicars: Raymond, then John Collins, and finally Sandy Millar. It was a great privilege to be a part of a church growing from quite small and traditional to one of the largest in the UK, playing a major part in the renewal of the Anglican Church and subsequently affecting the worldwide church through the Alpha Course. In the early 80s we experienced the arrival and impact of John Wimber and the Vineyard movement. He had a profound affect on nearly every aspect of our church life, not least the emphasis on the kingdom of God, and intimacy with the Lord through worship. We learnt so much from conferences in the UK and California and the personal visits he and his teams paid to HTB, as the church became known. It was as if he gave us the confidence to act with expectation and faith on what we already believed, but perhaps had been hesitant about before.

Family

In 1977 I got married to Moyne, and within eight years we had four children: Harry and Edward (twins), Sam and Saskia. In 1988 we decided as a family to move out of London to Oxford. This meant the end of Cloud and leaving the church we had 'grown up' with, which was hard. We joined St.Aldate's Church under the ministry of David MacInnes (the same who spoke at the Chelsea Town Hall) and I began to get involved with the worship teams there. I continued to travel as and when I was asked, to lead and speak about worship on my own and with others, and went on to record various solo albums of my songs. I was invited to join Chris Bowater for a week at Spring Harvest, which was a new experience, playing in someone else's band, but it led to a lasting friendship with Chris who I am very fond of, and from whom I have learnt a great deal. We even met up for a couple of days to write songs together. There were subsequent weeks at Spring Harvest with my own band that I put together for the events and a tour with Chris and other worship leaders such as Noel Richards, Sue Rinaldi, Trish Morgan, Wes Sutton, Dave Hadden and others, called 'Together for Jesus'. It was an exciting time of seeking to work together with a varied group of leaders in their own right from different church backgrounds, just coming together to worship at the throne of God. We travelled to a number of cities around England, Scotland, Northern and southern Ireland with numbers from about 400 to 1,700 in leisure centres, halls and theatres. It was a wonderful experience and there was a live album released afterwards, but it also showed me that being 'on the road' is not necessarily something I would want to do too often!

The St Aldate's STARR service

One of the special periods during the early 90s in Oxford was when we were involved with an alternative service on Sunday mornings held in the church hall, The Rectory Room —hence **St. A**ldate's **R**ectory **R**oom service or STARR. They were very simple services – singing, a talk, and prayer ministry – and the Lord really seemed to bless what we were doing. For a term while the hall was being renovated we moved into St. Peter's College Chapel, which had plenty of space for growth, since it had originally been a local church. There were complaints from the students about the noise of the band playing at such an early hour (10.30!), as they said they were studying for their finals. I was convinced, however, that they just did not like being woken up! We compromised by agreeing to have the first half of the service in acapella form, using no instruments other than an occasional acoustic guitar. It created a real challenge to find the songs and hymns that would work well in that way, but it led to some very special times of singing and creative forms of worship. There were people who came in off the street and sat and listened and ended up in tears. There were others who were converted and filled with the Spirit, and numbers grew to about 250 at one point. Sadly, our time there was limited and we had to return to the hall which was renamed 'The Christopher Room', but it was difficult as there was no space for us to grow. The service was eventually ended at a time when the church went through a period when all ministries were laid down, as if the land was to be made fallow. I have to admit that we found it very painful to give up what we felt had blossomed into something that God was obviously blessing, but perhaps we had grown too fond of it and needed to let it go. This was 1994, and there were many unusual things happening in the churches, as what later was dubbed 'The Toronto Blessing' swept through the land and turned people's lives upside down.

Toronto

Many will have heard of the so-called 'Toronto Blessing', and will no doubt have strong opinions as to the veracity or validity of the phenomenon, which impacted much of the 'charismatic' wing of the church throughout the world. Without going through any of the arguments for and against it, I want to mention a little of how I was affected by what was going on and how God touched my life through it. I regard it as one of the stepping-stones in my spiritual journey. Early on in 1994, we went to a meeting in Oxford held by the Vineyard churches in the UK. We were fairly disturbed by some of the ways in which people were responding to the apparent movement of the Spirit in our midst; it was extremely noisy, and there were many strange sounds and screams coming from some and a lot of falling about. However, I had a great sense of God's presence and spent quite some time shaking and trembling, awestruck again by the glory and power of God. I was not afraid or worried, but believed God was genuinely at work. One of our children who were there found it all a bit much and went outside for a break. While he was there, someone leaned out of a window to ask him what on earth was going on, and he replied that people were just drunk in the Spirit!

Later that year, I decided to go to a conference in Toronto called *Catch the Fire*, to discover what really was going on over there. I went with two friends expecting that we would know no one and could therefore hide anonymously among the crowd. At the airport we met friends, and when we got to the conference discovered many others doing the same thing as us! It was an amazing experience. There were about 3,500 people from all over the world, including about 100 from the UK. There was a great sense of expectancy and the time we spent in sung worship and prayer was glorious, the talks being inspirational. Every session would end with prayer ministry and there was much falling or being 'slain in the Spirit', and people would spend anything up to an hour just resting on the floor. This happened to me several times and I felt very close to the Lord. Once, while I was on the floor, a British vicar prayed over me and asked for me to have a special anointing of God's compassion. Another time I was prayed for, without falling over, and my hands began to shake vigorously, and then my lips started to tremble. This went on for about fifteen minutes, then calmed down and stopped. I felt strongly that God was strengthening me in my hands for both engraving and music, and that he was touching my lips for speaking, writing and singing. I returned to England full of a new confidence in the Lord and readiness for whatever He had in store for me. I could see a freshness in my songwriting and a greater sense of clarity and authority whenever I spoke or led worship afterwards. The essence of the whole movement was summed up at the time as a reawakening of the awareness of God's nearness to us and our dearness to Him.

I do sincerely believe that it was the Lord, in spite of the strangeness of it all. There was a sense of His peace and presence at the centre of it despite the noisiness and apparent disorder. These movements of the Spirit seem to come and go in waves, and while there are casualties along the way and unwelcome extremes in some behaviour, one has seen abundant fruit in people's lives and increased faith and confidence in His power and grace.

Value Me

In 1995, I collaborated with Shelagh Brown to produce a book published by Bible Reading Fellowship, with an accompanying music album on the subject of finding our true value and worth in God. The book is comprised of stories of people from all walks of life who have had their sense of self-esteem destroyed or damaged through circumstances such as unemployment, homelessness, abuse, marital breakdown or eating disorders, etc. In each case, the people had begun to find healing and their lives being rebuilt through discovering the love of Jesus. The album has songs written by others and myself which reflect the truth of God's love being the way for us to find wholeness, with relevant scriptures read during instrumental passages. I recorded it with Helen Kucharek, a classical singer who had been in Cloud, who had been through various deep traumas in her own life.

VALUE ME

Tell me I'm valued, tell me I'm loved
And the child within my heart will cry
Who wants a reject? Who really cares
For a victim of self-hatred and fear?
A river dammed, a stagnant pool
Enclosed by death, polluted by sin
Still find me special?
Still call me loved?
For my heart finds it hard to accept
You value me

Tell me I'm needed, respected, affirmed
And the child within my heart will say
How can you value? How can You love
A captive locked in walls of clay?
A fountain dry, a garden sealed
And overgrown with thorn and weed
You tell me I'm special
You tell me I'm loved
Yet I still find it hard to accept
You value me

Is it deception, or is it a mask
Created by the power of lies?
If I'm forgiven, if it's the truth
It will only take one glance of Your eyes
And You'll steal my heart
You'll make me whole
Replacing my old heart of stone
Please, tell me I'm special
Please, tell me I'm loved
And my heart shall be free to accept
My heart shall be free to accept
You value me, You value me

Phil Lawson Johnston Copyright ©2001 IQ Music

Small rural churches

In recent years the main emphasis of my music/worship ministry
has been rather more small scale, but none the less rewarding and
encouraging. I have visited numerous churches and small fellowships
around the south of England, most of which have been Anglican and
rural. Many of the visits have been to encourage church music groups,
others have been to lead and teach about worship at fellowships and
post-Alpha groups who have a hunger for contemporary worship
music in church situations where they feel starved. I have also led
days for groups who just need to be refreshed spiritually. I love seeing
God at work in these places, more often than not in a very quiet and
gentle way; seeing others encouraged is such an encouragement to
me.

Worship in the Room

Having seen this hunger in people, I thought that one way to help was
to produce a series of albums specifically for small groups to sing
to when they have no musician to lead them. Called *Worship in the
Room*, each one has a number of familiar and new songs and hymns
recorded in a 'cottage industry' style with very simple arrangements;
voices, guitar and piano to sound as close as possible to us being

'in the room' leading the worship. These have seemed to prove popular with individuals and churches here and in the USA. They are available direct from me and a few Christian bookshops.

Conferences

I have, however, been involved in a number of larger conferences as well. I have led worship weeks at Lee Abbey several times, 'Message for Our Times' in Malvern, 'Kairos' in Northern Ireland and several Wycliffe Hall Summer Schools here in Oxford. I have enjoyed a number of visits to the USA to lead worship at conferences that introduce the Alpha course to church leaders. These have been immensely encouraging times, particularly as my fairly laid-back style is generally received very warmly there. They are also unused to having worship led by just one person, being more accustomed to big bands and choirs etc., and for those who come from smaller churches with fewer resources it is encouraging for them to see it can be done very simply.

St. Andrew's

Currently, we go to St. Andrew's Church in north Oxford, the vicar of which, Andrew Wingfield Digby, has become a great friend, and I lead worship there once or twice a month. In addition to this I still get regular invitations to go and speak and lead worship at churches and events. Some of the best times have been when my daughter, Saskia, who sings and plays the violin and my son, Harry, who plays the drums, have accompanied me.

Engraving glass is still my main occupation, so I have to be careful how I divide my time between glass and song. There are times during the day when I will be engraving away and an idea for a song will bounce across my mind; then I will put down my engraving drill and pick up my guitar. As you can imagine, a certain amount of self-discipline is needed here, and I am not always very good at getting it right! But to be in the position of having two occupations that I love is a rare privilege, even though I have no guarantee of constant work. For anyone who is interested, samples of my engraving can be seen on my website, www.glassengraver.net.

I am so thankful to my Lord and Friend, Jesus, who started me on this path, has walked with me along the way, and will be there at the end. I am grateful for all He has taught me, the many times He has rescued me from my own mistakes and shortcomings, and the way He has shown me time and time again that I really cannot do it very well without His help and strength.

This fairly recent song sums up what I feel:

GRATEFUL

Grateful for Your death
Upon the tree
Grateful for the life it's given me
Grateful I wasn't turned away
Grateful You invited me to stay
Close to You, by Your side
Face to face, eye to eye
Sharing in Your purposes
Seeking out Your will
Learning how to know Your voice
Learning how to follow You

Grateful You lift me when I fall
Grateful You don't condemn at all
Grateful for love so freely shared
Grateful my heart has been prepared
To be close to You, by Your side
Face to face, eye to eye
Sharing in Your suffering
Sharing in Your joy
Walking step by step in time
Learning how to follow You

Phil Lawson Johnston ©2001 IQ Music/Cloud Music

"Father, I pray that the story of my own journey will in some way encourage others in theirs. What you have done in my life is unique to me, and yet your grace is available to all and as a loving Father, you know the intimate details of all our lives. May You pour out that grace on all who are embarking on their journey and those who have travelled far already, for Jesus' sake. Amen."

Part One

The Nature of Worship

3

I HAVE LOVED YOU
—THE SONG OF THE FATHER'S HEART

BE STILL, MY CHILD

I have drawn you with loving-kindness
I will build you up again
I will hold you in My everlasting arms
I will restore you with loving-kindness
I will take you to My heart
Be still My child, be still My loved one
Be still My child, let Me love you
Be still My child, be still My loved one
Be still My child, let Me hold you in My heart

Jeremiah 31:3

Extract taken from the song "Be Still, My Child" by Phil Lawson Johnston
Copyright ©1993 Thankyou Music*

The eternal song of creation

The worship song that we sing to God is a response to the song that He has been singing to us since the beginning of time. Even as He was creating the world before man existed, there was singing; *"Where were you when I laid the foundations of the earth? ...When the morning stars sang together, and all the sons of God shouted for joy"* (Job 38:4,7).

All creation has a song to sing, and not just the birds: *The heavens declare the glory of God, and the firmament shows His handiwork. Day unto day utters speech, and night unto night reveals knowledge. There is no speech or language where their voice is not heard. Their line has gone out through all the earth, and their words to the end of the world* (Psalm 19:1–4a).

Let the heavens declare His righteousness (Psalm 50:6a).

I have been greatly encouraged to discover recently that my great-grandfather, John Lawson Johnston, the inventor of Bovril, had a strong faith. On seeing the stunning sight of Niagara Falls, his reaction was, "If there is a spot on earth calculated to draw our wandering thoughts from nature to nature's God.... The prismatic glory of numerous rainbows say, 'Behold I set my bow in the clouds' ...here certainly we find books in the running brooks, sermons in stones...."

Creation seems to be flush with its own songs, many of which will have their fulfilment in the future: *Let the heavens rejoice, and let the earth be glad; Let the sea roar, and all its fullness; Let the field be joyful, and all that is in it. Then all the trees of the woods will rejoice before the LORD. For he is coming, for He is coming to judge the earth. He shall judge the world with righteousness, and the peoples with his truth* (Psalm 96:11–13).

Let the rivers clap their hands; Let the hills be joyful together before the LORD, for he is coming to judge the earth. (Psalm 98:8–9a).

...The mountains and the hills shall break forth into singing before you, and all the trees of the field shall clap their hands (Isaiah 55:12b).

Alister McGrath has said that, 'It is part of the purpose of the creator that we should hear the music of the cosmos and, through loving its harmonies, come to love their composer.'[1] It is almost as if there is a song bursting to come forth from the very fabric of the universe, and, when people fail to express it, the rest of creation has to let it rip! Indeed, Jesus proclaimed that, *"the stones would immediately cry out"* if the praising disciples were made to keep quiet as the Pharisees wanted, (Luke 19:40). Paul wrote, *For the earnest expectation of the creation eagerly waits for the revealing of the sons of God. For the creation was subjected to futility, not willingly, but because of Him who subjected it in hope; because the creation itself also will be delivered from the bondage of corruption into the glorious liberty of the children of God. For we know that the whole creation groans and labors with birth pangs until now.* (Romans 8:19–21).

The state of the creation seems inextricably bound up with the state of mankind. The song creation is longing to sing is held back until the time when God's people are fully set free. The song at this time is a groan, almost a constipated groan waiting to be released! We have hints of it in the Old Testament, as we saw in Isaiah 55:12.

Again in Psalm 65 we read, *You crown the year with your goodness, And your paths drip with abundance. They drop on the pastures of the wilderness, And the little hills rejoice on every side. The pastures are clothed with flocks; The valleys also are covered with grain; They shout for joy, they also sing* (vv.11–13).

One could dismiss it purely as poetic language used to describe abundance and fruitfulness, but nonetheless one gets the sense of creation pregnant with praise: *Let the sea roar and all its fullness; Let the field rejoice, and all that is in it* (I Chronicles 16:32).

Even science seems to recognise that there is music in creation. In Elizabethan cosmology it was thought that the heavens were structured by the 'music of the spheres', the combined resonance of the planets. Pythagoras originally developed this concept and went on to describe it in mythological terms. Each planet had a siren attached to it, which rubbed the rim of the planet, creating a musical note, much as one does when rubbing the rim of a wine glass. Astrophysicists looking into the origin of the universe have now found evidence of pre- 'big bang' sound, which still can be heard! Apparently, they now even think that black holes hum in the key of Bb! I am reminded of this every time water is flushed in our house. Our quirky plumbing seems to hum in B or occasionally in Bb or C!

Others have described the original creation in musical terms. I have found that Calvin Miller's remarkable poem entitled The Singer expresses something of what creation and the Fall means to me personally, as an artist and musician. Miller writes, 'in the beginning was the song of love'. How rich is that metaphor, reminding us that God, the Father, the Son and the Holy Spirit, created all that is, out of —nothing! Before anything in the universe existed, God was there. For me, what the poet calls the 'song of love' evokes something of the amazing, infinite, inexhaustible love of God. The poet then writes movingly of the creation of man, and of man's terrible rebellion against the love which had brought mankind into being: '...He scooped the earth dust in His hand and worked the clay till He had molded man... ...laid him down beneath primeval trees and waited there.' Then the first man's self-awareness is depicted, again using the imagery of song: '"I am a man!" the sun-scorched being sang. He stood and brushed away the clinging sand. He knew from where his very being sprang.' Father, Son and Holy Spirit create man, yet how soon man rebels! —and Miller shows that rebellion, rejection of the rule of Divine love, and the resulting death, for soon man is 'strident' —and, 'the new man aged and died and dying grew a race of doubtful, death-owned sickly men. And every child received the planet's scar and wept for love to come and reign.'[2]

And we have a similar image in C.S.Lewis's 'The Magician's Nephew', where the Lion sings the song of creation. We read that the deeper notes of the Lion's song create something like a row of fir trees, while light, shorter notes produce primroses. Polly realises that the created things were emerging from Aslan's head. This speaks strongly of the fact that creation was in God's mind and when He spoke (or sang), it came into being.[3]

The song of heaven
Forever, O LORD, Your word is settled in heaven (Psalm 119:89). The song of heaven bursts forth at the birth of Jesus, and the ordinary shepherds are privileged to hear it. At first a single angel comes into view and gives them the good news, then, it is as if all the other angels cannot contain themselves any longer and they explode into praise: *And suddenly there was with the angel a multitude of the heavenly*

host praising God and saying: 'Glory to God in the highest, and on earth peace, goodwill toward men!' (Luke 2:13–14).

We get further glimpses of the worship of heaven in Revelation, where we read of the songs that are being sung continually before the throne of the Lamb. *And every creature which is in heaven and on the earth and under the earth and such as are in the sea, and all that are in them, I heard saying, "Blessing and honor and glory and power be to Him who sits on the throne, and to the Lamb, forever and ever!" Then the four living creatures said, "Amen!" And the twenty-four elders fell down and worshiped Him who lives forever and ever* (Revelation 5:13–14).

Whether it be the first cry of a new-born baby, the dawn chorus, or the last trumpet call at the Second Coming, there is an eternal song resonating at the core of creation.

The power of music

There is great power in music. The sounds that tell a story, make a point, or express feelings and emotions are one of the major ways in which culture can be reflected. It can portray a way of life, a doctrine of life, and provide common ground for people of similar beliefs and values to convey ideas and longings where words alone would be inadequate. There are many siren voices singing their songs to us from the world, and today we hear many of the pagan and humanist philosophies being propagated through popular songs. 'I will do it my way', 'search for the hero inside yourself', 'do what you want, why worry?', 'be tolerant, there are no absolute truths', etc., together with songs of ambition, success, sexual gratification, pleasure, no rules or responsibilities. Music is a powerful and effective language, which communicates and teaches.

A church's or people's theology is expressed through the songs and hymns that they sing. Many of what we call traditional hymns were written to teach biblical truths to illiterate people. William Cowper heard workmen singing in the fields and thought to give them similar songs to sing, but with lyrics full of Christian truth. Martin Luther spoke of the power of music: 'Next to the word of God, music deserves the highest praise. She is mistress and governess of those human emotions... which control men or more often overwhelm them... whether you wish to comfort the sad, to subdue frivolity, to encourage the despairing, to humble the proud, to calm the passionate, or to appease those full of hate... what more effective means than music could you find?'[4]

Famously, William Booth, founder of the Salvation Army, said, "Why should the devil have all the good tunes?" He recognised the influence that music has on people. Even false doctrines such as the Arian heresy were spread and taught to people through song. But church leaders have not always thought so highly of music. 'Music sullies the divine service, for in the very sight of God, in the sacred recesses of the sanctuary itself, the singers attempt, with the lewdness of a lascivious singing voice and a singularly foppish manner, to feminise all their spellbound little followers with the girlish way they render the notes and end the phrases.'[5] This was written by John of Salisbury in the 14th century, when there was a movement from plainsong to the use of harmony. There are still some churches where singing is still frowned upon. Some Scottish Presbyterians still forbid singing in worship and allow only the readings of Psalms. Of course there can be a danger of allowing music to become more important than the truths we are trying to express. Those of us who have been involved in the spread of contemporary praise and worship music have sometimes got close to worshipping worship itself more than the One to whom all worship should be directed.

God's song

I believe God created music as a means for us to learn about Him and to express our love for Him. Praise music is an effective way of making God known and of glorifying Him. As it says in Psalm 50:23, *Whoever offers praise glorifies Me*; and in Psalm 89:1–2, *I will sing of the mercies of the Lord forever, With my mouth will I make known Your faithfulness to all generations. For I have said, "Mercy shall be built up forever; Your faithfulness You shall establish in the very heavens."* For worship music to be acceptable it needs to be theologically correct; telling the truth about God according to what He has said about Himself in the Bible, not our opinion or fanciful ideas. Tozer reminded us that worship was theologically sharply defined, must contain truth, and if it did not take place within the confines of eternal truth, it would be rejected.[6]

Even the world's greatest music—from the passion of Italian opera, through the drama and tragedy of Wagner, the grandeur of Beethoven, the joy and fun of Mozart and the humour of Gilbert and Sullivan—cannot compare with God's amazing song to mankind. His song can satisfy the ideals of every culture and the needs of every person; and He sings not a theory, or philosophy or set of rules, but a person. The Bible as a whole, and the life of Jesus in particular, sing of the love and passion that is in God's heart for the children He has created. It is a song about Himself, for God *...has in these last days spoken to us by His Son, whom He has appointed heir of all things, through whom also He made the worlds; who being the brightness of His glory and the express image of His person, and upholding all things by the word of His power, when He had by Himself purged our sins, sat down at the right hand of the Majesty on high* (Hebrews 1:2–3).

God's song is a song of invitation: Come to Me and let Me love you, forgive you, heal you, make you whole. It is not a song like many others with three verses and a chorus, but more a symphonic song, full of emotions and truths, varied dynamics and colours. It is a song from the heart of the Father.

The Father's song

One great difference between the God we worship and the gods of other religions is that our God is a Father, and we relate to Him as His children. We inevitably transfer our own perceptions of parenthood on to God, positively or negatively according to our experiences. Some of us will have had strict fathers who seem to be only interested in our behaviour, meting out punishment liberally. Others have had fathers who have a carrot and stick approach, where favour and love has had to be earned, threatening dire consequences for failure. Others will have only known unconditional love and acceptance. Whatever our experience of fathers and mothers, it will have coloured our view of God and how we think He might relate to us. Many barriers need to be broken down by the loving ministry of the Holy Spirit to change our perception and enable us to receive the unconditional love, acceptance and affirmation that our Father in heaven wants us to enjoy.

For you did not receive the spirit of bondage again to fear, but you received the Spirit of adoption by whom we cry out, "Abba,

Father." The Spirit Himself bears witness with our spirit that we are children of God (Romans 8:15–16).

We need to hear His song and become those who Michael Green describes as 'Abba worshippers'.

The Father's song is—

A song of truth that tells us who He is and what He has done for us. It proclaims His eternal purposes, designs and desires.

A song of mystery

It tells of His otherness, His majesty, power and glory, His omniscience, immutability, holiness, purity and transcendence. It silences our chatter as we stand or bow before His glorious presence. The Bible tells us that He dwells in obscurity hidden behind a cloud of unknowing and we cannot see Him through our own understanding or emotions. But He has revealed Himself to us through Jesus and through His Spirit given to us: *But as it is written: "Eye has not seen, nor ear heard, nor have entered into the heart of man the things which God has prepared for those who love Him." But God has revealed them to us by His Spirit. For the Spirit searches all things, yes, the deep things of God* (I Corinthians 2:9–10).

The Bible gives us some glimpses of the hidden realms of mysterious angelic beings, many of which are shown in heavenly worship. Windows into heaven are opened for us at certain times: at the birth of Jesus, His transfiguration, and throughout Revelation. And yet, the mystery of God is the fact that He has decided to come and live within us. Paul speaks of, *the mystery which has been hidden from ages and from generations, but now has been revealed to His saints. To them God willed to make known what are the riches of the glory of this mystery among the Gentiles: which is Christ in you, the hope of glory* (Colossians 1:26–27).

Jesus called God the Father 'Holy', and, 'Father' —so we can understand something of the balance of God's otherness and yet desire for an intimate Father/child relationship with us.

A song of love

Richard Foster describes worship as a response we make to God's wooing us. God reaches out to us with His 'overtures of love', and we reciprocate with our adoration. It is a song-story of Him pouring His love out by giving Jesus to us: *For God so loved the world that He gave His only begotten Son...* (John 3:16a). It is a story of us becoming His children: *Behold what manner of love the Father has bestowed on us, that we should be called children of God!* (I John 3:1).

The Song of Songs is a glorious celebration of the intimacy between husband and wife, giving us also a picture of the love of Christ, the Lover, towards the believer, the beloved. Because of its explicit and even erotic language, it is a book that some would rather not be in the canon of Scripture at all. But because it captures something of the very nature of the love relationship that God wants with us, I believe it is a vital book to have at the centre of the Bible. It is a song of love that fills us, compels us, and impassions us to be full of compassion. When Jesus saw the crowds He had compassion on them.... God's love for us does not come and go in fickle ways like ours —it endures forever.

For me the song of love is best portrayed in the well-known parable of the prodigal son (Luke 15:11ff), where we see a father who is committed to loving his son even though their relationship is broken. The story begins with the younger of two sons demanding his share of the estate. This was tantamount to saying, 'I wish you were dead, give me my inheritance now!' It is most likely that the father knew what his son would do, yet he let him go ahead and do it, and later we realize that it did not seem to affect his love for him. God agonises over those who walk away from Him, yet He still loves and He still waits for them to come to their senses (v.17). The son blows his inheritance and ends up being prepared to eat pig cast-offs. For a Jew to even touch a pig was considered totally unclean, and so, we see that this man is plumbing the depths of degradation. When there is nowhere deeper for him to sink to, he wakes up to the possibility of returning as a servant to his father's household. He plans a speech for his father, not expecting forgiveness, nor even to be regarded as a son, and heads for home.

We then return to the picture of the father scanning the horizon in the hope of seeing his son returning. We do not know how long he had to wait, but it must have been months if not years, and still he did not write him off. How patient God was with me, mercifully waiting throughout the years of my wanderings. Peter emphasises the point in his letter, for God, *...is longsuffering toward us, not willing that any should perish but that all should come to repentance* (II Peter 3:9b). Every day the father would look in hope, and then one day he spots a far-off figure approaching. The father's heart leaps and he cannot contain himself: *But when he was still a great way off, his father saw him and had compassion, and ran and fell on his neck and kissed him* (Luke 15:20).

The father did not stand with his hands on his hips and wait for his son to come crawling up to him. No, he ran! For a man of his position it was the height of indignity to run, because to do so, he would have had to lift his clothes and his legs would have been seen.

I wonder what the son must have felt to see his father throwing dignity to the wind and racing towards him. The son must have been in rags, dirty and very smelly with the lingering pong of pigs about him, and yet his father did not screech to a halt and say, 'Phworr! Go and have a bath at once!' Instead, he flung his arms around him and embraced him. It is the equivalent of the Queen running and embracing a tramp. To me, this portrays the utter grace of God towards us. He does not wait for us to get cleaned up before He reaches out to us, although I expect very soon after, the father would have sent him off for a bath!

The greatest example of this kind of grace can be seen in prison. I have been helping at an Alpha course at a local prison, and have seen God reach out to men who have hit the bottom. There have been some who have responded warmly to God's embrace, asked Jesus to come into their lives, and have shown a determination to live differently with His help. I know that they have not got everything straightened out in their lives, and no doubt will fail many times, but just to know that God still loves them, is prepared to live in them and bring about change, has been such a reminder of His unconditional love.

When the son says his prepared speech, the father responds by quickly dressing him in the best robe, giving him a fine ring and new shoes and calling for a celebratory feast. One is left in no doubt about his re-acceptance and re-instatement as a son: *...for this my*

*son was dead and is alive again; he was lost and is found. And they
began to be merry!* No wonder that Jesus says that there is rejoicing
in heaven when one sinner repents.

The story ends with the rather sad scene of the older son angrily
objecting to his father's display of grace towards his sibling, and
refusing to join in with the celebrations. Although he had had all
the opportunities available to him at home, he clearly did not know
he was loved and could have enjoyed celebrating with his friends
whenever he wanted. Although the older son represents the Pharisees
of the time, this is a great reminder to those 'churchy' people who
have not necessarily rebelled against God by rejecting the Christian
faith, but who easily get their noses out of joint when 'sinners' are
welcomed in to the church. Suspicion can lead to a lack of acceptance
and forgiveness, even though God has accepted and forgiven them.
One can be just as 'lost' at home as in a 'distant country', and yet the
Father clearly loves both sons, and wants both to enjoy the fullness
of His grace.

YOU STILL LOVE ME

Though I sometimes fail You and though I often turn away
There's still mercy for me
Though I disappoint You, falling into compromise
Your grace covers my sin

And You still love me, You still love me
In spite of all, You still love me

When I fail to follow, when I wander from the path
Your love beckons me back
When I fail to listen, my stubborn will blocks out Your voice
Your word guides me back to You

Though I often fail to trust and cease to live expectantly
You're still faithful to me
When I fail to speak for You, holding back because of fear
Your voice urges me on

Phil Lawson Johnston Copyright ©1999 Cloud Music/IQ Music

A song of agony

The love of God involves pain and sadness; the Father letting His Son go and giving Him up to die. It is the excruciating cry of, "*My God, My God, why have You forsaken Me?*" —and it is the triumphant cry of, "*It is finished!*"

Death brings the agony of separation and that is an experience that we all go through to a greater or lesser extent at certain times in our life. The loss of my father was, for me, an unexpectedly difficult thing to come to terms with, even though he was nearly 91 and I had plenty of time to prepare. It was emotionally exhausting. I went through some of the same feelings when our dog died. I walked over the ground where I had taken her every day, and I was a wreck! But I sensed God speaking to me through it all, showing me again that death is separation. One minute someone is there, the next they are not. It is as if a wall rises up between us. If death is separation then what is life, if it is not being together with God and with others. The shortest verse in the Bible, *Jesus wept* (John 11:35), shows us Jesus' own pain at losing Lazarus, even though He knew that He was going to bring him to life again. Death was never God's intention; it came because of sin and rebellion. And God Himself experienced the very thing that was alien to His own nature, of being separated from His own Son through His death. Creation itself expressed the agony of that pain, through the earthquake that shook and the darkness that covered the earth at the moment Jesus died.

God also agonises over broken relationships. Time and again, God bemoans the unfaithfulness of His people. "*O Ephraim, what shall I do to you? O Judah, what shall I do to you? For your faithfulness is like a morning cloud, And like the early dew it goes away*" (Hosea 6:4). Likewise, in Isaiah 5, God laments over the vineyard He has planted, representing His people: "*Now let Me sing to my Well-beloved a song of my Beloved regarding His vineyard:*

My Well-beloved has a vineyard on a very fruitful hill.... but it brought forth wild grapes. What more could have been done to My vineyard that I have not done in it? Why then, when I expected it to bring forth good grapes, did it bring forth wild grapes? ...For the vineyard of the LORD of hosts is the house of Israel, and the men of Judah are His pleasant plant. He looked for justice, but behold, oppression; For righteousness, but behold, a cry for help."

I HAVE LOVED YOU

SONG OF THE VINEYARD

I will sing a song to the one I love
The one who planted a vineyard
Surrounded by a wall and tended with care
Guarded from above by a watchtower
He looked for a harvest of fruit, fresh and pure
Fruit from the choicest vine
But why were the branches that should have borne fruit
Laden with grapes that were wild
Laden with grapes that were wild?

Could you not have stayed with Me?
How could you be so blind?
What more could I have done
To keep your first love as Mine?
I would hear a song from the one I love
As I walk in the cool of My garden
The song that I can hear is a song I know
But the words have lost all their meaning
I looked for a bride that was spotless and pure
To walk with me in love
But why has My beloved who should have been Mine
Turned to follow a lover
Turned to follow a lover?

You may hear a song from the one you love
Sung with the voice of reason
Turn and see the one who walks with you
See whose hand you are holding
Do you feel the scars that paid such a price?
Or is it the grip of another?
While you honour Me with lips that sound full of praise
Your heart is courting a stranger

Extract taken from the song "Song of the Vineyard"
by Phil Lawson Johnston & Colin Rank. Copyright ©1985 Thankyou Music*

The book of Lamentations, written by Jeremiah, is a funereal song of mourning over the destruction of Jerusalem as a consequence of the people's sin, anger mingled with hope of God's mercy and restoration. In the same way, Jesus wept over Jerusalem at her blindness and refusal of what was being offered to her through Him. He grieved over her, knowing that destruction was coming her way again.

A song of anger

Those who limit the wrath of God to the Old Testament forget the anger Jesus expressed when He saw His Father's house being abused. Taking a whip, he overturned tables and drove out the crooked money-changers. The character of God does not change between the two testaments; He still has a hatred of sin, rebellion, injustice, oppression, hardness of heart, and death itself. The devil and all his works will receive the brunt of God's wrath, as we see in Revelation. Revelation 18:4ff speaks about the judgment of Babylon: *...her sins have reached to heaven, and God has remembered her iniquities. Render to her just as she rendered to you, and repay her double according to her works....* And, in v.22, *The sound of harpists, musicians, flutists, and trumpeters, shall not be heard in you any more.*

A song of deliverance and freedom

The songs of Moses and Miriam, Deborah and Barak celebrate the victory of God over His enemies. He wants each of us to know His deliverance as well: *You are my hiding place; You shall preserve me from trouble; You shall surround me with songs of deliverance* (Psalm 32:7). The enemies most of us face are not generally flesh and blood but are in the form of fears, anxieties, doubts, and, in some, depression in varying degrees. The promises are still there for us to hold on to because we know that the Lord wants freedom for us: *Stand fast therefore in the liberty by which Christ has made us free, and do not be entangled again by a yoke of bondage* (Galatians 5:1).

And the weapons we use are not worldly ones, but divine. *For the weapons of our warfare are not carnal but mighty in God for pulling down strongholds, casting down arguments and every high thing that exalts itself against the knowledge of God, bringing every thought into captivity to the obedience of Christ* (II Corinthians 10:4–5).

In these verses, Paul is showing us that our warfare is conducted in the realm of thought and argument, and we can see the battle for the Truth raging all around us today, as different philosophies and teachings contend for our allegiance.

It involves knowing the truth about ourselves and our standing before God that brings that freedom. *"And you shall know the truth, and the truth shall make you free"* (John 8:32).

Isaiah reassures us of the victory we have: *"In righteousness you shall be established; You shall be far from oppression, for you shall not fear; And from terror, for it shall not come near you. Indeed they shall surely assemble, but not because of Me. Whoever assembles against you shall fall for your sake"* (Isaiah 54:14–15).

A song of victory over Satan, sin and death

"Death is swallowed up in victory." "O death, where is your sting? O Hades, where is your victory?" (I Corinthians 15:54b–55).

Therefore if the Son makes you free, you shall be free indeed (John 8:36).

O wretched man that I am! Who will deliver me from this body of death? I thank God – through Jesus Christ our Lord! So then, with the mind I myself serve the law of God, but with the flesh the law of sin. There is therefore now no condemnation to those who are in Christ Jesus, who do not walk according to the flesh, but according to the Spirit. For the law of the Spirit of life in Christ Jesus has made me free from the law of sin and death (Romans 7:24 –8:2).

A song of new creation

Therefore, if anyone is in Christ, he is a new creation; old things have passed away; behold, all things have become new (II Corinthians 5:17). *For in Christ Jesus neither circumcision nor uncircumcision avails anything, but a new creation* (Galatians 6:15).

Then He who sat on the throne said, "Behold I make all things new!" (Revelation 21:5).

A song of peace

"Peace I leave with you. My peace I give to you; not as the world gives do I give to you. Let not your heart be troubled, neither let it be afraid" (John 14:27).

It contains the message of reconciliation between God and man and peace through the cross, putting to death hostility between people.

Therefore, having been justified by faith, we have peace with God through our Lord Jesus Christ, through whom also we have access by faith into this grace in which we stand, and rejoice in hope of the glory of God (Romans 5:1–2).

Now all things are of God, who has reconciled us to Himself through Jesus Christ, and has given us the ministry of reconciliation, that is, that God was in Christ reconciling the world to Himself, not imputing their trespasses to them, and has committed to us the word of reconciliation (II Corinthians 5:18–19).

His peace brings us wholeness and contentment in all circumstances. *Be anxious for nothing, but in everything by prayer and supplication, with thanksgiving, let your requests be made known to God; and the peace of God, which surpasses all understanding, will guard your hearts and minds through Christ Jesus* (Philippians 4:6–7).

A song of hope

Hope in Him is the antidote to disappointment. *Hope does not disappoint, because the love of God has been poured out in our hearts by the Holy Spirit who was given to us* (Romans 5:5).

We have the certainty of God's faithfulness and ultimate justice and salvation. And the final triumph of God over all sorrow and pain is assured, for all those who know and trust in Him: *And I heard a loud voice from heaven saying, "Behold, the tabernacle of God is with men, and He will dwell with them and they shall be His people. God Himself will be with them and be their God. And God will wipe away every tear from their eyes; there shall be no more death, sorrow, nor crying. There shall be no more pain, for the former things have passed away"* (Revelation 21:3–4).

Our hope in God is centred on the sure fact that Jesus will return to judge the world in fairness. We are *..looking for the blessed hope and glorious appearing of our great God and Saviour Jesus Christ* (Titus 2:13).

A song of delight

At every stage of the creation, God, 'saw that it was good'. He was pleased with what He had made.

Mankind, the pinnacle of His creation, was created specifically for His pleasure and delight. *For the LORD takes pleasure in His people* (Psalm 149:4a).

The LORD takes pleasure in those who fear Him, In those who hope in His mercy (Psalm 147:11).

The LORD your God in your midst, the Mighty One, will save; He will rejoice over you with gladness, He will quiet you with His love, He will rejoice over you with singing. (Zephaniah 3:17).

Here is a song of His delight over us:

HE WILL REJOICE

Do not fear, O child, lift up feeble hands
Do not be afraid, strengthen feeble knees
Say to those with fearful hearts, be strong and do not fear
For your God will come to you, He will save

The Lord Your God is with you, He is mighty to save
He will take great delight in you
He will quiet you with His love
He will rejoice over you, He will rejoice over you
He will rejoice over you with singing
He will rejoice with a singing heart

Phil Lawson Johnston Copyright ©1995 Cloud Music/IQ Music

Many of us find it hard to believe that we are truly loved and that God sincerely delights in us. This can be the result of poor parenting which may have created for us a distorted father image. If no one has ever told us we are valued for who we are rather than for what we do or achieve, it can be hard for us to accept that our Father in heaven feels any delight in us. I once was deeply moved at a service I attended at the Anaheim Vineyard Fellowship when they were singing a song I knew well called, 'Lord, You are more precious than silver....'. They turned the words round to sing, 'My child, you are more precious than silver....' as if God Himself was singing to us.

I found I had to stop and just listen to it, receiving the truth of what the Father felt about me. It struck me that I found it easy enough to accept that God 'loved' me, but it had never occurred to me that He might 'like' me as well. I thought that because He is God, He almost had a duty to love me, but to like me was a different thing altogether. I confess that I can love people without liking them. To like someone is to genuinely enjoy being with them and miss them when apart. To think that God might feel that about me was and is an amazing thought. However, the more I read His word the more I realise how true it is that He delights in us all the time, and wants to pour His love upon us, not just when we are in dire need.

It is good news for all of us, especially when we feel alone or abandoned; *You shall also be a crown of glory in the hand of the LORD, and a royal diadem in the hand of your God. You shall no longer be termed Forsaken, nor shall your land any more be termed Desolate. But you shall be called Hephzibah, and your land Beulah; for the LORD delights in you, and your land shall be married* (Isaiah 62:3–4). He makes promises—and rejoices in doing good—to His people; *"Yes, I will rejoice over them to do them good, and I will assuredly plant them in this land, with all My heart and with all My soul"* (Jeremiah 32:41).

He delights in those who obey and follow Him with all their heart and soul; *The LORD your God will make you abound in all the work of your hand, in the fruit of your body, in the increase of your livestock, and in the produce of your land for good. For the LORD will again rejoice over you for good as He rejoiced over your fathers, if you obey the voice of the LORD your God, to keep His commandments and His statutes which are written in this Book of the Law, and if you turn to the LORD your God with all your heart and with all your soul* (Deuteronomy 30:9). His delight in us should fill our hearts with a song of gratitude and love.

God is still speaking and singing to His creation, and there is no place on earth where His voice cannot be heard: *Then I saw another angel flying in the midst of heaven, having the everlasting gospel to preach to those who dwell on the earth—to every nation, tribe, tongue, and people—saying with a loud voice, "Fear God and give glory to Him, for the hour of His judgment has come; and worship Him who made the heaven and earth, the sea and springs of water"*

(Revelation 14:6–7). His song will not be silenced, whereas many of our songs need to be. My prayer is that all of us would understand the song that the Father has been singing from the beginning, is singing now, and will sing throughout eternity. May our response be; *Oh, give thanks to the LORD, for He is good! For His mercy endures for ever* (Psalm 136:1).

He has been singing that song to mankind since the beginning of time; He has sung to us through a person, Jesus Christ; and He has called us to sing His song to a lost world. As our hearts begin to beat in time with His, as we start to feel as He feels; we become His minstrel ambassadors, allowing His appeal to be heard through us.

Now then, we are ambassadors for Christ, as though God were pleading through us: we implore you on Christ's behalf, be reconciled to God (II Corinthians 5:20).

I LOOK FOR A MAN

Could you not watch with me?
Could you not pray?
I look for a man who will build up the wall
I look for a man who will stand in the gap
Who will listen to My word
Who will give warning to My people

I look for a man
Who will watch and pray

Could you not wait on Me
and speak of the things I tell?
I look for a watchman who will stay alert
I look for a man who will stay at his post
Who will open his eyes
Who will give warning of the enemy

Who is prepared to weep with me
To see the things I see?
I long for a people who will lift their eyes

THE SONG OF THE FATHER'S HEART

I long for a people who will be on their guard
Who will stay awake with Me
Who will stand full of courage in adversity

Whoever would listen, let him listen
Whoever would refuse, let him refuse

(Ezekiel 22:30; 33:7)

Extract taken from the song "I Look for a Man" by Phil Lawson Johnston
Copyright ©1985 Thankyou Music*

Notes

[1] Alister McGrath, *The Re-enchantment of Nature*, 2003 p.13. Reproduced by permission of Hodder and Stoughton Limited.

[2] Taken from *The Singer* by Calvin Miller. Copyright © 2001 by Calvin Miller. Used with permission of InterVarsity Press, P.O. Box 1400, Downers Grove, IL 60515, USA.

[3] See C.S. Lewis, *The Magician's Nephew*, Harper Collins pp.119–123.

[4] Quoted in F. Blume, *Protestant Church Music*, London 1975, p.10.

[5] Quoted in P. Weiss and R. Taruskin, *Music in the Western World*, London 1984 p.62.

[6] A.W. Tozer, *Worship, the Missing Jewel of the Evangelical Church*, Christian Publications.

4

WE WERE MADE FOR WORSHIP

WE WERE MADE FOR WORSHIP

We were made for worship
Created for Your praise
We are called to serve You
And love You all our days

We were made for worship
To follow You alone
No foreign god besides You
No rivals on Your throne

You will not share Your praises
There's no room for idols in our hearts

To be for the praise of Your glory
To be the salt of the earth
Our lives telling Your story
We are the light of the world
We are the light of the world

THE SONG OF THE FATHER'S HEART

We were made for worship
Created to be free
To love You as our Saviour
Throughout eternity

We were made for worship
To walk with You alone
To be loved as Your children
To find in You a home

You will not share Your praises
There's no room for idols in our hearts

To be for the praise of Your glory
To be the salt of the earth
Our lives telling Your story
We are the light of the world
We are the light of the world

You will not share Your praises
There's no room for idols in our hearts……..

Phil Lawson Johnston
Copyright ©2004 Cloud Music

Before starting this book I wrote to a number of friends and asked for their view of worship. Here is one of the responses, from John Irvine, Dean of Coventry Cathedral:

"To worship is to attribute worth to something or someone; to reverence, respect and honour. Humanity must worship. It is the most basic of instincts planted there by God and if we don't worship God we will find something else to worship. I love the fundamental question posed in the Scottish Catechism – 'Why was I created?' and the answer, 'I was created in order to worship God and enjoy Him forever.' Christian worship should be joyful, reverent and Christ-centred."

God decided to create all things purely because it was His desire. *For You created all things, and by Your will they exist and were created* (Revelation 4:11). We were intended for God's own pleasure. *He chose us in Him before the foundation of the world, that we should be holy and without blame before Him in love, having predestined us to adoption as sons by Jesus Christ to Himself, according to the good pleasure of His will* (Ephesians 1:4–5). And He takes great delight in us especially when we worship and trust Him: *The Lord delights in those who fear Him, who put their hope in His unfailing love* (Psalm 147:11).

A.W. Tozer, who had a knack of putting things most succinctly, said that we were made to worship God and have an eternal preoccupation with Him. Even anthropologists acknowledge the fact that we have an instinct for worship of some kind. If it is true that God has put into every single human being that has ever lived the inbuilt ability and desire to worship, then everyone must indeed worship. They may not call it that nor attribute it to God, but just as babies are born with the potential to walk and talk, and as they grow they begin to do so, so all people will naturally turn towards something or someone onto which they will pour their affection. Everyone looks for something on which they will try to centre their lives and through which find their value. Many have called it 'the God-shaped blank'. Ultimately all people are yearning for something, and most of the time they cannot identify it and will try to fill the void inside with anything they can find. What has been aptly termed 'the chill wind of loneliness' still blows through their lives.

People will fill their lives with drugs, drink, and other excesses, or put their faith in horoscopes, crystals, therapies, life coaches or gurus, clairvoyants and on and on. They often seem to be gripped by fear and superstition, yet at the same time, summarily dismiss the Christian faith as irrelevant. Others, who outwardly appear to have no needs at all and do not fall into such practices, will self-sufficiently go though life full of pride, arrogantly proclaiming that they have no need of a deity or outside help. The Bible calls them fools: *The fool says in his heart, "There is no God"* (Psalm 14:1), and speaks of the wickedness of ignoring God: *An oracle within my heart concerning the transgression of the wicked: There is no fear of God before his eyes* (Psalm 36:1; see Romans 3:18).

One should not be too surprised, I suppose, when Jesus explained to Nicodemus the 'verdict' that is hanging over mankind:

"And this is the condemnation, that the light has come into the world, and men loved darkness rather than light, because their deeds were evil. For everyone practising evil hates the light and does not come to the light, lest his deeds should be exposed. But he who does the truth comes to the light, that his deeds may be clearly seen, that they have been done in God" (John 3:19–21).

It still remains, however, that many of one's friends who seem to be basically good and kind to others, continue to find it so hard, if not impossible, to become worshippers of Jesus. Maybe it has to do with the need to humble oneself, to admit one has been wrong. For to admit to any kind of need is seen by many as a sign of weakness and is therefore anathema to them. The key, of course, is to be willing to be made willing, and for many the only way they can come to this point is for some crisis to happen which they are powerless to change. Illness, relationship break-down or economic melt-down, however unpleasant, can all bring people to the point of admitting need and the preparedness to be vulnerable.

That, coupled with the fact that these things are spiritually discerned and that one needs to have one's eyes opened, seems to keep people at a distance. *But the natural man does not receive the things of the Spirit of God, for they are foolishness to him; nor can he know them, because they are spiritually discerned* (I Corinthians 2:14).

Also, one must not forget the part that Satan plays in keeping people blind: *...whose minds the god of this age has blinded, who do not believe...* (II Corinthians 4:4).

Blaise Pascal put it like this, 'The Christian religion teaches two truths: that there is a God who men are capable of knowing, and that there is an element of corruption in men that renders them unworthy of God. Knowledge of God without knowledge of man's wretchedness begets pride, and knowledge of man's wretchedness without knowledge of God begets despair, but knowledge of Jesus Christ furnishes man's knowledge of both simultaneously.' The amazing thing is that when our eyes are opened and we understand both our own need and all that God has done for us, particularly how much He loves us, those things that seemed so important before somehow appear to lose much of their significance.

Significance, identity, destiny

It has been said that the greatest three needs that people have are to find significance, identity and destiny. They will search for these things wherever they think they can find them. Magazines are full of references to identity crises, depression and low self-esteem among the young. Britain seems to have one of the worst records in Europe for teenage pregnancy, drug taking, drunkenness, abortion and divorce, all signifying that our society has thoroughly lost its way. This search is exemplified by the current popularity of various quasi-religions, which have enjoyed considerable publicity through the numbers of celebrities who have bought into their mainly self-orientated philosophies. Sadly, the church will, all too often, not be their first port of call, or even be disregarded altogether as irrelevant. But ultimately the only way they will have their hunger fulfilled is through a worshipping relationship with God. If there is no God and we are just 'accidents' in a world of random chance, then there is no reason to search for such things; they simply do not exist. Without God as a starting point, there is no reason to love or expect love, no purpose to aim for, and no end to look forward to. And still people search! Why? Because that is the way they were created. [God] ...*has put eternity in their hearts.* (See Ecclesiastes 3:11).

Eternal novelty

God is the only one who can provide the eternal 'novelty'—or, perhaps we should rather say newness—which we long for; moreover, we are only satisfied in Him, and He requires that we only worship Him. As St Augustine puts it, *Our souls are restless until they find their rest in Thee.*

There is, I believe, a 'homesickness' for the divine which is built into each one of us, and which can only be fully 'healed' by a relationship with God. There is a longing for 'home' or completeness, which is given us by God, and He is the one who can lead us there even though it seems to lie more dormant in some than in others. It is, of course, easier to want 'home' when one has tasted it first, as we see in the story of the prodigal son. But I am certain that just as some birds and animals have a homing instinct, it is also present in all of us. With the birds it is activated by a combination of the earth's magnetic fields and the position of the sun, and with us it can be influenced by circumstances as well as an exposure to the light of God, and is ultimately quickened in us by the Holy Spirit. Having twin boys myself, I have always been fascinated by the special relationship they have. I have read stories of twins who have been separated at birth and never been told of their other 'half', and yet have experienced a sense of loss or incompleteness throughout their lives. In the cases where they have eventually met up with their lost brother or sister, there has been, apart from the obvious emotions, a glorious sense of them being made complete again.

The longing for God's 'home' is wonderfully expressed in various psalms, particularly 27:4, 42:1–2 and 63:1–5, but perhaps most supremely in Psalm 84.

How lovely is Your tabernacle, O LORD of hosts! My soul longs, yes, even faints for the courts of the LORD; My heart and my flesh cry out for the living God. Even the sparrow has found a home, and the swallow a nest for herself, Where she may lay her young – even your altars, O LORD of hosts, My King and my God. Blessed are those who dwell in your house; They will still be praising you (vv.1–4).

Home, to me, now speaks of a place of rest and safety, where I am known and loved; a place of intimate relationships and shared hopes and dreams. For the men and women of faith, the *great cloud of witnesses* listed for us in Hebrews 11, it was a place of the future, a heavenly country promised by God to all who trust in Him. Paul describes it in terms of earthly tents and heavenly dwellings and how, *...we groan, earnestly desiring to be clothed with our habitation which is from heaven.* (See II Corinthians 5:2). He also says that, *...our citizenship is in heaven, from which we eagerly wait for the Saviour, the Lord Jesus Christ, who will transform our lowly body that it may be conformed to His glorious body...* (Philippians 3:20–21).

Not only will we have the home that we long for, but also the perfect bodies that most of us long for too!

Everyone is searching for a home of some kind, some intimacy to fill that void which yearns to love and be loved, to know and be known. As the Irish band, The Corrs sing, 'Everybody's searching for intimacy, oh, everybody's hurting for intimacy.'

Here is a song I wrote some time ago, in which I try to express something of the 'strain and struggle', of life and the longing to be at rest with the Lord.

TO REST IN HIS LOVE

Hello strain, hello burden
Hello struggle and strife
No much rest not much freedom
Where is the peace on my mind?
What do I see? A bit confusing
Twilight, foggy and grey

Hollow smiles, empty phrases
I'm trying hard to be free
I 'praise the Lord', I 'Alleluia'
But somehow there's something between us
I look for a sign, I look for an answer
But why am I so slow to see?
It's simple and pure, it's sitting right here in front of me

Come let me return unto Jesus
Come let me lay my burden down
Come let me return
Unto the love I knew at first
Come let me return to rest in His love

Extract taken from the song "To Rest in His Love" by Phil Lawson Johnston
Copyright ©1978 Thankyou Music*

Celebrity worship

I have been fascinated by a series of articles that appeared recently in various newspapers and magazines, which reported that psychologists had identified a new condition called Celebrity Worship Syndrome. It is an obsessive interest in famous people, which shows itself through a belief that they know and are known by their chosen celebrity, and a desire to become like them by dressing or trying to behave like them; even through collecting articles that have been touched by them, in a bizarre throw-back to the mediaeval practice of collecting religious relics. It is thought to be caused by a lack of real relationships in their own lives, and it seems that many people are now suffering from it! It has led to depression and psychoses in some, and is even now being studied by evolutionary biologists. Although one may laugh disparagingly about such poor, inadequate souls, confirming all that we ever thought about hero-worship and our love affair with fame, it speaks volumes about the basic human desire to worship.

Some people have described football as the new religion in the UK, not without some reasons: calling the pitch the 'sacred turf', the 'religious' anthems that are sung, and the symbols used, such as flags. And yet there are still, on average, four and a half times as many people in Anglican churches on Sunday in England than those watching a match! The British public's adoration of Princess Diana was a prime example of this new kind of secular religiosity, if we may call it that. The extraordinary scenes in the week following her tragic death were nothing short of mourning the death of a 'goddess', with the mountain of flower 'offerings', which were laid at the 'shrine' of her Kensington home. Another explanation of such a huge outpouring of grief is that her death enabled people to express bottled-up feelings that they had been unable to release over their own losses or tragedies. The desire to express such an outpouring of mourning has been described recently as 'emotional incontinence'. Whatever term is applied, it was a remarkable phenomenon. We are not surprised though, when we note how disillusioned people can become when flaws appear in their celebrity 'gods', whether it be the disclosure of some extra-marital affair, or when patience is lost and photographers get punched!

I wonder, also, if you have noticed how often you hear blasphemous exclamations using the name of God, in plays, films and reality television, as well as in everyday life? It seems to be the most common response to good or bad news, but lacks any sincerity. As they blaspheme, those who do not know God personally do not seem to know what they are saying. And why would the name of Jesus be misused as a common swear word in our society? It exhibits a total lack of respect for our Lord, and it furthers Satan's intention to take the good things of God and corrupt them; but could even that casual taking of God's name in vain point to a 'God shaped gap' in so many lives which are being lived without awareness of His presence?

G.K.Chesterton once said that when people stop believing in God, they do not believe in nothing but will believe in anything, and the same can be said about worship.

Praise as boasting

Likewise, a very human instinct is to praise. People are only really following their natural tendencies when they express their enthusiasm over anything that they are passionate about. C.S. Lewis wonderfully describes this in *Reflections on the Psalms*. He observes that the most humble, well–balanced people praise most, and 'cranks, misfits and malcontents' praise least.

To praise is to speak well of a person, thing or activity; in short, to speak positively. In Christian terms, to praise is to release blessing with our lips. To be bursting with excitement about a relationship is such a normal thing for those who have experienced being in love. You simply cannot stop talking and thinking about your beloved, sometimes to the extent that your friends get thoroughly bored! And so it can be when one discovers the wonder of getting to know God.

Praise has been described as 'excited boasting' about God, and that fits well with Psalm 44:8, *In God we boast all day long, And praise Your name forever.*

I was brought up never to boast about myself, and the Bible certainly reinforces this. The only personal boast that seems to be allowed is boasting about one's own shortcomings. *...Therefore most gladly I will rather boast in my infirmities, that the power of Christ may rest upon me* (II Corinthians 12:9). However, we are encouraged to 'glory in' [or, as it is sometimes translated, 'boast about'] God.

Thus says the LORD: "Let not the wise man glory in his wisdom, Let not the mighty man glory in his might, Nor let the rich man glory in his riches; But let him who glories glory in this, That he understands and knows Me, That I am the LORD, exercising lovingkindness, judgment, and righteousness in the earth. For in these I delight," says the LORD (Jeremiah 9:23–24).

THE FOOLISHNESS OF GOD

God has chosen foolishness to shame the wise
The weak things of the world to shame the strong
He has chosen lowliness and things that are despised
For to Him all might and power belong
So, let not the wise man boast of wisdom

THE SONG OF THE FATHER'S HEART

Let not the strong man boast of strength
Let not the rich man boast of riches
Let him who boasts, boast of this
That he understands and knows the Lord
And he puts his trust in God alone

Christ is our righteousness and wisdom
It is by grace we have been saved
Through faith and not by works to earn His love
It is the gift of God
We have this treasure as in jars of clay
To show that this power is from God
His grace is sufficient for us so that we may boast
That when we are weak then we are strong
And we understand and know the Lord
And we put our trust in God alone

Phil Lawson Johnston Copyright ©1995 Cloud Music

Not boasting about oneself, but about God, is a good antidote to pride, which is the greatest hindrance to our coming to know Him and yielding ourselves totally to Him.

Submission of all our nature

William Temple helpfully described worship in terms of submitting or surrendering ourselves to God; as we worship Him, the mind, imagination and heart is profoundly affected by Him, and we are opened to His love in a selfless way.

Worship involves every part of our being. Although the idea of submission or surrender may seem to imply something passive, or have negative connotations, surrendering our lives to God is the most positive and active thing we could ever do; just as an eagle 'surrenders' itself to the thermals, in order to rise to the heavens. It enables us to begin to obey the first commandment, to love the Lord our God with all our heart, mind, soul and strength. This does not mean that God is looking for us to spend our entire life sitting in a haze and just thinking about Him, but that in every area of our life, occupation, relationships, leisure, etc., He is wanting us to honour and please Him, putting His will first.

Many might think that this restricts or curtails our freedom to be and do whatever we want, and feel that God is really just a killjoy. To think that is to show a lack of understanding of how much God loves us and wants the best for us. He created us to live in a certain way according to His eternal principles, and just as a car will eventually cease to work with the wrong fuel in it, so will we cease to function properly if we do not live as we were intended. He wants us to be free and live abundantly, but in His way. *And I will walk at liberty, For I seek Your precepts* (Psalm 119:45).

He does truly know what is best for us, and the key to it is, simply, love —His love, and our love expressed in a secure relationship. *We love Him because He first loved us* (I John 4:19).

This is made possible not by us trying to be better, but by our hearts being filled with His own Spirit, who gives us that love and enables us to live in a way that is pleasing to Him. Therefore, to worship God is to seek to please Him in everything we do. *Therefore we make it our aim, whether present or absent, to be well pleasing to Him* (II Corinthians 5:9). *For you were once darkness, but now you are light in the Lord. Walk as children of light (for the fruit of the Spirit is in all goodness, righteousness, and truth), finding out what is acceptable to the Lord* (Ephesians 5:10).

Though we must be very clear that we cannot earn salvation, we can only receive it by accepting His mercy and forgiveness through His substitutionary death, we do not just please Him by what we believe but also by what we do. *And whatever you do in word or deed, do all in the name of the Lord Jesus, giving thanks to God the Father through Him* (Colossians 3:17).

A life of service

Worship is more than singing songs; it is a *life* of service. Worship definitely involves singing and making music with our voices and in our hearts to God, and it indeed pleases God when we do this.

I will praise the name of God with a song, And will magnify Him with thanksgiving. This also shall please the LORD better than an ox or bull... (Psalm 69:30–31).

But it cannot be restricted to an hour or two on Sunday when we are in church. It must be expressed continually in the way we live for God and as we serve others. I want to emphasise the point that when we do sing, it is in the context of worship being at the very core of our whole walk with God. *From the rising of the sun to its going down the LORD's name is to be praised* (Psalm 113:3).

Recently, I saw an apt notice on the inside of a church door, which read, 'The worship has now ended; the service now begins.' Paul, in Romans 12:1, links worship and service: ...*present your bodies a living sacrifice, holy, acceptable to God, which is your reasonable service*. And in German we find the word for worship itself is *Gottesdienst*, meaning 'service of God'.

Reflections

Our worship should be reflected in our behaviour. Our words, too, should reflect what is in our hearts. *"These people draw near to Me with their mouth, And honour Me with their lips, But their heart is far from Me. And in vain they worship Me"* (Matthew 15:8–9).

And Paul, in Ephesians 1:12, calls us to honour God, just as much by the way we are as by the words we say or sing, for, ...*we who first trusted in Christ should be to the praise of His glory.*

Light is to shine in us. *"You are the light of the world.... Let your light so shine before men, that they may see your good works and glorify your Father in heaven"* (Matthew 5:14,16). *For it is the God who commanded light to shine out of darkness, who has shone in our hearts to give the light of the knowledge of the glory of God in the face of Jesus Christ* (II Corinthians 4:6).

We cannot achieve this by our own effort, but by Him living in us and giving us the inner ability to love and obey Him.

Now hope does not disappoint, because the love of God has been poured out in our hearts by the Holy Spirit who was given to us (Romans 5:5). *"...I will put My law in their minds, and write it on their hearts..."* (Jeremiah 31:33).

When we are truly in love with Him, obedience to Him and His laws ceases to be such a problem. It is not a case of us bowing down to an unreasonable dictatorial power, but rather a delight in pleasing one who loves us beyond measure. If we love God, we will not want to have any other 'gods' but Him; we will not want to 'make for ourselves an idol', or 'misuse the name of the Lord', or 'murder', or 'commit adultery', etc., etc. He is not a harsh taskmaster demanding instant compliance, but the adoring Father who only wants the best for His children. Living His way is the only way to truly experience life as it was always meant to be: full of satisfaction, enjoyment and fulfilment. By pleasing Him, we will also always bring great pleasure to ourselves; 'It is our duty and our joy....', as the Book of Common Prayer puts it.

Until now we have been looking at worship from our perspective and what it might mean to us. Perhaps it is now time to look at God's perspective on it.

A jealous God

We understand from the Bible that God created us so that He might love us and be loved by us, and we can see that worship is the way in which that love affair is kept alive. Just as a husband feels a fierce protective jealousy over his bride, so God feels intense jealousy over us, particularly when He sees us rejecting Him and turning to other objects of worship. I find Tozer's picture helpful: he likened God's action to His giving man a harp, with more strings and wider range than was available to any other created being. At the Fall, it is as though man took the harp he had been given and discarded it. Man became self-centred; in his fallen state, true worship and real joy is absent.

Perhaps it can be illustrated also by this song:

TURN, TURN AGAIN

"Why do you stray, My sheep, why do you roam?
Why look for pastures new, when I have given you a home?
By lusting with your eyes, you have become so blind
Now you are wondering why I seem so hard to find

Turn, turn again; it's time you realised
Turn, turn again; you've swallowed only lies
From the world, from the world

By accepting compromise, you've turned away from Me
You've set up idols in your hearts with divided loyalty

While flirting with the world and chasing after gold
Your eyes have lost their light, your heart has now grown cold

Turn, turn again; cease your flirting there
Turn, turn again; stop this love affair
With the world, with the world

I burn with jealousy, I long with all my heart
To see us restored again and no longer drifting apart
I've no desire to see you lost; I have no wish to hide
But I will not force a change; it's up to you to decide

Turn, turn again; it's time you realised
Turn, turn again; you've swallowed only lies
Turn, turn again; cease your flirting there
Turn, turn again; stop this love affair
With the world, with the world"

Phil Lawson Johnston Copyright ©1988 Cloud Music

The Bible is very clear about God's jealousy: *...for you shall worship no other god, for the LORD, whose name is Jealous, is a jealous God* (Exodus 34:14). The first of the Ten Commandments states: *"You shall have no other gods before me"* (Exodus 20:3); and the second extends it: *"You shall not make for yourself a carved image—any likeness of anything that is in heaven above, or that is in the earth beneath, or that is in the water under the earth; you shall not bow down to them nor serve them. For I, the LORD your God, am a jealous God, visiting the iniquity of the fathers upon the children to the third and fourth generation of those who hate Me, but showing mercy to thousands, to those who love Me and keep My commandments."*

Idolatry or false worship
Idolatry, or false worship. is a major cause of God's anguish and anger at His people throughout the Old Testament, rising out of jealousy for His people's love. An idol is anything that takes the place of God

in our heart and affections. Idols are usually self-created, whether they be physical or something that we allow to grip our hearts. Isaiah often speaks about the worthlessness of idol worship. *Those who make an image, all of them are useless, and their precious things shall not profit; They are their own witnesses; They neither see nor know, that they may be ashamed. Who would form a god or mould an image that profits him nothing?* (Isaiah 44:9–10). Throughout the Old Testament they are continually described as worthless idols, in contrast to the worthiness of God, that we read of in Revelation: *You are worthy, O Lord, to receive glory and honour and power* (Revelation 4:11).

It is said that the English word for worship derives from the Anglo-Saxon word *weorthscipe* (lit. 'worthship'), which helps us understand how worship is all about the worthiness of God. Ravi Zacharias speaks of worship as affirming God's inestimable worth, and John Piper has described worship as being a way in which we gladly reflect back to God the radiance of His worth.[1]

The New Testament is just as clear as the Old Testament about idols; *...we know that an idol is nothing in the world, and that there is no other God but one. For even if there are so-called gods, whether in heaven or on earth (as there are many gods and many lords), yet for us there is one God, the Father, of whom are all things, and we for Him; and one Lord, Jesus Christ, through whom are all things, and through whom we live* (I Corinthians 8:4–6). And John finishes his first letter by saying, *Little children, keep yourselves from idols* (I John 5:21). Likewise, Paul says, in I Corinthians 10:14, *Therefore, my beloved, flee from idolatry.*

Even greed is equated with idolatry in Colossians 3:5. Money and all that comes with it can be the source of much of the idolatry in many societies. Jesus warns us that we cannot follow two masters: *"You cannot serve God and mammon"* (Matthew 6:24). And Paul writes: *men will be lovers of themselves, lovers of money...lovers of pleasure rather than lovers of God.* (See II Timothy 3:2–3.) *For the love of money is a root of all kinds of evil...* (I Timothy 6:10).

We perhaps think most readily of idolatry in terms of bowing down to images of animals or strangely shaped human forms. But it is just as prevalent today in forms of our obsession with material things, or personalities as we have already noted above in the 'Celebrity

Worship Syndrome' or even in the way we name television shows such as 'Pop Idol'. Money, sex, power and ambition can become idols if they consume our thinking and goals. That is not to say that all ambition, for example, is wrong. There are goals and desires in all of us, many of which have been placed there by God Himself. The problem arises either when our ambition is set on something ungodly or when an ambition becomes a ruling obsession in our lives.

Even science itself can become an idol in the scientist's life, particularly when the search for knowledge and discovery is limited to a purely naturalistic world-view and science is thought of as reigning supreme over all. The stubborn refusal of some scientists to even contemplate the possibility of a Designer of the universe can become idolatrous; though there are many who acknowledge that recent discoveries keep pointing them to the existence of a Creator being a feasible explanation for the origins of the universe.

Isaiah 65:11 speaks of the ideas of 'fortune' and 'destiny', idols which seem to have just as much a following today as ever, whether it be through the lottery or horoscopes. Material things can become objects of worship as well. I recently test drove the latest Rolls Royce Phantom, (no, I am not thinking of buying one, even if I could; besides, I really prefer Bentleys!), and I can see how such an extraordinary machine, even momentarily, could become an idol.

Both James and John give strong warnings about being too friendly with worldliness. *...Do you not know that friendship with the world is enmity with God? Whoever therefore wants to be a friend of the world makes himself an enemy of God* (James 4:4). *Do not love the world or the things in the world. If anyone loves the world, the love of the Father is not in him. For all that is in the world – the lust of the flesh, the lust of the eyes, and the pride of life – is not of the Father but is of the world* (I John 2:15–16).

A. W. Tozer maintained that to entertain thoughts about God which are unworthy of Him is the essence of idolatry.[2] It is nothing less than the exchange of truth for lies, or the worship of God Himself being exchanged for something created or man-made. They, *...exchanged the truth of God for the lie, and worshipped and served the creature rather than the Creator, who is blessed for ever. Amen* (Romans 1:25).

To gain some idea why God is so angry at our leaning towards idolatry, one needs to see the damage it can do to one's life. Paul leaves us in no doubt about this. *For this reason, God gave them up to vile passions.... And even as they did not like to retain God in their knowledge, God gave them over to a debased mind, to do those things which are not fitting; being filled with all unrighteousness, sexual immorality, wickedness, covetousness, maliciousness; full of envy, murder, strife, deceit, evil-mindedness; they are whisperers, backbiters, haters of God, violent, proud, boasters of evil things, disobedient to parents, undiscerning, untrustworthy, unloving, unforgiving, unmerciful; who, knowing the righteous judgment of God, that those who practice such things are deserving of death, not only do the same but also approve of those who practice them.* (See Romans 1:26ff).

Idolatry not only displeases God, but leads to our own ultimate destruction; Deborah sings of how it led to war: *They chose new gods, Then there was war in the gates* (Judges 5:8). Judges tells a story of God's people continually falling away from Him, worshipping idols and being brought into subservience to other nations. They cry out to God and He has compassion and rescues them. When we fall into disobedience, it is as if He removes a degree of His protection and allows us to be enslaved by sin until we come to our senses and cry out to Him again. Thus He shows us, yet again, our desperate need of Him. What He desires above all is that we keep a sincere and pure devotion to Christ, which will guard us from allowing anything else to take His place in our hearts.

Can we begin to understand what God must feel when He sees us putting something other than Him at the centre of our hearts? We hear Him warn us not to put anything in His place —not out of desperation, but anger that we should forsake Him, mixed with longing for our relationship to be restored to everything it was meant to be: *"For My people have committed two evils: They have forsaken Me, the fountain of living waters, And hewn themselves cisterns —broken cisterns that can hold no water..."* (Jeremiah 2:13).

He longs to hear us say, *Whom have I in heaven but You? And there is none upon earth that I desire besides You. My flesh and my heart fail; But God is the strength of my heart and my portion forever...* (Psalm 73:25).

THE ONE AND ONLY

The one and only begotten Son
The one and only God and Saviour
The one and only soon coming King
Our Lord Jesus Christ

The only perfect sacrificial Lamb
The only Holy One
The only God who loved the world so much
He gave His only Son

The only name by which we can be saved
The only Living One
The only Mediator who can stand
Between man and a holy God

The only One who speaks in our defence
The only Righteous One
The only Judge of the whole world
Who holds the keys of life and death

The only One who made the universe
The only Mighty One
The One who holds the future in His hands
The King of time and space

The one and only begotten Son
The one and only God and Saviour
The one and only soon coming King
Our Lord Jesus Christ

Phil Lawson Johnston Copyright ©2003 Cloud Music

You shall be as gods
Perhaps the greatest idolatry of all is self-worship. Satan in the form
of the serpent promised to Eve, *"You will be like God"* (Genesis 3:5),
if she would only go against God's specific command. This original

promise of Satan, and acceptance of it by Adam and Eve, has had a devastating effect on all creation, and we can trace virtually all the suffering and evil that has taken place in the world to this one act of rebellion and defiance against God and His love. No wonder it is called the 'original sin', which led to the inherited fallen nature of mankind from which every one of us needs to be rescued. All praise to God for sending Jesus to be the perfect sacrifice that saved us from the effects of this great fall from grace, giving us a new nature with the propensity to love and follow God instead of disobeying Him.

We can see how much of the world's thinking and religious philosophy owes its origin to this promise of Satan's. Secular humanism and most postmodern philosophy have this self-centredness at its core. This is manifest, for example, in 'situation ethics', in which one's behaviour and moral choices is evaluated only by reference to the situation one is faced with, not by any external absolute standard. As soon as you abandon unchanging, absolute truths, you become the judge who decides between what is right and wrong; in other words, you make yourself 'god'. Read again what God commanded, and compare that with what Satan promised. *And the LORD God commanded the man, saying, "Of every tree in the garden you may freely eat; but of the tree of the knowledge of good and evil you shall not eat, for in the day that you eat of it you shall surely die..."* (Genesis 2:17). When the serpent said to the woman, *"You will not surely die,"* and, *"For God knows that in the day you eat of it your eyes will be opened, and you will be like God, knowing good and evil"*, the lie was offered: that you do not need God, that you can do it without him, make your own decisions; that you are the master of your own destiny, so do not be restricted by codes and morals; whatever suits you will be fine, and so on.

Most of what goes under the title of 'new age' philosophy is basically following that very same promise: 'Find your full potential, search for the god within you', is the cry. It is much the same as classic pantheism, which sees god in everything and everything as god. The antidote to such self-worship is to discover the mystery of *Christ in you, the hope of glory.* (See Colossians 1:27). The mystery referred to is not something hidden or 'mysterious' in the modern sense of the word, but literally *a secret revealed,* something that is made known by God Himself. Receiving Christ as Saviour and Lord enables us to truly worship Him —the One who promised believers that He would dwell in us and we in Him.

They will be like them

One can discover what someone's god is by seeing what they sacrifice most for – money, sex, power, ambition, sport and ideology, even family and career, are classic 'gods' of our day, and society tends to resemble its idols. Graham Tomlin, Vice Principal of Wycliffe Hall, Oxford says: "The kind of person I am or am going to become, is governed by what I worship."

Those who make them are like them; so is everyone who trusts in them (Psalm 115:8).

If one's 'god' is aggressive and vindictive, then one will show similar characteristics. One can see this throughout history most clearly in those dictators and emperors who have been almost deified by their followers. Many Roman emperors, Hitler, Stalin, Amin, Saddam etc., were all exalted figures who created societies which mirrored their own vile personalities. Ideologies themselves can become gods, such as Nazism, communism and even capitalism in its worst forms. Psalm 115 goes on to exhort the people of God to instead, *...trust in the LORD... trust in the LORD... trust in the LORD.* (See vv. 9 – 11).

In true worship we dethrone the idols that attract us so much, and the gods we have put our trust in, and turn to the one true God revealed to us in Jesus Christ. Why settle for second-best when the best is readily available to us? There are not many people who have studied Jesus who would deny that He is the most perfect person who has ever lived. Believers and non-believers alike have admired him, whether or not they have put their trust in Him; and there cannot be a better character by whom to allow one's life to be shaped. If we have a desire to be like Him, then one way to start is to worship Him alone. Having Him living in us means that He puts within us the power within to become like Him.

JESUS THE LOVELINESS OF GOD

My Lord is higher than the mountains and the stars.
My Lord is more glorious
Than the sunset, sky on fire;

Jesus, the loveliness of God,
Shining brighter than the sun;
Jesus, the glory of God,
Revealed to man,
Revealed to man.

My Lord is mightier than
Thunder and the sea,
My Lord is closer than
A brother to you and me.

My Lord is greater than
All other gods known to man;
My Lord is more precious than
The jewels in your hand.

O Lord, how lovely You are….

Phil Lawson Johnston Copyright ©1998 Cloud Music/IQ Music

Sacrificial worship

We read much about the requirement of sacrifice in worship under the old covenant, which has been surpassed by the once-for-all sacrifice of Jesus Himself on the cross, but the principle of not counting anything above God remains an important aspect of our worship: *I also count all things loss for the excellence of the knowlege of Christ Jesus my Lord, for whom I have suffered the loss of all things, and count them as rubbish, that I may gain Christ* (Philippians 3:8).

Whether we live or die, Jesus is our lasting treasure; *"For where your treasure is, there your heart will be also"* (Matthew 6:21). And He is worth sacrificing everything for. Amazingly, Abraham even regarded the prospect of sacrificing his own son as worship. It is not really worship until you lay something you value before God. David recognised this: *"...nor will I offer burnt offerings to the LORD my God with that which costs me nothing"* (II Samuel 24:24).

C.T. Studd gave up the pleasures and comfort of home to go to China as a missionary, and he was asked whether he felt the sacrifice was worth it. He replied that it was no sacrifice at all and that it would have been if he had stayed at home and missed out on all God had for him.

We can see how Jesus values costly sacrifice in the way He responded to the widow who gave all that she owned. (See Mark 12:43), and to the woman who broke the alabaster bottle and anointed Him with perfume that was worth a year's wages. (Matthew 26:6ff). She gave what amounted to her entire inheritance.

More than offerings, though, God looks for mercy and for us to acknowledge Him. *"For I desire mercy and not sacrifice, and the knowledge of God more than burnt offerings"* (Hosea 6:6).

We are called to offer spiritual sacrifices of praise and thanksgiving: *Therefore by Him* [Jesus] *let us continually offer the sacrifice of praise to God, that is, the fruit of our lips, giving thanks to His name. But do not forget to do good and to share, for with such sacrifices God is pleased* (Hebrews 13:15–16). *Coming to Him as to a living stone, rejected indeed by men, but chosen by God and precious, you also, as living stones, are being built up a spiritual house, a holy priesthood, to offer up spiritual sacrifices acceptable to God through Jesus Christ.* (I Peter 2:4–5).

A glad response of praise and thanksgiving for all that God has done for us is not much of a sacrifice to make, if our hearts are full of the Spirit and in love with Jesus. However there are the times when we do not feel like giving praise, when we are hurt, or going through tough circumstances, and to lift our hearts is something of an effort. Perhaps we have questions of God, asking why He seems to be silent or inactive, and praise almost seems inappropriate. Those are the times that it becomes a sacrifice.

I remember the weekend when David Watson, the well-loved teacher, author and evangelist, died after a fight against cancer. I was leading the worship on the Sunday evening at Holy Trinity Brompton and, as was the practice then, we had chosen and printed all the songs earlier in the week. I saw that they were songs full of majestic praise and wondered how on earth we were going to sing them in the light of his death, but there was nothing much we could do. The announcement of his death was made at the beginning of the service and then we began to praise. Rather than seeming inappropriate, the songs just seemed to express all that we wanted to say to God in thanks for David's life, and it was one of the most wonderful services I can remember. It also showed me how the Holy Spirit can influence our choices in advance of unforeseen events.

The greatest sacrifice we can give is the offering of ourselves in response to all that God has done for us. *I beseech you therefore, brethren, by the mercies of God, that you present your bodies a living sacrifice, holy, acceptable to God, which is your reasonable service* (Romans 12:1).

Moreover, God loves our obedience far above whatever we sacrifice: *Has the LORD as great delight in burnt offerings and sacrifices, as in obeying the voice of the LORD? Behold, to obey is better than sacrifice, and to heed better than the fat of rams. For rebellion is as the sin of witchcraft, and stubbornness is as iniquity and idolatry* (I Samuel 15:22–23).

A surrendered life is a beautiful and pleasing thing to God and is the kind of worship that He seeks from us. He is calling us to live a life like Jesus: *Therefore be imitators of God as dear children. And walk in love, as Christ also has loved us, and given Himself for us, an offering and a sacrifice to God for a sweet-smelling aroma* (Ephesians 5:1–2).

The beauty of holiness

He is a holy God, and is calling us to be holy as He is: *...As obedient children, not conforming yourselves to the former lusts, as in your ignorance; but as He who called you is holy, you also be holy in all your conduct, because it is written, "Be holy, for I am holy'* (I Peter 1:14–15). *Oh, worship the LORD in the beauty of holiness! Tremble before Him, all the earth* (Psalm 96:9).

How can we, being unworthy, flawed and weak begin to be holy like Him? The answer is that of ourselves we cannot, but He has made it possible by giving us everything we need. Peter gives us the full answer: *...His divine power has given to us all things that pertain to life and godliness, through the knowledge of Him who called us by* *glory and virtue, by which have been given to us exceedingly great and precious promises, that through these you may be partakers of the divine nature, having escaped the corruption that is in the world through lust.* (II Peter 1:3). J.C. Ryle, in his book entitled *Holiness*, described holiness like this: 'Holiness is the habit of being of one mind with God... hating what He hates, loving what He loves and measuring everything in this world by the standard of His word. He who most entirely agrees with God, he is the most holy man. A holy man will endeavour to shun every known sin and to keep every known commandment. He will have a decided bent of mind towards God, a hearty desire to do His will — a greater fear of displeasing Him than of displeasing the world, and a love to all His ways.... A holy man will strive to be like our Lord Jesus Christ.'

God wants us to be dead to the world and alive to Him, not living separated *from* the world, but living distinctively *in* it with Him. Jesus prayed, *"I do not pray that You should take them out of the world, but that You should keep them from the evil one"* (John 17:15). Paul elaborates on this: *For you died, and your life is hidden with Christ in God* (Colossians 3:3). We must never think that we can make holiness our 'way' to God. Holiness is not the way *to* God but the way *of* God, and our holiness is founded on His holiness. It is a gift that we do not deserve or earn, but which He planned for us to have before the world began: *...He chose us in Him before the foundation of the world, that we should be holy and without blame before Him in love* (Ephesians 1:4). The source of that holiness is His life in us, and the only way to maintain that life is through a relationship dependent on Him, of intimate obedience and love in the power of His Holy Spirit. It is following the principle of 'WWJD', as many now wear on a wristband, asking, 'What Would Jesus Do?' —and then trusting Him for the strength to do it.

Jesus Himself is our model for holiness. and gives us perhaps the most perfect 'worship cry' in the Garden of Gethsemane, when faced with His greatest trial: *"...nevertheless not My will, but Yours, be done."* Holiness is impossible without His help, but it is a beautiful thing to see in others. Unless our lives begin to show something of the beauty of His holiness flowing from our hearts, then the words that we say and sing will lack real meaning. However 'religious' we may seem on the outside, God is not fooled if the truth is not really living in us, and the people we meet are not fooled either, as a rule. God does not consider the outward appearance as we do; He looks at the heart. (See I Samuel 16:7). Jesus was very harsh with those religious people whose outward veneer did not match what was going on inside. He condemned their vain attempts to fool others by saying the right words whilst their hearts were not engaged, and he quoted the Scripture that says, *"...in vain they worship Me."* (See Matthew 15:9).

To please God we have to exercise faith. This implies belief in His existence and the fact that He created us and loves us, but faith also means personal trust. Faith includes having no other gods but Him; our worship of Him being lived out in action and not just words, and believing that He wants to reward us as we seek to come close to Him. *But without faith it is impossible to please Him, for he who comes to God must believe that He is and that He is a rewarder of those who diligently seek Him* (Hebrews 11:6).

We have been created to give God the worship of our lives. We will not be satisfied—and God's requirement of us will not be satisfied—until we begin to fulfil that which we were made for.

Don McMinn underlines the point that God made us to please Him with our praises, likening this to the making of a musical instrument; and our worship of God involves the whole person: body, mind and spirit.[3]

There is much work still to be done in all of us, which one day will be completed. Paul declares this: *...being confident of this very thing, that He who has begun a good work in you will complete it until the day of Jesus Christ* (Philippians 1:6).

Every human being who has ever lived, and everyone who will live, is unique and yet made in the image of the one holy God who made all things. We are all called to worship that one God, whatever nationality, culture, tongue or ethnic group we may be. Our souls will not find their true resting place until we do indeed worship the only one who is worthy of our lives and our highest praise. That is the song He wants to sing to us. This song, which was inspired by Isaiah 40, expresses that truth for me:

To whom will you compare Me?
Who is my equal? Says the Holy One

THE SONG OF THE FATHER'S HEART

Lift your eyes and look to the heavens
Who created what you see?

Why do you say, O Jacob
And complain, O Israel
My way is hidden from the Lord
My cause is disregarded by my God?

Do you not know? Have you not heard?
The Lord is the everlasting God
Do you not know?
Have you not heard?
He is Creator of the ends of the earth
He is Creator of the ends of the earth

Who has measured the waters
In the hollow of His hand?
Who has held the earth in balance
Or weighed the mountains on the scales?

Who has understood the mind of the Lord
And whom did He consult?
Before Him all nations are as nothing
They are regarded as dust

Do you not know?
Have you not heard?
Have you not understood since the earth was made
Do you not know?
Have you not heard?
He sits enthroned above the circle of the earth
He sits enthroned above the circle of the earth

To whom then will you compare God?
What image will you liken Him to?
He reduces rulers to nothing
He blows on them, the whirlwind sweeps them away

Yet He gives strength to the weary
And increases the power of the weak
Those who hope in the Lord
Will renew their strength
They will soar on eagles' wings

Do you not know?
Have you not heard?
Has it not been told you from the beginning?
Do you not know?
Have you not heard?
He is the sovereign Lord
The everlasting God
He is the sovereign Lord
The everlasting God

Extract taken from the song "To Whom Will You Compare Me?"
by Phil Lawson Johnston
Copyright ©1985 Thankyou Music*

"Father, You alone created the heavens and the earth and are worthy of all our worship. We know that You are a jealous God and will not share Your glory and Your place in our lives with any other so-called god or idol. Give each of us an undivided heart and help us to keep You at the very centre of our lives, in the way we think, speak and act, that we may be for the praise of Your glory, in the name of Jesus. Amen."

Notes

[1] John Piper, *Desiring God* 1986, 1996, 2003 Multnomah Publishers © Desiring God Foundation.
[2] *The Knowledge of the Holy*, James Clarke & Co, London, p.80.
[3] See Don McMinn *The Practice of Praise* 1992, Word Music, p.95.

5

TRUTH AND LOVE—
WORSHIP IN SPIRIT AND TRUTH

There is a word unshakeable
That nothing can destroy
Which has stood forever and will be
Unchanged eternally
The world may pass away
But the truth will never die
There is a word unshakeable
That no-one can deny

The world will tend to love the lie
That Satan has employed
To cast a doubt upon the Truth
And keep us in the dark
But God has made it firm
Not built on shifting sand
His very word unshakeable
The Rock on which we stand

There is a love unquenchable
That hate cannot destroy
A love that drives away all fear
And warms the coldest heart
A love that is prepared
To suffer and to die
A love that heals the deepest wound
And heeds the faintest cry

There is a bond unbreakable
That none can tear apart
That will hold together for all time
A fortress for the heart
For God has made it so
That truth and love go hand in hand
Love has spoken to the world
And His truth will ever stand

Phil Lawson Johnston Copyright ©2003 Cloud Music

One of the interesting things about the Bible is that there are very few instructions on how we should conduct a service of worship. We see many instances of individuals and groups at worship, but there is no set liturgy or pattern that we are told to follow. In the Old Testament there are very detailed directions on how to build the tabernacle or temple and how to conduct sacrifices, but none that gives us much of a clue as to how much singing, praying, preaching there was to be. It is a wonderful thing that God has entrusted to us the responsibility of choosing how we want to create a service of worshipful significance.

The only direct teaching that Jesus gave us about worship other than, perhaps, the first commandment, is found in John chapter four during His dialogue with the woman of Samaria. He has been talking about her dubious marital status and she responds by raising historical differences between the Jews and the Samaritans over worship. She says, *"Sir, I perceive that you are a prophet. Our fathers worshipped on this mountain, and you Jews say that in Jerusalem is the place where one ought to worship."*

Jesus replies to her, *"Woman, believe Me, the hour is coming when you will neither on this mountain nor in Jerusalem, worship the Father. You worship what you do not know; we know what we worship, for salvation is from the Jews. But the hour is coming, and now is, when the true worshippers will worship the Father in spirit and truth; for the Father is seeking such to worship Him. God is Spirit, and those who worship Him must worship in spirit and truth"* (John 4:19ff).

In this chapter, we will unpack this theme of worship in spirit and in truth.

The place of worship

One of the first things we learn from this passage is that worship of the Father is no longer dependent on a place. As we read elsewhere, we (believers) are now the temple of the Holy Spirit, individually and corporately, when we come together. (See I Corinthians 3:16; II Corinthians 6:16; I Peter 2:5; I Corinthians 6:19.) Wherever we are becomes the place of worship. It has been pointed out that we no longer go to the sanctuary, we take the sanctuary with us. However, there can be a sense in which a revelation of the Truth can drive us to approach God and worship Him. *Oh, send out Your light and Your truth! Let them lead me; Let them bring me to Your holy hill, And to Your tabernacle. Then I will go to the altar of God, To God, my exceeding joy; And on the harp I will praise you, O God, my God* (Psalm 43:3–4).

The Father seeks worshippers

Note that what Jesus says is that the Father is seeking *worshippers*, not only worship. In other words He is seeking relationship with a people, rather than performance of a particular ritual. It is the most wonderful relief to me that worship is relational and not a set of regulations from which we must not deviate. Of course, when we come to put together a meeting or service, we seek to give God the best we can in terms of quality of music, talk, prayer etc., but the underlying priority is for us to meet with Him —personally, and as a people.

Furnace, fuel, heat, fire

Worship in spirit and in truth has been aptly described in terms of a furnace of fire. The human spirit, or the renewed heart, is the furnace; the truth about who God is and what He has done is the fuel; the heat generated is our expression of adoration, thanks, praise, repentance, obedience, and living a life of love —but it is all nothing without fire, which is the work of the Holy Spirit, without Whom no genuine heat can be produced. Truth without fire becomes dry and arid, whereas fire without truth becomes chaotic and burns itself out. It is only the Holy Spirit who can quicken our worship as He takes the Truth and ignites it within us. He makes it real. A. W. Tozer writes movingly of the ingredients of worship being present at the point of adoration of God; that fire which comes from the Holy Spirit providing the 'heat'.[1]

Strong feelings for God, held and shaped by the truth, become the core of real worship. Just like marriage, worship is an affair of the mind and the heart. The form of our worship should provide opportunities for us to understand in our minds the truth of God's glory and reality, but also for our hearts to respond to His beauty and be set on fire. How we express ourselves in worship, whether exuberantly or quietly, needs to reflect both.

Word and Spirit

There are two very similar and parallel passages, in which Paul shows the link between God's word, the Spirit and worship. Firstly, in Ephesians 5:18f, he commands that we, ...*Be filled with the Spirit, speaking to one another in psalms and hymns and spiritual songs, singing and making melody in your heart to the Lord, giving thanks always for all things to God the Father in the name of our Lord Jesus Christ.* Secondly, in Colossians 3:16, he encourages us: *Let the word of Christ dwell in you richly in all wisdom, teaching and admonishing one another in psalms and hymns and spiritual songs, singing with grace in your hearts to the Lord. And whatever you do in word or deed, do all in the name of the Lord Jesus, giving thanks to God the Father through Him.*

By the inspiration of God's Spirit and His truth, Paul links singing with teaching, admonishing, giving thanks, and extends them all into our daily lives in everything we do. Incidentally, the word 'psalm' literally means the plucking of a stringed instrument, a sacred song accompanied by an instrument or a song of praise; 'hymn', a song of praise to God, and 'spiritual songs' are songs (*lit.* Gk. Ode) inspired by the Spirit.

The combination of Spirit and Word is powerful and life giving, as Jesus says to His disciples, *"The words that I speak to you are spirit, and they are life."* (See John 6:63). Again, we read in James 1:18, *Of His own will He brought us forth by the word of truth, that we might be a kind of firstfruits of His creatures.*

It is a highly creative combination, as we see from the beginning of creation. Genesis 1:1–2 tells us: *In the beginning God created the heavens and the earth. The earth was without form, and void; and darkness was on the face of the deep. And the Spirit of God was hovering over the face of the waters. Then God said, "Let there be light"; and there was light.* Here we have God, the Spirit and His Word, commanding something into being from nothing and it bursting forth into existence. In a worship gathering when the power of the same Holy Trinity is at work, we can begin to see what potential there is for God's creativity and new creation to break forth in people's lives. We could then have the situation described in I Corinthians 14:24, which must be the dream of every evangelistically minded church leader: *But if all prophesy, and an unbeliever or an uninformed person comes in, he is convinced by all, he is convicted by all. And thus the secrets of his heart are revealed; and falling down on his face, he will worship God and report that God is truly among you.* The image comes to my mind of the Spirit of God hovering over a congregation as He did at creation, and the Word of God dwelling richly in people's hearts as they worship Jesus before the throne of God; there is expectancy of something powerful happening in their midst that would cause believers and non-believers alike to fall on their faces before Him in awe and wonder as they do in countless passages in Revelation, or as they did at the time when the cloud of God's glorious presence filled Solomon's temple. Then something so dramatic took place that, *...the priests could not continue ministering because of the cloud; for the glory of the LORD filled the house of God* (II Chronicles 5:14). How often have you seen a service stopped by the presence of God? Before I get too carried away, let us now consider what is meant by 'Spirit' and 'truth' in more detail.

In Spirit

I have read some writers who interpret 'worship in spirit' as only referring to the human spirit, the inner place where we now meet God, and then others who say it refers to the Holy Spirit and the importance of His inspiration and presence for our worship to be true. I am sure it is both. I sometimes think of it as our spirits reaching out to touch God's Spirit, or our hearts reaching out to His. Our worship is more an attitude of heart than an outward performance, and the Holy Spirit, who indwells every believer in Jesus, can take worship from being a dead external formalism and ritual and turn it into something that is alive, vibrant and life-changing. Worshipping in spirit is the opposite of worshipping in merely external ways, which can be nothing more than empty traditionalism. Worship must have 'heart' and 'head', engaging emotions and intellect. Truth without heart produces dead orthodoxy, whereas heart without truth can be empty and shallow, or even worse, lead to heresy. The Bible continually links love and the law, for example in Romans 13:10, *love is the fulfillment of the law*. It is more than just an effort of the will, but the quickening of the heart to respond to the truth of God with joy. It is in the Spirit that we meet God the Trinity. The Spirit reveals Jesus and the Father to us, leads us into all Truth and changes us into the likeness of Christ. The Holy Spirit turns worship from being a formality to a feast, involving every part of us including the emotions. Tozer said, 'The work of the Spirit is among other things to rescue the redeemed man's emotions, to restring his harp and open up again the wells of sacred joy which have been stopped up by sin.'

There seems to be great fear of emotions, particularly amongst some British Anglicans, even though it was Bishop Cuthbert Bardsley who said that emotionalism was not the chief problem of the Church of England! Emotions are a part of our make-up as human beings, and one only has to go to a football match to see that even the British can get excited. It seems we fear the extremes of emotionalism, which have beset some sections of the church at certain times, but if we are to follow the Bible in all its fullness, abundant joy and exuberance are commonplace, and more often than not a result of the activity of God's Spirit. In Philippians 3:1–3, Paul exhorts us to, *...rejoice in the Lord*, because we are those who *...worship God in the Spirit, rejoice in Christ Jesus, and have no confidence in the flesh*. From this we learn that worship in spirit is to be Christ-centred, and dependent on the Spirit, with ample reason for us to express joy.

We can spend a lot of time and energy getting very worked up about what we want from worship, as if it were purely for our own benefit, without much consideration of what God might want. Warren Wiersbe has wisely pointed out that we are to worship God because He is worthy, not for what we might get out of it. If we are just seeking what we can get from it, Wiersbe reminds us, then we are making God our servant rather than our Lord. 'Selfish gratification' becomes the goal.[2]

Worship is primarily for God not for us, but at the same time we can also make the mistake of thinking that it is more holy to have no self-interest at all in our worship of God. I believe firmly that God is more pleased when we delight in His magnificence than when we are so unmoved by it that we scarcely feel anything. Without such delight in Him, 'worship' can become just a duty. To take your wife out to dinner and say, "It's my duty", would be an insult, but to say, "It's my joy" would be just what she wants to hear. David tells us to delight ourselves in the Lord, and ...*He shall give you the desires of your heart.* (See Psalm 37:4); and, *You will show me the path of life; In Your presence is fullness of joy; At Your right hand are pleasures forevermore* (Psalm 16:11). Paul says, *Rejoice in the Lord always. Again I will say, Rejoice!* —repeating himself to add emphasis.

When you see something that causes you to be awestruck, like being caught up in stunning music or a beautiful painting, you are not thinking: to what end am I experiencing this? There will be no thought in your head other than wonder and exhilaration. Self-consciousness can kill joy, because as soon as you begin examining your emotions and motives they have gone like the wind. Real joy is self-forgetful, because it is when we take our eyes off ourselves and focus them on to Him that our hearts can be affected with joy. The one who has all our attention is the One who is being glorified, not ourselves, whereas the one who sets himself above God is the one who comes just to give rather than to get — making himself the benefactor rather than God. John Piper develops this theme in many of his writings and I am immensely grateful for how he has helped me understand that there is no shame in our enjoyment of God. It is through the Spirit that we have access to this great joy, and it is He who makes it real for us. We do not come to worship God in order just to feel good, but it is part of our faith to believe Him, for: *...without faith it is impossible to please Him, for he who comes to God must believe that He is, and that He is a rewarder of those who diligently seek him* (Hebrews 11:6); and we could be accused of being churlish not to accept all that He wants us to have, for, *My soul shall be satisfied as with marrow and fatness, And my mouth shall praise You with joyful lips* (Psalm 63:5).

One of the keys to effective worship is expectancy. What are we expecting of God as we come to Him? Does He really want to meet with us and bless us, or should we expect nothing of Him? It is the Spirit who gives us a thirst and a yearning for Him which can only be satisfied by Him. *My soul thirsts for God, for the living God. When shall I come and appear before God?* (Psalm 42:2). Without a Spirit-given thirst and an expectancy based on what God has promised, our worship of Him can become lacklustre and dry. One of the main reasons we come together is to encourage one another, and our ability to genuinely affect each other's lives will be governed very much by how much we ourselves have received as we meet with God. As we receive from Him encouragement and blessing, so we will be able to encourage and bless others more effectively. *Blessed be the God and Father of our Lord Jesus Christ, the Father of mercies and God of all comfort, who comforts us in all our tribulation, that we may be able to comfort those who are in any trouble, with the comfort with which we ourselves are comforted by God* (II Corinthians 1:3–4).

WINGS OF THE WIND

The wind blows where it pleases
The wind blows where it wills
No man can direct it
The tempest or the still
You hear the sound
Feel the breeze
Yet you cannot tell
Where it comes from
Or where it goes

The wind of God is rising
Blowing where He wills
Stirring up His people
Making dry bones live
You hear the sound
Feel His breath
Move your heart
Out of slumber into life

Jesus, ride on the wings of the wind
Breathe on us and we shall live
Spread abroad through us
The knowledge of Your name
Spread abroad through us
The fragrance of life

Come blow on Your garden
Spirit give the increase
That the world may know
And taste its fruit
Take delight
In its Saviour's love
Find salvation and find life

Jesus, ride on the wings of the wind
Breathe on us and we shall live
Spread abroad through us
The knowledge of Your name
Spread abroad through us
The fragrance of life

Jesus, ride on the wings of the wind
Jesus, ride on the wings of the wind
Jesus, ride....

Extract taken from the song "Wings of the Wind" by Phil Lawson Johnston
Copyright ©1997 Thankyou Music*

In truth

If our worship is just all heart and feelings, with no reference to the Bible, we can very easily fall into the trap of losing touch with the truth about God. This is how heresies start and how strong, domineering leaders, supposedly the inspired spokespeople of God, can take groups down a false trail which inevitably ends up being destructive, sometimes horrendously so. Ill-discipline in study of Scripture can lead to breakdown of affective worship. Our concept of God is crucially important to our worship, and we get our concept of God from His Word, the Bible, as Tozer and many others have pointed out. When the substance of God's truth is corrupted and falls into liberal interpretation, then the reality of worship suffers also. If the difference between a liberal pilot and an orthodox pilot is that one believes the manual and the other does not, I know which one I would rather trust!

Jesus regarded God's word as sacrosanct; and, as the Holy Spirit Himself is the author, it is not surprising that Spirit and truth cannot be separated from each other.

The account of the woman of Samaria who did not know whom she was worshipping, nor who Jesus was, teaches us that true worship must rest on a true perception of who God is. Paul teaches us to let the word of Christ dwell in us richly, and there is indeed richness in the word of God. There are untold blessings and promises to be found and experienced, like a pearl of great price. The psalmist affirms this repeatedly, writing of the statutes, judgments and commandments of God: *More to be desired are they than gold, Yea, than much fine gold; Sweeter also than honey and the honeycomb* (Psalm 19:10).

The apostles recognised that the truth they had in Jesus was more valuable than anything else. When many disciples turned away from Him because of His challenging teaching, Jesus asked the apostles whether they were going to leave as well, and Peter answered for them, *"Lord, to whom shall we go? You have the words of eternal life. Also we have come to believe and know that You are the Christ, the Son of the living God"* (John 6:68–69).

TIMELESS WORDS

We sit here at Your feet
Where else could we go
To hear the Master speak
Words that feed the soul?
Grace and favour, wisdom and truth
Are on the Master's lips
Ready to eclipse ungodly thought
Grace and favour, wisdom and truth
Timeless words of life
Timeless words of life

We look up to Your face
With open ready hearts
To hear the Shepherd's voice
Shed light upon our path
Love and mercy, purity and peace
Are in the Shepherd's face
So, turning, we retrace our wayward steps
Love and mercy, purity and peace
Timeless words of life
Timeless words of life

So give us ears to hear
The still small voice of calm
The subtle and the clear
The warning and the balm
Word of Jesus
Piercing like a sword
In the Master's hand
Helping us to stand and overcome
Word of Jesus, piercing like a sword
Timeless word of life
Timeless word of life

Extract taken from the song "Timeless Words" by Phil Lawson Johnston
Copyright ©1997 Thankyou Music*

What is truth?

Many people have been influenced by the utterances of high profile public figures who have spoken dismissively of truth, or who have demonstrated little regard for truthfulness, whether in public or private matters. So it is scarcely surprising that our claim to the absolute truth of God, revealed in His Word, meets with sceptical minds. Pontius Pilate asked, at Jesus' trial, "What is truth?" Much philosophical speculation has involved questioning the veracity of universal truth claims of any sort other than those of formal logic, and, in today's popular thought, truth is all too often seen as whatever you want to make it: 'whatever is *true for you* is true'! Postmodern philosophy tends to discount any absolutes, and anybody who dares to say that there is such a thing as eternal, unchanging truth, runs the risk of being accused of arrogance and intolerance. But it is not arrogant to state the revealed truth of God's Word —because it is not *ours* as such; rather, it has been given to us. There is no shortage of people who—despite the prevailing mood of philosophical and practical scepticism concerning truth claims in general—really are searching for purpose and meaning, and want to have definite answers to life's big questions; hence, for example, the popularity of the Alpha Course throughout the world. Nonetheless, it remains the case that God's revealed truth is under attack, especially the truth of statements regarding the uniqueness of Jesus, His divinity and His being the only Way to God the Father. Many liberal thinkers would see it as intolerant to deny that other religions are true. But Jesus Himself has left us no alternative. *"I am the way, the truth, and the life. No one comes to the Father except through Me"* (John 14:6).

Singing the truth

The singing of hymns and songs plays a huge part in the proclaiming of the truth, and one can learn a lot about a church's theology by listening to what they are singing. Praise declares the truth about God, and many of the great hymns were written as a means of teaching those truths to people who were illiterate. Singing the truth about God reminds us of who is in control and our utter dependence on Him. It reminds us of how great and holy He is, and our desperate need of forgiveness and grace. For example: *Honour and majesty are before Him; Strength and beauty are in His sanctuary. Give to the LORD,*

O families of the peoples, Give to the LORD glory and strength. Give to the LORD the glory due His name; bring an offering, and come into His courts. Oh, worship the LORD in the beauty of holiness! Tremble before Him, all the earth (Psalm 96:6–9).

Praise also reminds our enemy, Satan and all his minions, of who is our Lord. Praise silences the lies of the enemy with the truths of God.

Another meaning of the Greek word used for truth in John chapter four (*aletheia*) is *reality*. Our worship must be real. It must relate to real life and not just be an imaginary escape from reality, an interlude in the week before we get back to the 'real' world. It is important not only that our own individual worship feeds our corporate worship, but that we take care that corporate worship does not become a substitute for personal worship. There is sometimes a danger of our corporate worship becoming an escape from the realities of the world, rather than a place where the realities and pain in people's lives can be brought together and expressed, knowing that God is not untouched by them. The Psalms are full of real feelings of despair as well as joy, complaint as well as thanksgiving. In John chapter four, the story is not detached from reality, but is all about adultery, hunger, thirst and racial prejudice. The Jews avoided all contact with Samaritans, regarding them as inferior. The Father is seeking worshippers, even those who have been exposed as adulterers and outcasts in society. The woman became an effective evangelist, telling the whole town to come and meet Jesus, many of whom became believers and thus worshippers. So often, those who have the greatest awareness of their needs—moral, spiritual and physical—have the most passionate hearts for worship.

It must be real, also, in the sense that when we draw near to God we must believe He is truly there, and longing to meet with us; as we saw from Hebrews 11:6, expectancy is vital! If we do not expect anything to happen, or do not believe we are really going to meet with God, then we should not be surprised if little happens. But if God wants us to come to worship *face to face* with Him, as Moses did in the Tent of Meeting (see Exodus 33:11), then we, for our part, cannot be content with anything less. We can almost feel the expectancy amongst the believers in Acts when they met together to worship and pray. They knew experientially that God was going to act, because they had seen Him act before. We are encouraged to come confidently: *Therefore, brethren, having boldness to enter the Holiest by the blood of Jesus, by a new and living way.... ...let us draw near....* (See Hebrews 10:19–22.)

So we are to come to worship *knowing* that we are welcome; this is knowledge based on God's self-revelation in His written word; it is founded on Jesus, who is Himself the Truth; and we are spurred on by the urging and assurance given by the Holy Spirit.

As in so much of the Christian life, we can see true worship has a perfect balance: between love and truth; feelings and facts; heart and mind. God feeds and blesses us in the true worship that is marked by these things; and when we begin to get the balance between them right, the worship that we offer will deepen, and we will find a new freedom to *be* and to *do* as God desires.

The words of a Puritan, John Preston, sum this up aptly: 'O show me yourself that I might love you.'

I PRAY

I pray that out of His glorious riches
He may strengthen you with power
Through His Spirit in your inner being
So that Christ may dwell in your hearts through faith
That Christ may dwell in your hearts

I pray being rooted and established in love
You may have power with all saints
To grasp how wide and long and high
And deep is the love of Christ
How deep is the love of Christ

I pray you'd know this love that surpasses knowledge
That you may be filled
To the measure of all the fulness of God
With all the fulness of God

And now to Him who is able to do
Immeasurably more than all we ask
And now to Him who is able to do
Immeasurably more than we imagine
According to His power that is at work within us
To Him be glory in the church
And in Christ Jesus throughout all generations
For ever and ever Amen
For ever and ever Amen

Ephesians 3:16–21

Extract taken from the song "I Pray" by Phil Lawson Johnston
Copyright ©1997 Thankyou Music*

"Father, we thank you that You have provided for us not only a revelation of Yourself, so that we might know what You are like, but also You have given us Your Spirit to enable us to live the truth. Help us to find the right balance in our worship between our knowledge of the Truth and our experience of the Truth. Help us to become the worshippers in spirit and in truth that You are seeking, for Jesus' sake. Amen."

Notes

[1] See A.W.Tozer, *Whatever Happened to Worship*, 1985, Kingsway. p.69.
[2] See Warren Wiersbe, *Real Worship*, 2000 Baker Books.

6

THE FEAR OF THE LORD

THE FEAR OF THE LORD

Where is the wise man who fears the Lord
Who walks in all His ways
Following God with all his heart
And serving all his days?
For the fear of the Lord teaches wisdom
The fear of the Lord leads to life
The Spirit of the Lord will rest upon him
Who makes the fear of the Lord his delight

Let the fear of the Lord be upon us
Let godly fear be before our eyes
Let the fear of the Lord be our wisdom
Let godly fear be to us the light of life

The Lord God has shown us what is good
What He requires of us;
To act justly and to love mercy
To walk humbly with our God
The fear of the Lord is a refuge
A fortress in which we can hide
His mercy extends to those who fear Him
They are those in whom He confides

So who from among us will fear the Lord
And obey His every word?
No longer walk blindly in darkness
But trust in the name of God?
To fear the Lord is wisdom
To fear His name is life
O Spirit of God rest upon us
As we make the fear of God our delight

Phil Lawson Johnston
Copyright ©1997 Sovereign Lifestyle Music Ltd

Fear is one of the most powerful controlling factors in our lives. We generally fear something that is beyond our control, that which can have a detrimental effect on us, or can force us to do what we do not want to do. Evil regimes rule by fear; domineering parents and those in authority can enslave us through fear. People fear being vulnerable; they fear emotions, particularly here in northern Europe; they fear failure, and hate not being master of their own destiny. People fear for themselves, or for others who are close to them. It can stifle activity or drive one to respond irrationally or positively. Fear can be one of the reasons that determine why some people turn away from giving their lives to God, partly because it means surrendering control. The fear of what others may say can also cause paralysis of faith. As the Bible puts it, *The fear of man brings a snare, But whoever trusts in the LORD shall be safe* (Proverbs 29:25).

Biblical fear

The Bible speaks much about fear. There are good fears and bad fears; fears that are right to have and those which we have to get rid of. There is a healthy form of fear which warns us of danger, but should lead to us being prepared to face up to it rather than run from it. There are fears which all people experience at some stage, fears that enslave us, such as the fear of death: *...those who through fear of death were all their lifetime subject to bondage* (Hebrews 2:15); or fear of what the future may hold —which can be replaced with trust in God, through an understanding of His love for us. *There is no fear in love; but perfect love casts out fear, because fear involves torment. But he who fears has not made been made perfect in love. We love Him because He first loved us* (1John 4:18–19).

We can see from this that fear is overcome by love, and we only have to see our own children threatened to understand the truth of it. If they were in danger, one would not hesitate to act, however fearful the situation may be, because love is stronger than fear. And knowing we are God's children takes away the dread we might otherwise have of Him: *For you did not receive the spirit of bondage again to fear, but you received the Spirit of adoption by whom we cry out, "Abba, Father"* (Romans 8:15).

PERFECT LOVE

Perfect love, perfect love
Means that Jesus is near
Perfect love, perfect love
Leaves no room for my fear
Without warning a song
Seems to rise in my heart
As love finds a home
Seeking to set me apart
For Jesus alone

Perfect love, perfect love
Means that Jesus is here
Perfect love, perfect love
Is the cross I must bear

As a seed is sown
I must fall to the ground
And I must learn to die
Surrender myself to the sound
Of Jesus first not I

Extract taken from the song "Perfect Love"
by Phil Lawson Johnston
Copyright ©1978 Thankyou Music*

Anxiety

He does not want us to worry about anything; *"Therefore I say to you, do not worry about your life, what you will eat or what you will drink; nor about your body, what you will put on..."* (Matthew 6:25). *Be anxious for nothing, but in everything by prayer and supplication, with thanksgiving, let your requests be made known to God; and the peace of God, which surpasses all understanding, will guard your hearts and your minds through Christ Jesus* (Philippians 4:6–7).

And although He wants us to trust wholly in Him, He does not want us to live unconfidently. *For God has not given us a spirit of fear, but of power and of love and of a sound mind* (II Timothy 1:7).

It has been aptly said that, 'Both faith and fear sail into the harbour of your mind, but only faith should be allowed to anchor' and, 'We fear man so much because we fear God so little.'

The fear of God

The fear of God is what the Bible commends. It does not mean being scared of God, even though He may be scary to those who are in fear of judgment, but it does signify a holy, godly fear which comes from an understanding of God's greatness and power. The proper fear of God is characterised by awe and reverence in worship. *Therefore, since we are receiving a kingdom which cannot be shaken, let us have grace, by which we may serve God acceptably with reverence and godly fear. For our God is a consuming fire* (Hebrews 12:28–29).

It is described as the beginning of both knowledge and wisdom (see Proverbs 1:7; 9:10), and as the whole duty of man. *Let us hear the conclusion of the whole matter: Fear God and keep His commandments, for this is man's all* (Ecclesiastes 12:13).

It is what God requires of His people; *"And now, Israel, what does the LORD your God require of you, but to fear the LORD your God, to walk in all His ways and to love Him, to serve the LORD your God with all your heart and with all your soul, and to keep the commandments of the LORD and His statutes which I command you today for your good?"* (Deuteronomy 10:12–22). And it is an integral part of the closeness of our relationship with the Lord: *The secret of the LORD is with those who fear Him, and He will show them His covenant* (Psalm 25:14). It is to be at the centre of our lives as Christians: *And if you call on the Father, who without partiality judges according to each one's work, conduct yourselves throughout the time of your stay here in fear* (I Peter 1:17). *Honour all people. Love the brotherhood. Fear God. Honour the king* (I Peter 2:17); *...work out your own salvation with fear and trembling; for it is God who works in you both to will and to do for His good pleasure* (Philippians 2:12–13).

It is promised that those who fear the Lord will receive great blessing, along with their family: *Blessed is everyone who fears the LORD, who walks in His ways. When you eat the labour of your hands, you shall be happy, and it shall be well with you. Your wife shall be like a fruitful vine in the very heart of your house, Your children like olive plants all around your table. Behold, thus shall the man be blessed who fears the LORD* (Psalm 128:1–4).

A response of awe

As Jesus performed miracles and displayed the glory of God in what He did, we constantly read of the people responding by being filled with awe. This continued as the young church carried on the ministry of Jesus and performed many mighty wonders through the power of the Spirit. In Acts we read, for example: *So great fear came upon all those who heard these things* (5:5); *So great fear came upon all the church and upon all who heard these things* (5:11). *Then the churches throughout all Judea, Galilee, and Samaria had peace and were edified. And walking in the fear of the Lord and in the comfort of the Holy Spirit, they were multiplied* (9:31). *This became known both to all Jews and Greeks dwelling in Ephesus; and fear fell on them all, and the name of the Lord Jesus was magnified* (19:17).

Lack of the fear of God is seen as a companion to sinfulness. *An oracle within my heart concerning the transgression of the wicked: There is no fear of God before his eyes* (Psalm 36:1).

The fear of the Lord is directly related to worship, as we see throughout the book of Revelation. On many occasions we read the description of worship in heaven as a scene of awe and wonder, of the elders falling on their faces before the throne, the multitudes of angels and people giving glory to the Lamb. Songs of glory and praise are sung and God's enemies are defeated. An angel is, ...*flying in the midst of heaven, having the everlasting gospel to preach to those who dwell on the earth.* He says loudly, *"Fear God and give glory to Him, for the hour of His judgment has come; and worship Him who made heaven and earth, the sea and springs of water.* (See Revelation 14:6–7.)

"Do not be afraid"

As with so much of the Christian life, it is a question of balance. On the one hand we are exhorted to live in the fear of God, in respect for His awesomeness, as we have seen. On the other hand, whenever an angel appears, causing much consternation and fear, the first words always spoken are, *"Do not be afraid"*, whether it be the shepherds on the hill at Jesus' birth (Luke 2:9–10) or Zechariah the priest (Luke 1:12), or Mary, when the angel Gabriel appeared to her in Luke 1:30. Jesus said the same thing to the terrified disciples when He walked on the water (Matthew 14:27), at His transfiguration (Matthew 17:1), or when He met the women after His resurrection (Matthew 28:10). When He appeared in His glory to John, who fell at His feet as though dead, Jesus gently placed His right hand on him and said, *"Do not be afraid"* (Revelation 1:17). It is good to reflect this balance in the songs and hymns that we sing, whether it be, '...Bid my anxious fears subside'; '...and grace my fears relieved'; or—

> These, though we bring them in trembling and fearfulness,
> He will accept for the name that is dear;
> Mornings of joy give for evenings of tearfulness
> Trust for our trembling, and hope for our fear.

John Samuel Bewley Monsell (1811–75)

God-fearers

Some of the first Gentiles to be converted were described as God-fearing people, and it was that attitude to God which prepared them for the visitation of the Holy Spirit. Peter, who had been summoned to Cornelius's house by a vision from God, started to speak to them: *"In truth I perceive that God shows no partiality. But in every nation whoever fears Him and works righteousness is accepted by Him." While Peter was still speaking these words, the Holy Spirit fell upon all those who heard the word* (Acts 10:34,44).

Lack of fear

I have a sense that we have lost something of the proper sense of the fear of God that was normal to those in the early church. We are familiar with the, "Do not be afraid" of God, but less so with the, 'tremble before Him all the earth'. We often act very casually towards our awesome God, and although we attempt to recapture it in some of the songs we sing, when we come together we seem to lack the expectation of God acting and speaking in the powerful way He did then. John Stott speaks of the need to maintain a balance between fear and love in our lives, holding that both fear and love are inseparable elements in true religion. He points out that fear prevents love from degenerating into presumptuous familiarity, whilst it is love which stops fear from turning into dread.[1]

Perhaps we need to pray that our churches would be seized with great fear, and the name of the Lord Jesus would be held in high honour. *Teach me Your way, O LORD; I will walk in Your truth; Unite my heart to fear Your name* (Psalm 86:11).

HIGH KING OF HEAVEN

Jesus, High King of heaven
We bring our high praise to You
Jesus, High King of heaven
To whom all high praise is due

Who could be compared to You, O Holy One?
None in heaven or earth is Your equal

THE SONG OF THE FATHER'S HEART

You will not share Your glory with another
Honour to Your name

O, Lord God Almighty, who is like You?
Yesterday, today and forever
Power, mercy, faithfulness surround You
Eternal is Your name

You are the image, the radiance of God's glory
Through You the universe was made
You are the Alpha, Omega, the First and the Last
You are the Beginning and the End

Jesus, High King of heaven
Jesus, High King of heaven

Extract taken from the song "High King of Heaven" by Phil Lawson Johnston
Copyright ©1997 Thankyou Music*/1995 Cloud Music

Notes

[1] See John Stott, *Favourite Psalms*, Word UK, p.124.

7

THE KISS OF LOVE
—A FEARFUL INTIMACY

THE KISS OF LOVE

The kiss of love I offer You
Though my heart seems near empty
Wash me through with living streams
And fill my cup with plenty

How I long to love You more
How I long to please You
The love I have may seem so small
But what I have I offer You

Jesus, I love You
I've nothing left to hide
Jesus, I love You
My heart is open wide

Jesus, You are standing here
With arms open wide to welcome
Please accept what I can give
The kiss of love I offer You

Extract taken from the song "The Kiss of Love" by Phil Lawson Johnston
Copyright ©1993 Thankyou Music*

Serve the LORD with fear, and rejoice with trembling. Kiss the Son, lest He be angry, and you perish in the way, when His wrath is kindled but a little. Blessed are all those who put their trust in Him (Psalm 2:11–12).

It is an awesome thing to discover that the holy, almighty, majestic Creator of heaven and earth is not an unapproachable, terrifying figure, but a loving Father who longs to have a relationship with the children He has created for His pleasure. On the one hand, He is *a consuming fire* (Hebrews 12:29), on the other, *He will rejoice over you with gladness, He will quiet you with His love, He will rejoice over you with singing* (Zephaniah 3:17). Fear of God and intimacy with God has to be held in balance. Sometimes we veer one way, sometimes the other, but to keep both in equal measure will lead to a healthy walk with Him.

I know that some people find the term, 'intimacy with God', a difficult one to accept, particularly as the word 'intimacy' can have sexual connotations in other contexts and usages. It is possible that the word, 'closeness' may be better, but I feel that 'intimacy' has a greater depth to it, and speaks of a knowledge of the secret and hidden thoughts of a person's heart as well as a physical closeness. For that reason, in spite of the discomfort of some, I will continue to use it. In fact, in the biblical sense, 'knowledge' of someone implies intimacy, and is even a cause for us to boast. (See Jeremiah 9:23f, and discussion in chapter four above.)

It is possible to love at a distance, but it needs to be fed by intimacy and time spent together. Our daughter, Saskia, when she was on her gap year project in Tanzania, was away from us for four months. We only spoke once by phone on her birthday and otherwise communicated by email and letter for all that time. Our love for her and her love for us did not diminish because of the distance; we enjoyed moments of closeness when we chatted online and spoke, but it could not replace the joy of seeing her again when she returned.

It is quite possible to love Jesus in gratitude for all He has done for us, but still keep Him at arm's length and not enjoy the intimacy that He wants us to experience. Sin, of course, creates a barrier between us, just as a grudge or lack of forgiveness causes us to keep our distance from others, but the Lord wants to remove the gap through forgiveness and grace to bring us close again. Fear can also keep us from enjoying His love. Fear of vulnerability, exposure, emotion, embarrassment and even punishment can prevent us entering into the place of intimacy where God wants us to be. Knowing we are loved and valued by our heavenly Father is the starting point of freedom from all fear for: *There is no fear in love, but perfect love casts out fear* (I John 4:18). John tells us that we have fellowship with the Father and the Son (I John 1:3), while Paul writes of Christians having communion or fellowship with the Holy Spirit (see, for example, II Corinthians 13:14), so the love relationship we have with God is with each person of the Trinity.

We can learn much about the intimacy between the Bridegroom, Jesus, and the bride, His Church, from God's love poem, the Song of Solomon. Some people, I am sure, would rather it was not in the Bible at all, and are embarrassed by the love language and sensual imagery used; for example, it starts, *"Let him kiss me with the kisses of his mouth"* (1:1), and later, *"His left hand is under my head, and his right hand embraces me"* (2:6). And, *"His mouth is most sweet, Yes, he is altogether lovely. This my beloved, and this is my friend"* (5:16).

It was the discovery of friendship, growing into intimacy with God that attracted and drew me into a relationship with Him in the first place. I have always loved the simplicity of the gospel; the Father's love has never been an intellectual exercise for me. I have never had to work it all out in my mind, and the simplicity of 'Jesus loves me, this I know' really has been enough for me. As the psalmist says, *The Lord preserves the simple* (Psalm 116:6).

NOW I KNOW YOU LOVE ME

Now I know You love me
Now I know You care
I feel Your arms around me
Now I know You're there
Now I hear You speaking
I hear You call my name
I know Your love has freed me
From all fear and shame
Father, Father, You loved me first

THE SONG OF THE FATHER'S HEART

My heart is burning with desire
An all-consuming thirst for You Father
You are my Father

Now I know You see me
I can sense Your smile
You've shone Your face upon me
You have called me, "Child"
Now my heart is yearning
Just to know You more
A new-felt passion burning
To worship and adore

Extract taken from the song "Now I Know You Love Me"
by Phil Lawson Johnston. Copyright ©1993 Thankyou Music*

However, more recently I have become excited about filling in the gaps in my knowledge and understanding. Having discovered the writings of Ravi Zacharias and his associates, I have started a new journey of discovery to explore the background reasons for the validity of the gospel and the process that has brought some people to think in the way they do. Although I have not had trouble believing the fundamentals of God's truth, I am now beginning to understand how it has been undermined by a succession of philosophers over the ages who have sought arrogantly to disprove the existence of God and dismiss the whole notion of absolute values and truths. One just has to see in the public arena how any mention of a belief in the supernatural reality of God is so often ridiculed and dismissed as irrelevant, having been supposedly disproved long ago. It is wonderful to see that there are a growing number of seriously intelligent minds, which are able to put across an intellectual defence of the gospel that is valid and who can show the illogicality of much of the prevailing secular humanism, which has been swallowed hook, line and sinker by so many.

As I have grown in understanding of the Truth, that sense of being loved and having His undeserved favour rest upon me has increased; *For Your lovingkindness is before my eyes, and I have walked in Your truth* (Psalm 26:3). I have found this best expressed in the many songs that enable us to pour out our adoration and love. It was one of the great messages brought to us through the visits to Britain of John Wimber throughout the 1980s, when he and his worship leaders emphasised the need for intimacy in our worship; and their songs have helped many draw nearer to God. There is always a danger of imbalance, of course, and one has to beware of singing too many of what some people call 'girlie' songs, which as Lyndon Bowring (Chairman of *CARE*) puts it, 'make some men think more about women than Jesus!' Having said that, many British men have long had problems with intimacy, touch and emotion, and need to experience the 'hug' of their heavenly Father, with Him whispering in their ear the words, 'I love you'. It changes with the generations and, as a counter-balance to my parents' general lack of tactile expression of love (they made up for it in many other ways!), I have made a point of always hugging my sons and daughter whenever I see them, regardless of age. Hopefully, they will never need to go through the process of wondering whether their heavenly Father truly loves them and wants to hold them in His arms.

Understanding that the Lord knows us so intimately, that we cannot hide ourselves from Him or pretend before Him, can be a fearful thing, particularly if we think that by ignoring Him we can successfully make Him go away. Psalm 139 is the most glorious poem, unravelling the Lord's knowledge of our innermost make-up and being, as well as all our comings and goings. There is nowhere we can go and not find Him there waiting for us, no thought we have that He does not perceive *from afar*. We can try and run from this or fully embrace it as we allow Him to embrace us and have His way with us. Artist Charlie Mackesy has painted a number of wonderful pictures of the Prodigal Son and Prodigal Daughter, but has also marvellously sculpted the scene —to be seen at Holy Trinity Brompton. For me, the most powerful element is that the son's arms are completely limp. He is not holding on at all, but is being held and supported entirely by the arms of the Father. This speaks to me so strongly that we have nothing in ourselves that we can use to hang on to God; it is He alone who holds on to us. The sense of safety, security and being utterly loved without a word needing to be said is evident.

We so often think that we have to prove something to God, to earn His favour, when there is nothing we can do; it is all by His grace. We have been so conditioned by the world to think that we are valued by what we do, achieve, own, or even look like, that when something happens to cause us to fail or lose out in these areas, our sense of worth can easily be diminished or even destroyed. God does not love us because we are valuable; we are valuable because He loves us. To know that He is mindful of us and interested in us as people is wonderful. In the Magnificat, Mary exclaims, *"My soul magnifies the Lord, and my spirit has rejoiced in God my Saviour. For He has regarded the lowly state of His maidservant"* (Luke 1:47–8).

Although I have only marginally known lack of self-worth compared to some who have struggled with it all their lives, there have been times when I have found it hard to believe that God really likes me. As I have said elsewhere, I find it easier to believe that He loves me because somewhere at the back of my mind, I am aware that it is His nature as God to love. But to *like* is a different thing; it implies a choice of wanting to be with, to share and to enjoy things with me —which, when I think about it and begin to believe it, fills me with wonder and joy.

The following song was written in order to try and put myself in the place of perhaps many who find it nearly impossible to allow themselves to be loved by God, because they have been conditioned to believe that they are not worthy of anyone's affection or affirmation.

VALUE ME

Tell me I'm valued, tell me I'm loved
And the child within my heart will cry
Who wants a reject? Who really cares
For a victim of self-hatred and fear?
A river damned, a stagnant pool
Enclosed by death, polluted by sin
Still find me special? Still call me loved?
For my heart finds it hard to accept
You value me

Tell me I'm needed, respected affirmed
And the child within my heart will say
'How can You value, how can You love

A captive locked in walls of clay?'
A fountain dry, a garden sealed
And overgrown with thorn and weed
You tell me I'm special,
You tell me I'm loved
Yet I still find it hard to accept
You value me

Is it deception, or is it a mask
Created by the power of lies?
If I'm forgiven, if it's the truth
It will only take one glance of Your eyes
And You'll steal my heart
You'll make me whole
Replacing my old heart of stone
Please tell me I'm special
Please tell me I'm loved
And my heart shall be free to accept
My heart shall be free to accept
You value me, You value me,
You value me

Phil Lawson Johnston Copyright ©2001 IQ Music

God wants to sing a duet with us; for us to enjoy Him as He enjoys us. I always remember David Watson saying that our embrace of God is our worship, and His embrace of us is the filling of His Spirit. The Bible often speaks of the mutual delight and pleasure that we can have with God: *Let Israel rejoice in their Maker; let the children of Zion be joyful in their King. Let them praise His name with the dance; let them sing praises to Him with the timbrel and harp. For the Lord takes pleasure in His people; He will beautify the humble with salvation. Let the saints be joyful in glory; Let them sing aloud on their beds* (Psalm149:2ff). *In Your presence is fullness of joy; At Your right hand are pleasures forevermore* (Psalm 16:11). *Delight yourself also in the LORD, and He shall give you the desires of your heart* (Psalm 37:4). And see again Zephaniah 3:17.

His command to us to delight in Him is His invitation to us to enjoy Him. What greater desire of one's heart could there be than to know that He delights in us? There is great satisfaction in enjoying Him and all that He has provided for us. John Piper has pointed out that God is glorified when we are most satisfied in Him. As the theologian Jonathan Edwards put it, 'the happiness of the creature consists in rejoicing in God, by which also God is magnified and exalted.' Some may say, 'don't pursue joy, pursue obedience', but that is much like saying, 'Don't eat apples, eat fruit'! We are commanded to rejoice, therefore we should obey; *Be glad in the LORD and rejoice, you righteous; And shout for joy, all you upright in heart* (Psalm 32:11).

A little voice sometimes tells us that it must be wrong to enjoy our faith too much; that we, being unworthy creatures, (as indeed we are) should not expect anything from God, and that we should just come to give and not expect to receive. C.S. Lewis traced this notion back to Kant and the Stoics, contrasting such views with the amazing rewards offered in the Gospels.

We can run the danger of blasphemously placing ourselves above God by becoming the benefactor instead of God Himself. He alone is the Giver, and we should not assume His place. Joy and enjoyment of God burst out of the Scriptures at every point. Again John Piper says, 'The great hindrance to worship is not that we are a pleasure-seeking people, but that we are willing to settle for such pitiful pleasures.......you cannot please God if you do not come to Him for reward! Therefore worship that pleases God is the hedonistic pursuit of God. He is our exceedingly great reward! In His presence is fullness of joy, and at His right hand are pleasures forevermore. Being satisfied with all God is for us in Jesus is the essence of the authentic experience of worship. Worship is the feast of Christian hedonism.'[1] Andrew Brandon, likewise, in his book *Enjoying God* points out that the Bible encourages Christians to rejoice, for God Himself is the source of joy; as we enjoy God, we share His joy. Brandon contrasts the majestic living God depicted in the Scriptures with some 'austere' religion.[2]

One way in which we express our joy is through thanksgiving. Gratitude and appreciation are really the starting points of worship, and the death of gratitude for the love of God is the first sign of the extinction of worship. Who do we thank for life's pleasures or unexpected experiences, if we allow our relationship with God to diminish or descend into mere religion? G.K. Chesterton worried that religion can dampen romance, writing: 'Sometimes our worship is more of a theory that a love affair.'

Closeness with Jesus undoubtedly often brings feelings of emotional love and gratitude, but we must not forget that feelings come and go, whereas faith can remain unchangeable. In every marriage there are ups and downs, strong feelings of love, strong feelings of disappointment or irritation, but the fact that you are married does not alter. Mike Bickle in *Passion for Jesus* observes that when we seek intimacy with the Lord, we have to be aware that 'feelings' come and go; there are times of passion and times of spiritual dryness. We are not always aware of the presence of God, but persistence is essential, and we need not be concerned about the lack of 'feelings'.[3] Many other spiritual writers, through the ages, have affirmed the truth of this.

As with other things in the Christian life, the foundation is faith, not feeling; *Though now you do not see Him, yet believing, you rejoice with joy inexpressible and full of glory, receiving the end of your faith—the salvation of your souls* (I Peter 1:8).

Intimacy in our worship of Jesus can bring about a number of things in our lives. The first is that we become fruitful. Physical intimacy produces the fruit of children, and the spiritual equivalent produces the fruit of the Spirit, i.e. the character of Jesus in us. (See Galatians 5:22.) Jesus used the illustration of the vine to teach us that we can only bear fruit that will glorify the Father by abiding in Him; "*I am the vine, you are the branches. He who abides in Me and I in him, bears much fruit; for without Me you can do nothing*" (John 15:5). There is other fruit from intimacy with Jesus, and I want to examine it in some detail.

Intimacy in worship can make us be real with Him

There is a cry in the human heart for identity, intimacy, meaning, purpose, significance, and destiny, which can only be answered by a relationship with God. As far as I know, Christianity (and Judaism) is the only faith in which man is able to be real with God and God reveals Himself to man. We are allowed to question, complain or even shout to God in pain, as we read in the Psalms and elsewhere. *LORD... how long will the wicked triumph?* (See Psalm 94:3). Hannah, longing for a child, cried out in I Samuel 1:15, *"I... have poured out my soul before the LORD."* It was scarcely an unemotional outburst, as Eli, the priest, had thought she was drunk! David drenched his bed with tears (see Psalm 6). Again, in Psalm 56:8, he says, *"You number my wanderings; Put my tears into Your bottle; Are they not in Your book?"* God knows every tear we cry. It has rightly been said that the hand of God, which is strong enough to uphold the universe, is also gentle enough to wipe away tears.

It is hard to sing the Lord's song in the midst of suffering. One only has to hear about the persecution of Christians in countries such as Indonesia, Sudan, Pakistan, Nigeria, and many other territories, to realise how comfortable we are in the 'First World'. There is a place for the lament in our worship. It is a neglected area of songwriting because we have all tended to want to encourage, to express joy and gratitude, but there is a time to express grief and pain:

By the rivers of Babylon, there we sat down, yea, we wept when we remembered Zion. We hung our harps on the willows in the midst of it. For there those who carried us away captive asked of us a song, and those who plundered us requested mirth, saying, "Sing us one of the songs of Zion!" How shall we sing the LORD's song in a foreign land? If I forget you, O Jerusalem, let my right hand forget its skill! If I do not remember you, let my tongue cling to the roof of my mouth —if I do not exalt Jerusalem above my chief joy (Psalm 137:1–6).

Consider the contrast with Psalm 126:1–3, when the return from captivity takes place:

When the Lord brought back the captivity of Zion, we were like those who dream. Then our mouth was filled with laughter, and our tongue with singing.... The Lord has done great things for us, and we are glad.

B. W. Anderson has described the laments as being themselves expressions of praise 'offered in a minor key', reflecting confidence in the faithfulness of Yahweh.

YOUR GRACE WILL SUFFICE

How can I sing for joy
When sorrow has gripped my heart?
How can I sing of peace
In a land that is torn apart?
When hope has fled
And darkness looms
I'll search for the faintest light

I'll hang on to what I know
Of a God who is always there
I'll cling to that word of truth
That speaks of a God who cares
I'll stand on rock instead of sand
And trust in a God of grace

I'll sing of a God who cares
I'll trust in a God who never
Will abandon us to despair
I'll sing of a God who can
Walk with us through
The darkest night
In the furnace of our pain
Your grace will suffice

How can I sing of light
When godlessness holds the sway?
How can I sing the Truth
In a land that has lost its way?
With siren voices spreading lies
Claiming You've left the stage

You've walked the path of loss
Suffering all our pain
Giving Yourself to die
While carrying sin's dark stain

You've gone before
And paved the way
To heaven's eternal joy

I'll sing of a God who cares
I'll trust in a God who never
Will abandon us to despair
I'll sing of a God who can
Walk with us through
The darkest night
In the furnace of our pain
Your grace will suffice

Phil Lawson Johnston Copyright ©2004 Cloud Music

Intimacy in worship can make us contemplate the state of our relationship with God.
It can make us vulnerable, and this is perhaps one reason why people tend to avoid it. It can show up what is really there and who we really are, revealing our weaknesses and fears, which of course can be painful and embarrassing. We can try, but we cannot pretend with God, as we cannot really pretend with others when we are face to face with them. There is a need for emotional honesty and reality, allowing Him to reach behind the masks we wear, touch the real us, and love us as we really are. Are we made uncomfortable in worship? Richard Foster calls it, 'God's scrutiny of love'.

Intimacy in worship can lead us to an awareness of sin
Isaiah had a vision of the Lord high and lifted up in His utter holiness and his reaction was to become aware of his own sin and that of his people: *So I said: "Woe is me! for I am undone! Because I am a man of unclean lips, and I dwell in the midst of a people of unclean lips; For my eyes have seen the King, the LORD of hosts"* (Isaiah 6:5). He was cleansed by an angel and then could hear the conversation in heaven; *"Whom shall I send? And who will go for Us?"*

Intimacy in worship can lead us to security

There is a deep sense of safety and security from intimacy with Jesus. We sing 'safe in Your keeping tender', and Psalm 27:1 says, *The Lord is the stronghold of my life.* I used to think of this in terms of a castle where I can be safe, but now I tend to think of this as meaning, 'the Lord who holds me strongly'.

II Chronicles 16:9 says, *For the eyes of the Lord run to and fro throughout the whole earth, to show Himself strong on behalf of those whose heart is loyal to Him.* And Psalm 17, *Show Your marvellous lovingkindness by Your right hand, O You who save those who trust in You from those who rise up against them. Keep me as the apple of Your eye; Hide me under the shadow of Your wings.*

Intimacy in worship can lead to change

Now the Lord is the Spirit; and where the Spirit of the Lord is, there is liberty. But we all, with unveiled face, beholding as in a mirror the glory of the Lord, are being transformed into the same image from glory to glory, just as by the Spirit of the Lord (II Corinthians 3:17f). I look at this in more detail in chapter thirteen.

Intimacy in worship can lead to a restored passion for God

It can help us return to our first love. As we worship, we allow the Holy Spirit to change our hearts and to fill us again with the love of God, as Paul states in Romans 5:5, *Now hope does not disappoint, because the love of God has been poured out in our hearts by the Holy Spirit, who was given to us.*

Jesus spoke quite severely to the church at Ephesus about their lack of passion, in Revelation 2:4f. *"Nevertheless, I have this against you, that you have left your first love. Remember therefore from where you have fallen; repent and do the first works...."* This was a church that had previously been commended for her deeds, hard work and perseverance (see 2:2–3), and yet Jesus regarded the issue of first love as of paramount importance. So often in our churches we get so caught up in the 'deeds' we are doing—and even in the preaching—that we forget the vital priority of loving the Lord first.

I WILL RETURN

I will return to my first love
To know again that joy within
That raging flame your Word inspires
Changing all my heart's desires
The answer to my aching need is found
Right here by Your side
I will return to my first love
And with Your help will change be made

I will return to my first love
No looking back to what's gone before
A change of heart, a mind renewed
Turning every attitude
Towards the service of my Lord and King
I turn now to You
I will return to my first love
And with Your help will change be made

Phil Lawson Johnston Copyright ©1990 Sovereign Lifestyle Music Ltd

God complains of His people in Hosea 6:4, *"...what shall I do to you...? For your faithfulness is like a morning cloud, and like the early dew it goes away."* Sin and rebellion, apathy and lukewarmness, can cut off our passion for Jesus. He hates lukewarmness and passivity and longs for our wholeheartedness. Again Jesus, says to another church, Laodicea, *"I know your works, that you are neither cold nor hot. I could wish you were cold or hot! So then, because you are lukewarm, and neither cold nor hot, I will vomit you out of My mouth. Because you say, 'I am rich, have become wealthy and have need of nothing' —and do not know that you are wretched, miserable, poor, blind, and naked— I counsel you to buy from Me gold refined in the fire, that you may be rich; and white garments, that you may be clothed, that the shame of your nakedness may not be revealed; and anoint your eyes with eye salve, that you may see"* (Revelation 3:15–18).

Lukewarm liquid is disgusting. If it is a hot drink gone cold or a cold drink gone warm, it is only fit to be spat out, and our apathy is like that to the Lord. May He make us passionate again.

Passion means literally, 'to be affected by'. Thomas More described it as the essential energy of the soul. Spiritual passion is an all-consuming love for God. Andrew Brandon says that worship is, 'the attitude of the heart to God', and affirms that the Christian who is 'helplessly in love with God' will use every opportunity to express his adoration. It is the 'O...' of any heartfelt statement; a yearning to know and be known by God, to love and be loved. Tozer wrote most movingly of being 'captivated' with who God is, and of being 'struck with astonished wonder' by the splendour of God.

Thomas à Kempis put it like this: 'A loud cry in the ears of God is that burning love of a soul which exclaims, "My God and my love, You are all mine, and I yours.... Let my soul spend itself in Your praise, rejoicing for love. Let me love You more than myself, and myself for Your sake."'

Passion for God can lead one to drastic action, fuelled by righteous anger like Jesus, when He tore into the moneychangers who were abusing His Father's temple. When they saw this, the disciples recalled Psalm 69:9, *Zeal for Your house has eaten me up.*

Intimacy in worship can lead us to an awareness of the needs of others

When our passion for Jesus is genuine it will inevitably translate itself into compassion for others: *For the love of Christ compels us* (II Corinthians 5:14). *Therefore if there is any consolation in Christ, if any comfort of love, if any fellowship of the Spirit, if any affection and mercy, fulfill my joy by being like-minded, having the same love, being of one accord, of one mind.... Let each of you look out not only for his own interests, but also for the interests of others.* (See Philippians 2:1ff).

We read that John, the disciple Jesus loved, used to lean *on Jesus' breast* (John 13:25). I like to think that this closeness enabled him to feel Jesus's heart beating, and when we begin to sense God's heartbeat, and have 'the mind of Christ', we will begin to experience His compassion. The King James Version of the Bible uses, in different places, the expression 'the bowels of mercy', which has a much greater poignancy about it compared to other versions' *compassion*. It is to 'feel in the belly', to have a gut-wrenching urge, which forces one into action. Paul says in Philippians 1:8, *For God is my witness, how greatly I long for you all with the affection* [KJV 'bowels'] *of Jesus Christ*. The term used in the KJV may sound strange today, but it has much more power. The equivalent word in Hebrew is used in the story of the two women and the disputed child, who come before Solomon for his judgment. (See I Kings 3:26.) When he suggests dividing the child, the KJV says that the real mother's 'bowels yearned' upon her son. As a parent, I know that all-consuming feeling which rises up from somewhere deep within, when I see a child of mine threatened or in pain.

I confess that most of the time I have very little true compassion running through my inner being, and I know I need my heart to be constantly softened and re-sensitised. I tried to express this desire in a song.

KEEP MY HEART TENDER

Keep my heart tender
Keep my heart open
To the pain of those in despair
Keep my heart burning, filled with compassion
Cause my heart to beat in time with Yours

Don't let my heart grow cold, indifferent, hard or numb
Keep the fire of love burning deep within
Give me ears to hear, eyes to see, don't let me turn away
Cause my heart to beat in time with Yours

Keep my heart focussed, set to do Your will
Cause my feet to walk in step with Yours
Don't let me stay silent, let the cry of Your heart be heard
Cause my eyes to weep with Your tears

O My world, O My world
How often would I have gathered you under My wings
O My world, O My world
How often would I have given You comfort and joy

Phil Lawson Johnston Copyright ©1999 Cloud Music

Intimacy in worship can give us the aroma of Christ

Now thanks be to God who always leads us in triumph in Christ, and through us diffuses the fragrance of His knowledge in every place. For we are to God the fragrance of Christ among those who are being saved and among those who are perishing. To the one we are the aroma of death leading to death, and to the other the aroma of life leading to life... (II Corinthians 2:14–16).

Just as *the house was filled with the fragrance of the oil,* when Mary anointed Jesus (see John 12:3), the fragrance of worship is like the fragrance of love poured out upon us, enabling us to respond with adoration. I return to this theme in chapter ten.

"Father I know that You desire to have an intimate relationship with each one of Your children. I know that You long for us to recognize You as a loving Father, who knows the secret place inside us, the inner man where You want to dwell, and from where You can direct our lives and teach us how to please You."

Notes

[1] John Piper, *Desiring God,* Multnomah Publishers, ©1986, 1996, 2003 Desiring God Foundation.

[2] See Andrew Brandon, *Enjoying God*, Kingsway Publications, p.147.

[3] See Mike Bickle, *Passion for Jesus*, Kingsway Publications, p.149.

Part Two

God's Presence in Worship

8

HALLOWED GROUND — THE PRESENCE OF GOD IN WORSHIP

HALLOWED GROUND

Pausing, listening, hear the voice of Jesus
Resting in the presence of the Lord
Waiting, ready, spending time together
Holy Spirit, come anoint us as we pray

Touching, healing, like an ointment soothing
Breathing in the fragrance of the Lord
Speaking, revealing, guide us upward, believing
In triumph through heaven's open door

Remove the shoes from your feet
Lift your eyes to the mercy seat
Can't you see that the veil is torn in two?

For this is hallowed ground where we stand
Let us fall before His throne
For this is hallowed ground
Thou art holy
Thou art the Lord

THE SONG OF THE FATHER'S HEART

Gazing upward, into the face of Jesus
Basking in the presence of the Lord
Shekinah, glory, shining brighter than the sunlight
Chasing shadows from every corner of our lives

We take our place at the Father's feet
Ready for the marriage feast
Join with all creation in heaven's praise

For this is hallowed ground where we stand
Let us rise before His throne
For this is hallowed ground
Thou art holy
Thou art the Lord

**Extract taken from the song "Hallowed Ground"
by Phil Lawson Johnston, Colin Rank
Copyright ©1982 Thankyou Music***

Coming into God's presence is rather like coming home to the place that we have always meant to be, as there is an instinct in all of us to 'get back to the garden', to return to where we belong. It has been noted that the process of conversion to the Lord used to start with belief, then a change of behaviour and then a sense of belonging, but nowadays it seems that the order has changed. People need to feel they belong first, then they believe and then their behaviour changes. This sense of belonging usually comes through the community of Christians that welcomes them in, but the real 'homecoming' occurs as they encounter the living God.

There is a barrier created by sin which can only be crossed through faith in the death of Jesus at the cross where it was dealt with once and for all. As the prayer of humble access in the Anglican BCP Communion Service puts it, 'We do not presume to come to this Thy table, O merciful Lord, trusting in our own righteousness, but in Thy manifold and great mercies.' He opened the way for us to return from the exile of sin and to begin to enjoy again the privileges and blessings that Adam and Eve had in the Garden of Eden before the Fall. It requires us to seek God wholeheartedly and when we do,

He promises we will find Him (Jeremiah 29:13–14). In many places in the Bible we read of the sense of 'belonging' that we can enjoy in the Lord. Psalm 84 is a prime example of this: *How lovely is Your tabernacle, O LORD of hosts...! ...For a day in Your courts is better than a thousand. I would rather be a doorkeeper in the house of my God than dwell in the tents of wickedness.*

One reason that we can find a home in God is that His dwelling place has a permanence about it: I can live in the *house of my God,* whereas those without God dwell in *the tents of wickedness.* Having 'found' the Lord, we do not then call off the search, but continue to seek Him, to know Him better, and to discover His will and purposes for our lives.

I often hear a statement that we do not need to seek God's presence because we are daily living in it. I find myself being slightly irked by this, not because it is not true, but because I do not believe it gives quite the whole picture. It is true in the sense that God is everywhere and with all of us all the time and, for the believer, there is the wonderful assurance of the abiding presence in us; we are, indeed the temple of the Spirit, and Jesus promised He would be with His disciples always. But the Bible is full of instances when God reveals Himself in specific ways to people, making Himself known in a special way. Sometimes He appears to individuals and at other times to groups. We can 'practise the presence of God' whenever and wherever we are (in the sense of being more aware of what is already true for the believer, according to God's promise), but there are times when one has a *special* sense of His presence. It does not mean that He is not there when we are not feeling anything, but there are certain times during worship or in a particular place when it seems as though the 'veil is thin', as the Celtic Christians described it. I believe there can be a danger of complacency if we do not reach out for Him with hunger and even desperation at times. I want to explore both aspects in this chapter: His omnipresence and His manifest presence.

Instant access

We can turn to Him at any time because we have constant access to Him: *For through Him we both have access by one Spirit to the Father* (Ephesians 2:18). To have access implies a freedom to come and go as we please, not disrespectfully, but in the same way that a child has access to a father's presence. I am reminded of the story of the preacher who was struggling with his next sermon. As he prayed for God to help him, his young child came into his study and just sat on the floor playing with a toy. Instead of getting irritated at being disturbed, he found God speaking to him about the freedom we have to come into His presence and just dwell there without necessarily saying anything. He had his sermon.

In other places we read of the confidence we can have to come to Jesus, *...in whom we have boldness and access with confidence through faith in Him* (Ephesians 3:12). *Therefore, brethren, having boldness to enter the Holiest by the blood of Jesus, by a new and living way which He consecrated for us, through the veil, that is, His flesh, and having a High Priest over the house of God, let us draw near with a true heart in full assurance of faith, having our hearts sprinkled from an evil conscience and our bodies washed with pure water* (Hebrews 10:19–22). *Draw near to God and He will draw near to you* (James 4:8).

All these verses speak clearly of the confidence we can have with God, but also of the fact that we need to *approach, draw near, come,* which implies some kind of movement on our behalf.

We no longer have to go somewhere special to find God (like a temple or church building), because we can now meet Him in our hearts — *"...neither on this mountain, nor in Jerusalem...." "...true worshippers will worship the Father in spirit and truth..."* (See John 4:21–23).

There is a step of faith, though, that we need to take to positively turn towards Him and draw near.

God's invitations to come

Have you ever noticed how often the invitation to *come,* is repeated throughout Scripture? Here are some examples.

Come **to a place of safety:** *Then the LORD said to Noah, "Come into the ark..."* (Genesis 7:1).

Come **to praise and worship:** *Oh come, let us sing to the LORD! ... Let us come before His presence with thanksgiving.... ...Oh come, let us worship and bow down....* (See Psalm 95.)

Come **for refreshment:** *"Come to the waters..." (*Isaiah 55:1).

...Jesus stood and cried out, saying, "If anyone thirsts, let him come

to Me and drink" (John 7:37). *And the Spirit and the bride say, "Come!" And let him who hears say, "Come!" And let him who thirsts come. Whoever desires, let him take the water of life freely* (Revelation 22:17).

***Come* for rest:** *"Come to Me, all you who labour and are heavy laden, and I will give you rest."* (Matthew 11:28).

***Come* for cleansing:** *"Come now, and let us reason together,"* says the LORD. *"Though your sins are like scarlet, they shall be as white as snow; though they are red like crimson, they shall be as wool"* (Isaiah 1:18).

Many of these are direct invitations from God Himself to us.

To seek Him

Almost as many times as we are invited to come, we are also called to 'Seek Him', or 'Seek His face'. *Seek the LORD while He may be found, Call upon Him while He is near* (Isaiah 55:6).

To 'seek', in this sense, signifies looking for an audience with a king or ruler. It means to search, to hope for an encounter with the Living God, born out of a deep longing and yearning for Him: *O God, You are my God; Early will I seek You...* (Psalm 63:1).

It is not a half-hearted rummaging around for something or someone you do not expect to find, which, for example would happen if anyone tried to find anything in my workroom. (I, of course, know exactly where everything is!) It means looking hard until you find, not stopping until you do, in the way depicted in the parables of the lost coin and the lost sheep.

We can sense expectancy, an earnestness, or even desperation in many scriptures: *One thing I have desired of the LORD, that will I seek: That I may dwell in the house of the LORD all the days of my life, to behold the beauty of the LORD and to inquire in His temple.... When You said, "Seek My face," my heart said to You, "Your face, LORD, I will seek"* (Psalm 27:4,8).

There are many promises which tell us we will find if we seek: *"And you will seek Me and find Me, when you search for Me with all your heart"* (Jeremiah 29:13). *If you seek Him, He will be found by you* (I Chronicles 28:9). *"...seek and you will find..."* (Matthew 7:7).

He also promises great blessing when we seek Him seriously:

"But seek first the kingdom of God and His righteousness, and all these things shall be added to you" (Matthew 6:33). *Blessed are those who keep His testimonies, who seek Him with the whole heart!* (Psalm 119:2).

We are encouraged to *seek His face*, and I have made this a supplementary study in chapter nine.

Whether to *come,* or to *seek,* is a command or an invitation, He is calling us to draw near to Him in every way possible; and, when we respond, His promise is that we will indeed find Him.

SEEK HIM WHILE HE MAY BE FOUND

How often have you heard?
How many times have just simply turned away?
How much is your mind disturbed?
Seeing the changes, it must be more than idle play

Seeing it must be real
How many times will you say, 'wait until another day'?
How can you know for sure
That you even have another day to wait until?

This could be your last
This could be your last chance

God's Spirit will not always strive with man
There comes a time when He will go
How long will you go on rejecting Him
You must seek Him while He may be found
Call upon Him while he is near
Seek him while he may be found

How long will you resist?
How many golden chances will you toss away?
Are you so well prepared
Ready to meet the Lord

If He should come today?
Are you made of gold?
Could you stand before His throne?

God's Spirit will not always strive with man
There comes a time when He will go
How long will you go on rejecting Him
You must seek Him while He may be found
Call upon Him while He is near
Seek Him while He may be found

If you seek Him, you will find Him
If you search for Him with all your heart

Extract taken from the song "Seek Him while He May be Found"
by Phil Lawson Johnston
Copyright ©1982 Thankyou Music*

God's initiative

One of the elements that makes Christianity unique is that we learn that God has always taken the initiative to come towards us; in the garden He came looking for Adam and Eve, even though He knew that they had sinned; in the incarnation of Jesus, He came to earth to rescue mankind. In Zechariah's prophecy, it is declared that *He has visited and redeemed His people* (Luke 1:68).

In American English, 'visiting *with*', means sitting and talking with someone. What a picture of God: His wanting to come to us and sit and talk with us; or, as it is depicted in Revelation 3:20, to eat with us. *"Behold, I stand at the door and knock. If anyone hears My voice and opens the door, I will come in to him and dine with him, and he with Me."*

He has always looked for us, whereas in other religions people have tried to find a deity through pleasing or appeasing. We learn from John 4:23 that the Father is seeking worshippers who will worship Him in spirit and truth. What an amazing thought, that the Father is seeking us at the same time as calling us to seek Him!

Meeting with God

Meeting with God is one of the central aspects of corporate worship. We have already noted the boldness and confidence which flows from His promise in James 4:8. When we come to Him, He comes to us and meets us in our hearts. We see something of this principle in practice with Moses in the desert after the crossing of the Red Sea. In Exodus 33:7ff, we read, *Moses took his tent and pitched it outside the camp, far from the camp, and called it the tabernacle of meeting. And it came to pass that everyone who sought the LORD went out to the tabernacle of meeting which was outside the camp. So it was, whenever Moses went out to the tabernacle, that all the people rose, and each man stood at his tent door and watched Moses until he had gone into the tabernacle. And it came to pass, when Moses entered the tabernacle, that the pillar of cloud descended and stood at the door of the tabernacle, and the LORD talked with Moses. All the people saw the pillar of cloud standing at the tabernacle door, and all the people rose and worshipped, each man in his tent door. So the LORD spoke to Moses face to face, as a man speaks to his friend.* We are only shown here Moses actually entering the tabernacle for a meeting with God 'face to face', while the rest of the people, though they would still seek the Lord and worship Him, are not shown as enjoying that 'face to face' encounter. Now the situation has changed, in that all believers can come through the curtain into God's presence (Hebrews 10:22ff), no longer worshipping at a distance, but close to Him in the very Holy of Holies.

The tabernacle

The pattern of the tabernacle that God instructed Moses to make, and later the temple built by Solomon, is like a shadow of the worshipping relationship we now can have with God. The first object one would have been confronted with was the altar for burnt offering. This speaks of the sacrifice of Jesus through which we can now come near. Then there was the laver for cleansing, which speaks of our own washing with the blood of Jesus, imparting to us the holiness necessary for us to approach Him. Then there was the curtain into the holy place, where there was the table of the presence and the golden lamp stand, both signifying the presence of God. Finally, the curtain into the holy of holies, which was torn from top to bottom at the moment of Jesus' death, opening permanently the way for us to be able to enter. There we find the altar of incense and the ark of the covenant with the mercy seat above, where God was to meet with the high priest once a year. It was not until Moses had completed everything that God had commanded him that the glory of the Lord came and filled the tabernacle. *So Moses finished the work. Then the cloud covered the tabernacle of Meeting, and the glory of the Lord filled the tabernacle.* (See Exodus 40:33–35).

All this was highly symbolic and pointed towards Jesus and what was to come in the future. In Hebrews 8:5 we are reminded that priests of the old covenant served the *copy and shadow of the heavenly things.* And Hebrews chapter nine links the earthly tabernacle with what Jesus came to do as the great high priest who became the sacrifice to end all sacrifices.

The temple of the Holy Spirit

The pattern of the New Testament is that we become tabernacles or meeting places of God: *....Jesus Christ Himself being the chief cornerstone, in whom the whole building, being fitted together, grows into a holy temple in the Lord, in whom you also are being built together for a dwelling place of God in the Spirit.* (See Ephesians 2:20ff). *Coming to Him as to a living stone, rejected indeed by men, but chosen by God and precious, you also, as living stones, are being built up a spiritual house, a holy priesthood, to offer up spiritual sacrifices acceptable to God through Jesus Christ* (I Peter 2:4–5). *Do you not know that you are the temple of God and that the Spirit of God dwells in you? If anyone defiles the temple of God, God will destroy him. For the temple of God is holy, which temple you are* (I Corinthians 3:16). *For you are the temple of the living God. As God has said: "I will dwell in them and walk among them, I will be their God, and they shall be My people"* (II Corinthians 6:16). *Or do you not know that your body is a temple of the Holy Spirit who is in you, whom you have from God, and you are not your own?* (I Corinthians 6:19).

Moses was told by God, *"And let them make Me a sanctuary, that I may dwell among them"* (Exodus 25:8). This was a physical dwelling place, whereas now we are and will be the physical dwelling place of God. As many have said, we no longer go to the sanctuary;

we take the sanctuary with us. We are the sanctuary. As we saw in chapter three, when we considered 'a song of hope', what was lost in the Garden of Eden will be restored in the New Jerusalem, described as coming down out of heaven. (See Revelation 21:3–4.)

There are moments when the sense of God's presence is stronger than others. There are times when I have really felt close to Him and almost wanted time to stay still and not rush on to the next item on the 'service agenda'.

EYE TO EYE WITH JESUS

May the sun stay still
Like a kestrel hovering high
May the wind hold its breath
May this moment never die
Heart to heart, meeting here
Eye to eye with Jesus

As the clouds hold back rain
And the storm passes by
My heart skips a beat
As silent lightning fills the sky
Heart to heart, meeting here
Eye to eye with Jesus

But life will go on
Filled with joy or sorrow
Still I will stay close to You

As a branch bears its fruit
While abiding in the vine
So I'll guard my heart
As the well-spring of life
Heart to heart, meeting here
Eye to eye with Jesus

But life will go on
Filled with joy or sorrow
Still I will stay close to You

As a pool undisturbed
Becomes a mirror of light
So I long to remain
Quietly gazing at the sight
Heart to heart, meeting here
Eye to eye with Jesus

Phil Lawson Johnston Copyright ©2003 Cloud Music

Richard Foster describes worship as, '...to experience reality, to touch life. It is to know, to feel to experience the resurrected Christ in the midst of the gathered community. It is a breaking into the Shekinah of God, or better yet being invaded by the Shekinah of God.' [1]

The shekinah of God is the glorious cloud of His presence, as in the occasion when the temple was filled with a cloud (II Chronicles 5:14), or when Ezekiel met the glory of God (Ezekiel 1, 2:23, 8:4), or on the mount of transfiguration.

Meeting the glory of God

The word for glory in Hebrew means, literally, weight, heaviness or honour. There have been times during sung worship when I have felt a certain weightiness in the atmosphere, which was not negative but had a feeling of substance which inspired awe.

God's glory is His overwhelming presence

Whenever the 'cloud' of God's presence appeared, it was always a revelation of His glory, and often caused those who saw it to fall down on their faces: *Then Moses went up into the mountain, and a cloud covered the mountain. Now the glory of the LORD rested on Mount Sinai.... The sight of the glory of the LORD was like a consuming fire on the top of the mountain in the eyes of the children of Israel* (Exodus 24:15f). *And Moses and Aaron went into the tabernacle of meeting, and came out and blessed the people.Then the glory of the*

LORD appeared to all the people, and fire came out from before the LORD and consumed the burnt offering.... ...When all the people saw it, they shouted and fell on their faces. (See Leviticus 9:23f).

Ezekiel had a remarkable vision of God's glory: "*...And above the firmament over their heads on the throne was the likeness of a throne, in appearance like a sapphire stone; on the throne was a likeness with the appearance of a man high above it. Also from the appearance of His waist and upward I saw, as it were, the colour of amber with the appearance of fire all around within it; and from the appearance of His waist and downward I saw, as it were, the appearance of fire with brightness all around. Like the appearance of a rainbow in a cloud on a rainy day, so was the appearance of the brightness all around it. This was the appearance of the likeness of the glory of the Lord. So when I saw it, I fell on my face, and I heard a voice of One speaking....*" (Ezekiel 1:26ff).

The shepherds on the hill had a glimpse of it when heaven opened and they saw the angels at the birth of Jesus, as Stephen did just before he died from stoning. And, of course, we have the Revelation of John, in which the glory of God has its fullest description. John himself meets the glorified Christ and responds by immediately falling flat on his face. "*And when I saw Him, I fell at His feet as dead*" (Revelation 1:17).

God's glory is a display of who He is

God's glory is a manifestation of His power, majesty and character, as shown in Exodus 33:18–23, when Moses longs to see God's glory and to be reassured of His presence. God revealed His glory by causing all His goodness to pass before Moses, declaring His mercy and compassion. However, Moses still could not see God's face, "*for no man shall see Me, and live.*" There is a dying to be gone through before we can fully see God in all His glory. As we die to ourselves through a humbling of our pride in our own ability and achievement, we begin to see His glory.

God's glory is displayed in Jesus

Moses did finally see the glory of God, as we observe him appearing alongside Jesus on the mount of transfiguration. Both Peter and John witness to the fact that they saw the glory of God in Jesus. *For we... were eyewitnesses of His majesty. For He received from God the Father honour and glory when such a voice came to Him from the Excellent Glory: "This is my beloved Son, in whom I am well pleased." And we heard this voice which came from heaven when we were with Him on the holy mountain.* (See II Peter 1:16–18). *And the Word became flesh and dwelt among us, and we beheld His glory as of the only begotten of the Father, full of grace and truth* (John 1:14). And Hebrews 1:2 teaches us that the Son is the brightness of the Father's glory, and the express image of His person.

God's glory is reflected in His people

The more we see and experience the glory of God, the more we will reflect it in our lives. *For it is the God who commanded light to shine out of darkness, who has shone in our hearts to give the light of the knowledge of the glory of God in the face of Jesus Christ* (II Corinthians 4:6). *...Christ in you the hope of glory* (Colossians 1:27). *But You, O Lord, are a shield for me, my glory and the One who lifts up my head* (Psalm 3:3). *But we all, with unveiled face, beholding as in a mirror the glory of the Lord, are being transformed into the same image from glory to glory, just as by the Spirit of the Lord* (II Corinthians 3:18).

John Piper has pointed out that in worship we gladly reflect back to God the radiance of His worth.[2] It is through worship we have access into that place of meeting where we encounter Father, Son and Spirit, and we expose ourselves to the presence and glory of God.

To meet with God in this way can be a fearful thing and not to be treated lightly. Most of the individuals we read of as coming face to face with the Lord fell on their faces in terror or as if dead. When Joshua met the Lord before the taking of Jericho, his response was that he *fell on his face to the earth and worshipped* (Joshua 5:14). We recall, too, that when Isaiah was confronted by the glory of God, his reaction was to become painfully aware of his own sin and that of his people. (Isaiah 6:5). We read of similar reactions from Daniel (10:15) and John (Revelation 1:17) when they met the Lord in His glory. And Jacob was filled with awe after waking from his dream. *"...Surely the LORD is in this place, and I did not know it." And he was afraid and said, "How awesome is this place! This is none other than the house of God."* (See Genesis 28:16f).

In Hebrews 12:28, we are warned to, *serve God acceptably with reverence and godly fear. For our God is a consuming fire.* The Israelites were so frightened by the voice of God on the holy mountain that they begged Moses to ask God not to speak to them directly, but only through him. Even Moses himself was frightened: *...so terrifying was the sight that Moses said, "I am exceedingly afraid and trembling."* (See Hebrews 12:21.)

There were occasions when people fell in worship before Jesus. When He walked on the water and helped Peter do the same, it says that they worshipped Him as He climbed into the boat and the wind died down. After His resurrection when He appeared to the women we read that *...they came and held Him by the feet and worshipped Him.* Again, when Thomas saw Jesus and believed, he worshipped, and then just before His ascension, it says, *When they saw Him, they worshipped Him...* (Matthew 28:17). The word used for worship on these occasions means, literally, to prostrate oneself and kiss the feet.

God's glory will cover the whole earth

We only catch glimpses of God's glory now, since our vision is blurred and we see *in a mirror, dimly*; but there will come a day when we shall see *face to face* (I Corinthians 13:12).

There is a day coming when, *every eye will see Him* (Revelation 1:7), when some will react in horror and try to hide from Him, and, *...From the terror of the LORD and the glory of His majesty* (Isaiah 2:10); calling to, *...the mountains and rocks, "Fall on us and hide us from the face of Him who sits on the throne and from the wrath of the Lamb!"* (Revelation 6:16). Others will welcome Him as their King and Lord, as a bride welcomes her bridegroom. It will mean punishment for some and eternal joy for others. He will, *...in flaming fire take vengeance on those who do not know God, and on those who do not obey the gospel of our Lord Jesus Christ. These shall be punished with everlasting destruction from the presence of the Lord and from the glory of His power, when He comes in that Day, to be glorified in His saints and to be admired among all those who believe....* (See II Thessalonians 1:8–10.) What a day, when *...the earth will be filled with the knowledge of the glory of the LORD, as the waters cover the sea* (Habbakuk 2:14).

THE GLORY OF JESUS

Is this the day of visitation?
Is this the day we meet face to face?
Isn't it time for heart reflection,
Preparing ourselves
For His loving embrace?
Is this a time of revelation,
Is this the time when every eye will see?
Filled with anticipation,
When all of creation will come to be free.

Oh, the glory of Jesus
Will cover the face of the earth,
And the glory of Jesus
Will shine in the house of God.

Is this the time of His appearing?
Is this the golden age of light,
When He will call from every nation
A people of faith,
A bride dressed all in white?
Is this the time for consummation,
For being transformed by a holy kiss?
Isn't it time for celebration,
Of joyous abandon and heavenly bliss?

Is this a time to be distracted?
Is this a time for selfish gain?
Lust of the eyes and proud achievement,
Chasing the wind and striving in vain.
This is a day for consecration,
For living our lives on borrowed time,
Spending ourselves for His kingdom,
And dying to see His majesty shine.

Phil Lawson Johnston Copyright ©2001 Cloud Music/IQ Music

Meeting the love of God

With the reverence and awe, though, comes the intimacy and love that God wants us to know. He is awesome and yet delights in us, as we saw earlier, in Zephaniah 3:17.

He wants us to feel we are welcome in His presence and, while singing, I often imagine Him standing there with arms open wide to draw us close to Him. *LORD I have loved the habitation of Your house, and the place where Your glory dwells (Psalm 26:8). So I have looked for You in the sanctuary, to see Your power and Your glory. Because Your lovingkindness is better than life, my lips shall praise You. Thus I will bless You while I live; I will lift up my hands in Your name* (Psalm 63:2).

BETTER THAN LIFE

I search for You, I long for You
I earnestly seek Your face
My soul finds rest in You alone
For You are my only hope

Because Your love is better than life
My lips will glorify You
And in Your name I will lift up my hands
And I will be satisfied

I trust in You, I cling to You
Your right hand will hold me firm
I delight to sit in the shade of Your wings
Where I can sing my love to You

Your love is strong, it seals my heart
It burns like a blazing fire
Arise my love, and stir up my soul
Awaken my heart to sing

Meeting together

When Christians come together, we meet with God, but equally, we also meet with each other. Of course, we have a personal relationship with God and we can meet Him on our own in our devotions as we read His word or pray. However, Christianity is not a private religion, and too often we can make the mistake of going to a church service as though it were a private affair. It is like those who say they are, 'taking my communion', whereas the biblical pattern is that when we gather we are to relate to others in the Body of Christ. We meet to encourage, strengthen, support and love one another. *And let us consider one another in order to stir up love and good works, not forsaking the assembling of ourselves together, as is the manner of some, but exhorting one another, and so much the more as you see the Day approaching* (Hebrews 10:24–25).

In I Corinthians 14:26, Paul says, *Whenever you come together....* 'When', not 'if'! The word 'communion' implies not only our being together with God, but also togetherness with others. Gathering around the Lord's table is perhaps the most corporately intimate occasion in our life as Christians, as we remember His death and look to His coming again —having a foretaste of that heavenly banquet we will all enjoy when we meet Him face to face.

Walking with God

If meeting with God and others is a way of describing what we do when we worship corporately or individually, then 'walking with God' is a biblical way of describing our daily worship of God outside the gathering.

The expression 'walk the talk', underlines the need to live out what we say. We can be so good at saying all the right things, singing all the correct theology, but it does not really count if our hearts are not right and our lives do not live up to it. Jesus was harsh in His condemnation of this, quoting Isaiah, *"These people draw near to Me with their mouth, and honour Me with their lips, but their heart is far from Me. And in vain they worship Me, teaching as doctrines the commandments of men* (Matthew 15:8–9). To walk with God means to live righteously and humbly in relationship with Him. *He has shown you, O man, what is good; And what does the LORD require of you but to do justly, to love mercy and to walk humbly with your God?* (Micah 6:8).

Following

Walking, in a biblical sense, indicates more than simple physical exercise, it signifies following God, just as Jesus' disciples were called His followers. *Therefore be imitators of God as dear children. And walk in love* (Ephesians 5:1).

To 'walk with' someone suggests a picture of companionship, of friendship, of talking and listening. One can often have one's best conversations with people on a walk. In fact, I find the best way of spending time with the Lord is when walking on a local meadow. It clears my head, and I find I can hear Him speak to me and I feel I can talk to Him about anything.

Two disciples were walking on the road to Emmaus, when Jesus joined them without them recognising Him. The conversation they had with Him led to Him explaining from the Old Testament everything that related to Himself and the recent events in Jerusalem. Afterwards, they described the experience. *"Did not our heart burn within us while He talked with us on the road, and while He opened the Scriptures to us?"* (Luke 24:32).

In righteousness

The Bible describes walking with God in many different ways. It is a sign of righteousness, as we see in the case of Enoch and Noah: *And Enoch walked with God; and he was not, because God took him.* (Genesis 5:24). *...For before he* [Enoch] *was taken, he had this testimony, that he pleased God* (Hebrews 11:5). *Noah was a just man, perfect in his generations. Noah walked with God* (Genesis 6:9). Similarly, God says to Abraham: *"I am Almighty God; walk before Me and be blameless"* (Genesis 17:1). The Lord promises to those who are faithful to Him in the church at Sardis: *"...they shall walk with Me in white, for they are worthy"* (Revelation 3:4).

In light and truth

It is also described as walking in the light or truth. Proverbs puts it like this: *But the path of the just is like the shining sun, that shines ever brighter unto the perfect day. The way of the wicked is like darkness; They do not know what makes them stumble"* (Proverbs 4:18–19). Likewise, John: *If we say that we have fellowship with Him, and walk in darkness, we lie and do not practice the truth. But if we walk in the light, as He is in the light, we have fellowship with one another, and the blood of Jesus Christ His Son cleanses us from all sin* (I John 1:6–7).

The Psalms have a number of references to it: *Teach me Your way, O LORD; I will walk in Your truth...* (Psalm 86:11). *Blessed are the people who know the joyful sound! They walk, O LORD, in the light of Your countenance* (Psalm 89:15). We are also encouraged to follow in Jesus' footsteps. *He who says he abides in Him ought himself also to walk just as He walked* (I John 2:6). The promise is that we will be taught to be like Him. He will teach us His ways so that we may walk in His paths. (See Isaiah 2:3).

In safety

Walking with God also has the promise of safety and comfort: *Yea, though I walk through the valley of the shadow of death, I will fear no evil; For You are with me; Your rod and Your staff, they comfort me* (Psalm 23:4). *For You have delivered my soul from death. Have You not kept my feet from falling, that I may walk before God in the light of the living* (Psalm 56:13). And we can see that God has a desire to walk with us and among us. Adam and his wife, *...heard the sound of the LORD God walking in the garden in the cool of the day...* (Genesis 3:8). *"I will set My tabernacle among you, and My soul shall not abhor you. I will walk among you and be your God, and you shall be My people"* (Leviticus 26:11–12).

Spreading the gospel

Walking denotes the spreading of the gospel: *How beautiful on the mountains are the feet of him who bring good news, who proclaims peace, who brings glad tidings of good things, who proclaims salvation, who says to Zion, "Your God reigns!"* (Isaiah 52:7) *...and having shod your feet with the preparation of the gospel of peace* (Ephesians 6:15); and it is used as an illustration of God's promise to give victory to His people: *"Every place that the sole of your foot will tread upon I have given you, as I said to Moses"* (Joshua 1:3).

Jackie Pullinger-To, who has worked in Hong Kong ministering to drug addicts for many years, says that Christians too often have hard hearts and soft feet when they should have soft hearts and hard feet!

The One who walks beside

Jesus describes the Holy Spirit as the Comforter or Counsellor in John 14 and 16, and the word used, 'paracletos', literally means 'one who is called to come to one's side'. In Galatians 5:25, Paul writes, *If we live in the Spirit, let us also walk in the Spirit.* (See also Psalm 128:1). This speaks to me of being led by the Lord, being shown which way to go, and what to do. We have many promises that He will guide us as we walk with Him in humility and respect and yet in the closeness of companionship. *Your word is a lamp to my feet and a light to my path* (Psalm 119:105); *Your ears shall hear a word behind you, saying, "This is the way, walk in it"* (Isaiah 30:21).

There is a phrase, which is used mostly in Scotland, to describe adjoining country estates. They are said to 'march with' each other, no doubt coming from the time when neighbouring clans used literally to march together, but it now basically means to live alongside each other. In addition to walking with the Spirit in companionship, we are also expected to march with Him to confront the enemy, Satan, in intercession and praise, and to fulfil our calling, which was set out in Luke 9:1ff — *Then He called His twelve disciples together and gave them power and authority over all demons. He sent them to preach the kingdom of God and to heal the sick.*

BLESSED COMFORTER

Blessed Comforter, walk beside
Blessed Counsellor, be my guide
My Companion to the end
Spirit of Jesus, be my friend

Living water, flood my soul
Melt my heart, Lord, take control
Purify me with holy fire
The friendship of Jesus is my desire

Extract taken from the song "Blessed Comforter" by Phil Lawson Johnston
Copyright ©1989 Thankyou Music*

Running the race
As a well as being a walk with God, the Christian life is described
as a race that we run in order to gain the prize at the end: *...Let us
lay aside every weight , and the sin which so easily ensnares us, and
let us run with endurance the race that is set before us, looking unto
Jesus, the author and finisher of our faith, who for the joy that was
set before Him endured the cross, despising the shame, and has sat
down at the right hand of the throne of God. For consider Him who
endured such hostility from sinners against Himself, lest you become
weary and discouraged in your souls* (Hebrews 12:1–3).

Paul exhorts us: *Do you not know that those who run in a race
all run, but one receives the prize? Run in such a way that you
may obtain it* (I Corinthians 9:24). And at the end of his life, he
proclaimed, *I have fought the good fight, I have finished the race,
I have kept the faith. Finally, there is laid up for me the crown of
righteousness, which the Lord, the righteous Judge, will give to me on
that Day, and not to me only but to all who have loved His appearing*
(II Timothy 4:7–8).

Standing and sitting
In those Revelation passages which describe the worship in heaven, I
am always struck by the movement that takes place. One minute the
elders are standing before the throne, the next minute they are falling
face down. We stand in awe of His glory and ways: *O, LORD, I have
heard Your speech and was afraid; O LORD, revive Your work in the
midst of the years* (Habbakuk 3:2). *My flesh trembles for fear of You;
And I am afraid of Your judgments* (Psalm 119:120). And we stand
against the schemes of the enemy. (See Ephesians 6:13–14).

We are encouraged not to walk, stand or sit in the presence of the
wicked (Psalm 1:1), but to take our places alongside the Lord. *God...
raised us up together, and made us sit together in the heavenly places
in Christ Jesus* (Ephesians 2:6).

Following Mary's example, there is a time to be seated at Jesus'
feet to listen, and worship. (See Luke 10:39).

Desperation for His presence
Whether we talk of meeting, walking, running or simply sitting and
dwelling with God, we have a desperate need of His presence at all

times. Brother Lawrence's lesson of practising (or living in awareness of) the presence of God is something we all need to learn. Moses was desperate for God's presence, knowing it was the distinguishing feature of God's people. *"...If Your presence does not go with us, do not bring us up from here. For how then will it be known that Your people and I have found grace in Your sight, except You go with us? So we shall be separate, Your people and I, from all the people who are upon the face of the earth* (Exodus 33:15f). David showed a similar desperation: *My soul thirsts for God, for the living God. When shall I come and appear before God?* (Psalm 42:2).

As we draw near to worship the Lord, there is a very real possibility of experiencing His manifest presence, and this often enables us to receive what He wants to give us. Sometimes it is healing. I have often seen how God has met with people and released healing and deliverance into their lives, as they have opened themselves to Him in worship. Often, people hear Him speak to them during sung worship; others have been convicted of sin, like Isaiah, or have been shown how they need to forgive others who have wronged them. (See Matthew 5:23).

My aim when leading others in worship is, if possible, to take us beyond the material surroundings, to a place of intimacy balanced with awe in the presence of the Lord; a place where we can hear His voice, sense His touch and have our passion for Him reignited.

SURELY THE LORD IS IN THIS PLACE

Surely the Lord is in this place
Surely the Lord is in this place

Surely if the Lord, the Lord, is in this place
Let us wait and listen
Wait and listen
As we stand before Him we can say
This is the gateway to heaven
Gateway to heaven

HALLOWED GROUND

Lo, He rides on the wings of the wind
Let us join with angels, singing
Glory, glory, glory, glory
Sing glory to the Lord
Sing glory to the Lord
Emmanuel
The Lord is in this place

Extract taken from the song "Surely the Lord is in this Place" by
Phil Lawson Johnston. Copyright ©1977 Thankyou Music*

"Father, we are so thankful that Your desire is to be close to Your people. Help us to seek You, to draw near to You and to walk humbly with You."

Notes

[1] Richard J. Foster, *Celebration of Discipline*, 1978, p.138. Reproduced by permission of Hodder and Stoughton Limited.
[2] See John Piper, *Desiring God*, Multnomah Publishers.

9

TO BEHOLD YOUR FACE

TO BEHOLD YOUR FACE

To behold Your face
Just to feel Your touch
To know Your embrace
That would be enough
To satisfy my thirst for You
To satisfy my need
My heart is open to You now
And I reach out to receive
I reach out to receive Your love

Extract taken from the song "To Behold Your Face" by Phil Lawson Johnston
Copyright ©1987 Thankyou Music*

Following the theme of God's face throughout Scripture has always fascinated me. The words for 'face' in Hebrew and Greek, *panim* and *prosopon*, can also mean 'presence'. So, to seek God's face is to seek His presence. There are so many verses that refer to God's countenance, and which call upon us to seek His face or presence, and this is so vital for our understanding of worship, that this topic is worth special study.

Glory in His holy name; let the hearts of those rejoice who seek the LORD. Seek the LORD and His strength; Seek His face evermore. (I Chronicles 16:10f).

God looks and sees

First of all we know that He sees all things. From the beginning He observed what He had created and saw that it was good, and He continued to pay attention to what He created. We see Him looking for Adam and Eve in the garden after they had sinned; and we learn that He is watching us still: *"For My eyes are on all their ways; they are not hidden from My face, nor is their iniquity hidden from My eyes* (Jeremiah 16:17). *For the ways of man are before the eyes of the LORD, and He ponders all his paths* (Proverbs 5:21).

He can see our faith: *When He saw their faith...* (see Luke 5:20); and knows what is going on inside our thoughts. *But immediately, when Jesus perceived in His spirit that they reasoned thus within themselves...* (Mark 2:8).

Faces are significant in showing what is going on our hearts, just as the eyes are 'the window of the soul'. One can see contempt, determination, even friendship, in people's faces. Emotions of disappointment, fear, anger or elation can be clearly observed as in: 'his face fell', 'her face went white', 'they looked like thunder', or, 'their faces beamed'. God could see Cain's anger just by looking at his face: *So the LORD said to Cain, "Why are you angry? And why has your countenance fallen?"* (Genesis 4:6).

God looks with favour

We see this in Scripture too, where God's favour is often asked for, or shown, through the appearance of His face. *In the light of the king's face is life; and his favour is like a cloud of the latter rain* (Proverbs 16:15). *Look upon the face of Your anointed"* (Psalm 84:9). *Look upon me and be merciful to me* (Psalm 119:132).

We can see how God is watching over us and wanting to bless us: *The LORD looks from heaven; He sees all the sons of men. From the place of His dwelling He looks on all the inhabitants of the earth.... Behold, the eye of the LORD is on those who fear Him, on those who hope in His mercy, to deliver their soul from death, and to keep them alive in famine* (Psalm 33:13–14,18–19).

He wants to strengthen us: *For the eyes of the LORD run to and fro throughout the whole earth, to show Himself strong on behalf of those whose heart is loyal to Him* (II Chronicles 16:9).

He is watching and listening: *The eyes of the LORD are on the righteous, and His ears are open to their cry* (Psalm 34:15).

I love the picture one gets of God's beaming face in the great high priestly blessing of Numbers 6:24–26: *The LORD bless you and keep you; The LORD make His face shine upon you, and be gracious to you; The LORD lift up His countenance upon you, and give you peace."* And again, in Psalm 67:1, *God be merciful to us and bless us, and cause His face to shine upon us.*

Surely it is impossible for a person's face to shine without them smiling, and the image of God smiling as He looks on His children with favour and pleasure fills me with awe. It just reminds us of how much He adores us, as we recall from Zephaniah 3:17. As a father myself, I know that smile of delight. One cannot help it when one watches one's own children being born into the world, and as they grow up.

God's glory in Christ

It is indeed a consistent theme of Scripture that Jesus reflects the glory of the Father, as we saw in Hebrews 1:2 (see chapter three) and II Corinthians 4:6 (chapter four). *His face shone like the sun* (Matthew 17:2); and, *...His eyes like a flame of fire.... ...His countenance was like the sun shining in its strength.* (See Revelation 1:14,16.)

We read in Daniel 10:6 an Old Testament description of Christ-like glory. *His body was like beryl, his face like the appearance of lightning, his eyes like torches of fire, his arms and feet like burnished bronze in colour, and the sound of his words like the voice of a multitude.*

Eye to eye

One of the most meaningful verses that has helped me focus my heart in worship is Psalm 27:4 (See chapter eight, *Hallowed Ground.*) Often, as I begin to worship, I like to blot out everything else and just look into the face of Jesus, in my mind's eye. Then I look into His eyes and see if there is anything between us. You know how difficult it is to look someone in the eye if you are not completely right with that person. Dealing with it and receiving forgiveness, I am then able to look straight at Him with confidence. Again I turn to the prayer in Psalm 17:8, *Keep me as the apple of Your eye; Hide me under the shadow of Your wings.* I remember a speaker once saying he had wondered what the phrase, 'apple of Your eye', really meant. One understands it as being someone who is incredibly precious to us, but in the Hebrew, he saw that the word used for 'apple' actually means 'little man'! This seemed to make even less sense, until he began to think about it. When you look into someone's eyes, really close and straight in front of them, what do you see? A little reflection of yourself in their eyes, and they, likewise, see a reflection of themselves in yours. If we translate it into a worship context, and think about how we are in Christ Jesus and He is in us, then, looking into His eyes, we see a reflection of ourselves in Him and He sees a reflection of Himself in us. To me that speaks of intense intimacy with the Lord, and no wonder our hearts begin to melt and change when we have that kind of closeness to Him and gaze at His beauty in that way.

KEEP ME LORD

Keep me, Lord, as the apple of Your eye
Hide me in the shadow of Your wings
Hold me fast in the grip of Your hand
Keep me ever in Your sight
Keep me, keep me, keep me
As the apple of Your eye
Keep me as the apple of Your eye

Extract taken from the song "Keep Me Lord" by Phil Lawson Johnston
Copyright ©1989 Thankyou Music*

When God hides His face

There are times, though, when God 'hides' His face. This can be as a result of sin: *"And I will surely hide My face in that day because of all the evil which they have done, in that they have turned to other gods"* (Deuteronomy 31:18). *Behold, the LORD's hand is not shortened, that it cannot save; Nor His ear heavy that it cannot hear. But your iniquities have separated you from your God: And your sins have hidden His face from you, so that He will not hear* (Isaiah 59:1–2). So we have the great appeal in Psalm 27:9, *Do not hide Your face from me...*, and in 51:11, *Do not cast me away from Your presence, and do not take Your Holy Spirit from me.*

There are the occasions in every believer's life when God seems to be far away, and silent in the face of their prayers, and this not necessarily always caused by sin. I do not believe God generally wants to hide Himself from us or make it hard for us to find Him, but He sometimes withdraws from us when He wants to teach us something important. *"I opened for my beloved, but my beloved had turned away and was gone. My heart leaped up when he spoke. I sought him but I could not not find him; I called him, but he gave me no answer"* (Song of Solomon 5:6).

There are times when we cry out to Him. So in Isaiah 40:27 we read: *Why do you say, O Jacob, and speak, O Israel, "My way is hidden from the LORD, and my just claim is passed over by my God...."* And in 49:14, *But Zion said, "The LORD has forsaken me, and my Lord has forgotten me."*

It is wonderful that, as Christians, we can speak to God about our deepest concerns without His responding with condemnation or punishment but, rather, with understanding and comfort, though there is no licence to 'grumble', which is forbidden; and we are to rejoice *despite* the circumstances.

There is a freedom that we enjoy, to come to our heavenly Father with the pain we may be experiencing during deep suffering or confusion in our lives. Many have experienced an emptiness, which brings despair. Sometimes described as the 'dark night of the soul', or the 'soul's winter', there can be periods when God perhaps wants us to seek Him more earnestly, more desperately, even when we are only just holding on to our faith and trust. These can be times of great growth and strengthening. David expressed this when he was hiding from his enemies in the desert, isolated, lonely and probably afraid. In spite of having every human reason to accuse God of letting him down, he still cried out, *O God, You are my God, early will I seek You; My soul thirsts for You; my flesh longs for You in a dry and thirsty land where there is no water.... Because You have been my help, therefore in the shadow of Your wings I will rejoice. My soul follows close behind You; Your right hand upholds me* (Psalm 63:1,7–8). One can imagine him singing away in the darkness of the cave, needing to lift his spirits; and yet what faith he expresses in God's goodness when he sings, *Because Your lovingkindness is better than life, my lips shall praise You. Thus I will bless You while I live; I will lift up my hands in Your name. My soul shall be satisfied as with marrow and fatness* (vv.3–5). And he reminds himself of God's power: *So I have looked for You in the sanctuary to see Your power and Your glory* (v.2).

Elsewhere he desperately cries out to God to answer him and not to hide His face from him: *Answer me speedily, O LORD; My spirit fails. Do not hide Your face from me, lest I be like those who go down into the pit* (Psalm 143:7).

I can remember that once I was going through a confusing and difficult time. I called out to the Lord for help, and as I was writing this song I began to sense His comfort and peace:

COMFORT TO MY SOUL

You brought peace when I was in turmoil
You brought joy in my distress
You brought strength when I was disheartened
Swept away by fear and stress
I said, 'Lord, please come and rescue me'
You said, 'Come aside and rest'
You brought comfort to my soul
Comfort to my soul
You brought comfort to my soul

You brought hope in my uncertainty
You brought light when I'd lost my way
You brought sense to my confusion
Gently wiped my tears away
I said, 'Lord, how much more of this?'
You said, 'Come aside and rest'
You brought comfort to my soul

Comfort to my soul
You brought comfort to my soul

You forgave all my unworthiness
My guilty life has been redeemed
You've had me dressed in robes of righteousness
You restored my self-esteem
I said, 'Lord, I don't deserve all this'
You said, 'No, but the slate is clean'
You brought comfort to my soul
Comfort to my soul
You brought comfort to my soul

When my father died, I wrote another verse:

You reassured me in my sorrow
Knowing You are always near
I have hope for the future
I know that death will disappear
I said, 'Lord, can this really be?'
You said, ' Yes, there's no need to fear'
You brought comfort to my soul
Comfort to my soul
You brought comfort to my soul

Phil Lawson Johnston Copyright ©2001 IQ Music

When God sets His face against....

More awful still than when He hides His face because of sin, are the
occasions when God sets His face against people, cities or nations,
in judgment. *"And the person who turns to mediums and familiar
spirits, to prostitute himself with them, I will set My face against that
person and cut him off from his people* (Leviticus 20:6). *Therefore
thus says the Lord of hosts, the God of Israel: 'Behold, I will set
My face against you for catastrophe and for cutting off all Judah*
(Jeremiah 44:11).

Biblical judgment is an unpopular subject these days, and it is
regarded by so many as an exclusively Old Testament idea, coming

from a 'God of wrath', who was replaced by a 'God of love' in the New Testament. But that is a gross misrepresentation. God's wrath and God's love are both evident in both the Testaments. We would be extremely foolish to ignore what Jesus said about judgment; and what we read elsewhere in the New Testament concerning the anger of God at sin. Indeed, *...It is a fearful thing to fall into the hands of the living God* (Hebrews 10:31); and there are highly significant passages in Revelation, which are full of scenes of God's wrath being poured out on His enemies. We hear the multitudes of heaven shouting, *"Alleluia! Salvation and glory and honour and power belong to the Lord our God! For true and righteous are His judgments, because He has judged the great harlot who corrupted the earth with her fornication; and He has avenged on her the blood of His servants shed by her"* (Revelation 19:1–2).

It would be a frightening thing to fall into God's hands of judgment, and yet, although as believers who are trusting in Him we know we have passed through judgment already, the Bible warns us as God's children that we will be disciplined: *Do not despise the chastening of the Almighty* (Job 5:17). *For whom the LORD loves He corrects, just as a father the son in whom he delights* (Proverbs 3:12). *If you endure chastening, God deals with you as sons; for what son is there whom a father does not chasten?* (Hebrews 12:7). *Now no chastening seems to be joyful for the present, but painful; nevertheless, afterward it yields the peaceable fruit of righteousness to those who have been trained by it* (Hebrews 12:11).

As we lift our eyes to our God and Saviour, we know that His favour does indeed rest on us and whatever we go through, either at His hand or others'; we know He is faithful and trustworthy and will never let us down.

Although, of course, we can only 'see' the Lord in part now, there will come a time when we shall know Him fully. Now we can 'see' Him in His word and in our imaginations as we turn our faces to Him in worship and prayer. The more we gaze at Him and worship Him in His glory and beauty, a process of change will go on in our hearts, which is so beautifully described by Paul, in II Corinthians 3:16. *And we who with unveiled faces behold the Lord's glory, are being transformed into His likeness with ever increasing glory, which comes from the Lord who is the Spirit.*

As we 'behold the Lord's glory', we will begin to 'reflect the Lord's glory', and gradually become more like Him; a process that will be complete on the day when we see Him face to face.

Beloved, now we are children of God; and it has not yet been revealed what we shall be, but we know that when He is revealed, we shall be like Him, for we shall see Him as He is (I John 3:2).

As we see Him in part, it is like looking into a mirror that is in many pieces, and the more we see, the more that mirror comes together and the more we reflect His image. When we meet Him on that final day, the mirror will be complete and *...we shall all be changed – in a moment, in the twinkling of an eye, at the last trumpet....* (See I Corinthians 15:52.)

Moses' face shone from being in God's presence. (See Exodus 34:29–35); Stephen's face shone like an angel's when he was on trial (Acts 6:15), then spoke with boldness given by the Spirit: *But he, being full of the Holy Spirit, gazed into heaven and saw the glory of God, and Jesus standing at the right hand of God* (Acts 7:55).

As we lift our eyes to Him in worship, then perhaps our faces may take on some of the glow that comes from the Lord, for, *They looked to Him and were radiant, and their faces were not ashamed* (Psalm 34:5).

As you seek Him, may His face shine upon you!

"Father, we praise You for Your favour and Your smiling face as You look with delight upon Your children. As we seek Your face and behold Your glory, may we reflect Your beauty and character, for the honour of Your name. Amen."

10

TASTE AND SEE
— A SENSE OF GOD

TASTE AND SEE

Those who wait upon the Lord
Will soar with eagles' wings
They will know His strength
Those who come to rest
In the presence of the Lord
They will learn to be still

O taste and see that the Lord is good
His promises stand firm forever
O taste and see that the Lord is good
His word is forever true

Those who listen to His voice
And take His words to heart
Their joy will be complete
Those who seek His face
And follow where He may lead
They will learn to trust

THE SONG OF THE FATHER'S HEART

Those who know that they've been forgiven much
They will love Him all the more
Those who see Jesus as He really is
They will learn to glorify His name

It is through our five senses we test and authenticate what is real. We need them all to be functioning properly if we are going to be able to fully experience reality. There are, of course, those who from birth or through accident or disease lack one or other of their senses, and can survive perfectly well and lead a fulfilled life without them; but it seems that God has provided, ideally, all five for us to be able to enjoy everything that He has created in this world. In testing reality, more than one sense is usually needed. With one sense we can be mistaken; with two or three we can be convinced. 'I thought I saw you in the street', means I could have been wrong, but, 'I thought I saw you in the street and when you came close and spoke to me, I knew it was you', means you were definitely there.

In terms of faith, generally we believe by hearing the truth. *...And how shall they believe in Him of whom they have not heard? And how shall they hear without a preacher?* (Romans 10:14). However, some need more than one sense to be involved. When Thomas 'heard' about Jesus's resurrection from the other disciples, that was not enough for him. *"...Unless I see in His hands the print of the nails, and put my finger into the print of the nails, and put my hand into His side, I will not believe"* (John 20:25). He needed sight and touch as well as hearing, in order to believe —although Jesus went on to say that those who believe without seeing will be blessed; *"Blessed are those who have not seen and yet have believed"* (v.29).

Perhaps the hardest sense to deceive is smell. You can try and cover up unpleasant odours with something nicer, but no one is deceived! When our sons used to return from playing soccer or rugby, and their socks were so high they were practically walking across the floor of their own accord, the whole house was very soon filled with an abundance of spray deodorant! But even that did not succeed in disguising what was underneath! (I exaggerate, of course.)

The physical senses have been used in different ways as part of worship: incense, bread and wine, icons, music, listening to the word, etc., even the handshake during the peace, the modern equivalent of the 'holy kiss' in Scripture, I suppose. Similarly, there is a way in which we use our 'spiritual' five senses as well. We often sing of 'seeing' the Lord, or 'touching' or being 'touched' by Him, but what do we really mean by these terms? One could describe them as the 'senses of the heart', and it is to do with knowing, sensing and experiencing the Lord as we worship. As I say many times in this book, worship should involve every part of us: our whole mind, soul and strength. Sin deadens our spiritual senses, and we need His cleansing before we are able to know Him in these ways.

In some churches there is so much emphasis on just 'hearing' —reflected in the proportion of the service time allocated—that, vital as hearing the Word of God is, one can sometimes feel one has missed out on also being 'touched' by Him, or 'seeing' Jesus in His glory, 'tasting' His goodness or 'smelling' His fragrance of life. *That which was from the beginning, which we have heard, which we have seen with our eyes, which we have looked upon, and our hands have handled, concerning the Word of life—the life was manifested, and we have seen, and bear witness, and declare to you that eternal life which was with the Father and was manifested to us—that which we have seen and heard we declare to you, that you also may have fellowship with us; and truly our fellowship is with the Father and with His Son Jesus Christ* (I John 1:1ff).

We may not see, hear or touch as John did, but through the Spirit we can experience something of the same. We not only know *about* God through the Bible, but in relationship we come to know Him and are known by Him. We begin to recognise His voice in our hearts, experience the touch of His hand upon our lives and *taste and see that the Lord is good* (Psalm 34:8). In contrast to idols, which are unable to speak, hear, smell, feel, or walk (see Psalm 115:5–7), the God who created the senses is able to communicate with us through all of them. *The hearing ear and the seeing eye, the LORD has made them both* (Proverbs 20:12).

He not only sees and hears: *He who planted the ear, shall He not hear? He who formed the eye, shall He not see?* (Psalm 94:9); but He goes further and knows what is in our minds, too. (v.11).

He speaks through many means. He touches us through His Spirit; gives us His 'hug' of love and acceptance; He watches and looks to strengthen us when we are weak; He tastes whether we are 'hot' or 'cold', and smells the fragrance of our sacrifices.

Let us now look at each sense in more detail.

Sight

I have covered much of the ground regarding this particular sense in chapter nine, *To Behold Your Face*, but there are a few further thoughts I would like to express here.

First of all, we know that God is watching us: *The eyes of the LORD are in every place, keeping watch on the evil and the good.* (Proverbs 15:3). In fact, He can see right through us. Often we read of Jesus perceiving 'the thoughts of their hearts'.

Although our sight is thoroughly imperfect, we can 'see' something of God too. We 'see' something of His character through that which He causes and holds in existence: His creation. *For since the creation of the world, His invisible attributes are clearly seen, being understood by the things that are made, even His eternal power and Godhead, so that they are without excuse* (Romans 1:20). One can learn a certain amount about an artist by observing their art. It is important, though, that we understand that whilst He is present to His creation as Creator, the created order is not itself divine: it is distinct from the Creator, and it is fallen, marred by sin. To attribute divinity to the created order itself is the error of pantheism.

However, we only see God in part, like glimpses out of the corner of our eyes *as in a mirror*, and then only really by faith, *For we walk by faith not by sight* (II Corinthians 5:7). *Now faith is the substance of things hoped for, the evidence of things not seen* (Hebrews 11:1).

And yet, He shines His light into our lives so that we may begin to see His glory: *For it is the God who commanded light to shine out of darkness, who has shone in our hearts to give the light of the knowledge of the glory of God in the face of Jesus Christ* (II Corinthians 4:6).

We often say, 'I see', when we mean that we understand. We also speak of the 'eyes of faith', by which we understand His word and will: *Open my eyes, that I may see wondrous things from Your law* (Psalm 119:18). Paul prays for his readers that, *...the eyes of your* *understanding being enlightened; that you may know what is the hope of His calling, what are the riches of the glory of His inheritance in the saints* (Ephesians 1:18).

However, sin and rebellion can make us blind and deaf to the things of God: *"Son of man, you dwell in the midst of a rebellious house, which has eyes to see but does not see, and ears to hear but does not hear; for they are a rebellious house"* (Ezekiel 12:2).

We recall that, in Revelation 3:18, Jesus counsels the church that is blind to buy from Him salve to put in their eyes so that they could see.

Jesus spoke about His doing what He could see His Father was doing: *"Most assuredly, I say to you, the Son can do nothing of Himself, but what He sees the Father do, for whatever He does, the Son also does in like manner"* (John 5:19); and He told Paul He was sending him, *"...to open their eyes. in order to turn them from darkness to light, and from the power of Satan to God..."* (Acts 26:18). As we noted in chapter nine, as we look at the Lord we are being changed. (See II Corinthians 3:16).

Through the Spirit we can get a foretaste of what is to come (see again I Corinthians 2:9); and, finally, *...Beloved, now we are children of God; and it has not yet been revealed what we shall be, but we know that when He is revealed, we shall be like Him, for we shall see Him as He is* (I John 3:2).

CONTEMPLATE

When I lift my eyes to You
And contemplate Your beauty,
When I lift my eyes to see
The glory of Your face.

I love You, adore You, my one desire is You.
When I think about Your grace
And contemplate Your mercy,
When I lift my heart to taste
The beauty of Your peace.

When I listen to Your voice
And contemplate Your calling,
There's a burning in my heart
Knowing I belong to You.

When I rest secure in You
And contemplate the future,
I know I will never fall
While I'm holding on to You.

Phil Lawson Johnston Copyright ©2001 IQ Music/Cloud Music

Hearing

We know that He hears us when we pray: *Now this is the confidence that we have in Him, that if we ask anything according to His will, He hears us. And if we know that He hears us, whatever we ask, we know that we have the petitions that we have asked of Him* (I John 5:14–15). *The eyes of the LORD are on the righteous, and His ears are open to their cry* (Psalm 34:15). Yet, as we saw in chapter nine, sin can prevent our being heard. How does He hear our worship? Are there are times when it sounds so awful that He would say, *"Take away from Me the noise of your songs, for I will not hear the melody of your stringed instruments. But let justice roll down like water, and righteousness like a mighty stream!"* (Amos 5:23–24). Reading this, some might say, 'Ah, I told you so. This confirms that God hates your guitars and drums; away with them!' I think, however, it really means that whatever style we choose, if our hearts are far from Him and our lives do not reflect what we sing, then He finds it a vile sound.

What we hear affects us. Music has a profound effect on our mood; ambient, stirring, frenetic disco, smoochy nightclub, supermarket, water dripping, etc.... Listening to praise music can raise our faith, encourage us or help us to drive more considerately! Certain songs can evoke memories and feelings that we once had. What we take in with our minds – positive or negative, encouraging or discouraging thoughts – will inevitably influence the way we act. Similarly, when we listen to God and and take His words to heart, what we say and do will reflect them.

There are different ways in which we hear Him. Primarily, He speaks to us through His Word, the Bible, but we can also hear Him through others, and also the 'still small voice of calm' within our hearts.

We need to recognize His voice: *He who has an ear, let him hear* (Revelation 2:7,11,17,29 etc.); *"...and the sheep follow him, for they know his voice. Yet they will by no means follow a stranger, but will flee from him, for they do not know the voice of strangers"* (John 10:4–5). *Your ears shall hear a word behind you, saying, "This is the way, walk in it"* (Isaiah 30:21).

We need to listen and not harden our hearts to Him: *Today, if you will hear His voice: Do not harden your hearts...* (Psalm 95:7–8).

GIVE ME A HEARING HEART

O, give me a hearing heart O Lord
Give me the will to obey
Give me a desire to renew my love
To keep my heart open through the day
And give me a holy fear O Lord
Give me a hatred of sin
Cleanse me from secret and shameful thoughts
Brighten the eyes that have grown dim

That I may see, that I may hear
That I may love the things that You hold dear
That I may change that I may grow
That Your likeness may now begin to show
Give me a hearing heart, give me a hearing heart
Give me a hearing, hearing heart

And give me a faithful heart O Lord
Give me the nerve to believe
You give me confidence to draw near
Freedom to come and receive
And give me a waiting heart O Lord
To stay silent before Your throne

Give me a real and determined desire
To seek You and serve You alone

Extract taken from the song "Give Me a Hearing Heart"
by Phil Lawson Johnston
Copyright ©1987 Thankyou Music*

Touch

We often speak of being 'touched' by someone's kindness, or our hearts being touched as we are moved by a beautiful story, scene or piece of music. Likewise, there is a very real sense in which we can be 'touched' by the Lord during worship, prayer or listening to someone preach. Just as some people have heard God speak in an almost physical voice, and others have 'seen' Jesus in what is called an 'open-eye' vision, so still others have felt a physical touch on their shoulder or head, for example, during times of prayer. They have looked round and there has been no-one around. Many others have felt heat go through them when someone has prayed for healing and laid hands on them.

The warmth of God's embrace is something that many of us have experienced. When I am leading worship, I often like to think of it as us reaching out to touch Him, or our spirits touching His Spirit, or our hearts touching His heart. And when we pray for healing, sometimes it seems like us reaching out spiritually to touch the hem of His garment, and Him responding by reaching forth His hand and 'touching' us.

In the believers' prayer, in Acts 4:30, they cry out to Him: *"...grant to Your servants that with all boldness they may speak Your word, by stretching out Your hand to heal, and that signs and wonders may be done through the name of Your holy Servant Jesus."* Jeremiah experienced the Lord touching him. *"Then the LORD put forth His hand and touched my mouth, and the LORD said to me...."* (Jeremiah 1:9).

One could say that the Lord is 'touched' by our troubles, which can be a great comfort when we cry out to Him: *For we do not have a High Priest who cannot sympathize with our weaknesses, but was in all points tempted as we are, yet without sin. Let us therefore*

176

come boldly to the throne of grace, that we may obtain mercy and find grace to help in time of need (Hebrews 4:15–16).

Taste

As a sense, taste is very closely connected with smell. In fact, it is said that sometimes we think we are tasting something when we are really smelling it. Our taste buds are very sensitive, and there are tastes which we find attractive or repellent —and one person can have very different preferences to another. I find that I hate the taste of beetroots whereas others cannot cope with the taste of bananas. Tastes also change as one grows older. I used to hate olives; now I cannot get enough of them! Childhood memories are often triggered by the taste of certain sweets; for me, it is fruit gums. Taste falls into basically four categories: sweet, bitter, salty and sour. We use the word frequently in a figurative sense: for example, a bad situation or a disagreeable conversation 'leaves a nasty taste in the mouth', or we exult in, 'the sweet taste of victory', and we often express our preferences by saying such-and-such is 'not to my taste'.

The Bible speaks of us tasting the goodness of the Lord and His word: *Oh, taste and see that the LORD is good...* (Psalm 34:8); *...as newborn babes, desire the pure milk of the word, that you may grow thereby, if indeed you have tasted that the Lord is gracious* (I Peter 2:2); *...tasted the heavenly gift...tasted the good word of God....* (see Hebrews 6:4f). *How sweet are Your words to my taste, sweeter than honey to my mouth!* (Psalm 119:103). Wisdom, too, tastes sweet to the soul (see Proverbs 24:14).

There were times when a prophet experienced first a sweet taste in the stomach, and then a bitterness, when prophesying God's judgment. (See Ezekiel 3:3 and Revelation 10:8–11). Job, in his suffering, described his soul as bitter (Job 27:2).

The phrase, 'to taste death', is also used often. *"Assuredly, I say to you, there are some standing here who shall not taste death till they see the Son of Man coming in His kingdom"* (Matthew 16:28). *But we see Jesus, who was made a little lower than the angels, for the suffering of death crowned with glory and honour, that He, by the grace of God, might taste death for everyone* (Hebrews 2:9).

To 'suffer' death I can understand, but to 'taste' death I find a rather strange idea; yet it underlines that the 'cup' which Jesus drank included experiencing human death —for us.

Love of the Lord is prefigured in terms of fruit that we taste: *"Like an apple tree among the trees of the woods, so is my beloved among the sons. I sat down in his shade with great delight, and his fruit was sweet to my taste"* (Song of Solomon 2:3). The Holy Spirit produces in us the fruit of the Spirit (Galatians 5:22–23); and as we bear that fruit, the Father is glorified (John 15:8) —and fruit is full of wonderful taste!

Smell

Sensitive as taste is, it is crude compared to smell. Smell is supposedly the hardest sense to understand, explain or fool. It attracts or repels, and affects us more than any other sense. When I catch the smell of meat cooking, my stomach juices run wild and immediately I feel hungry! When there is a roast joint on the table I cannot stay silent: "Aaaaaah! Yum!" Different smells can be very evocative; mown grass epitomises summer, peat burning could only be Scotland or Ireland. Memories are triggered, and smell is used in therapy to aid recall in patients with amnesia. It is recommended that you put vanilla essence in the oven or brew some coffee when you are showing prospective buyers around your house! Some butterflies attract by emitting a tiny amount of scent, which can be picked up several miles away; perhaps this could be the greatest challenge for the perfume industry! You cannot ignore it. When there is smoke in the air, one has to discover whether it is a bonfire or something more worrying. When one has got 'something nasty' on one's shoe in the car, you cannot drive until you have dealt with it! —you cannot cover it up. And one can detect a healthy or unhealthy smell in people.

Death has a particularly unpleasant smell, which, of course, is why they were reluctant to open Lazarus's tomb. Dead ants give off a specific smell caused by oleic acid, so that the other ants carry them off to the ant cemetery. Experiments have been conducted where they have painted this acid on to live ants, so that even they have been carried off, in spite of their struggling!

Places, too, can have a smell of death. You can enter a church and be met by a smell of decay in the atmosphere, as opposed to others, which have the fragrance of life. There is a story of one church which had an unpleasant smell, as well as a heaviness in the air, which made it very hard for them to worship. It transpired that it had been desecrated by Satanists. The church decided to hold a service of communion and cleansing, and, during the prayer, people smelt a waft of flowers, which swept through the church building, bringing a freedom and new life to the congregation. I was reminded recently of another occasion when I was speaking at a London church about the fragrance of worship. At one point, a lady had to go out to help with the children. When she returned to the service she smelt a strong aroma of something like incense in the church, and it was not a church where it is used at all!

In Scripture, the smell of sacrifice is often mentioned. The expressions 'pleasing aroma' or 'fragrant offering' are used numerous times in Exodus, Leviticus and Deuteronomy to describe a sacrifice that is pleasing to God. I cannot believe that it was the smell of the meat that pleased Him, much more the devotion and purity of those giving it. There are occasions when people are regarded as a 'stench', or 'obnoxious' to others they have offended (e.g., Genesis 34:30).

The concept of the 'fragrant offering' is also mentioned several times in the New Testament. Giving is regarded as one: ...*having received from Epaphroditus the things sent from you, a sweet-smelling aroma, an acceptable sacrifice, well pleasing to God. And my God shall supply all your need according to His riches in glory by Christ Jesus* (Philippians 4:18–19).

Jesus Himself is declared to be the ultimate pleasing and fragrant offering to God: *And walk in love, as Christ also has loved us and given Himself for us, an offering and a sacrifice to God for a sweet-smelling aroma* (Ephesians 5:2).

In that fascinating passage II Corinthians 2:14–16, which we considered in chapter seven, there is the remarkable expression *the fragrance of the knowledge of Him.* We are *the aroma of Christ.* That we have a 'spiritual smell' which other people can detect is an extraordinary thought to me. It seems to say that as we are in Christ, then the fragrance of His life and death dwells in us. This is so that knowledge of Him can be spread abroad through us. We are reminded of the verse in the Song of Solomon that says, *"Awake O north wind, and come O south! Blow upon my garden, that its spices may flow out"* (4:16).

It is as if the Spirit 'blows' on the 'garden' of our lives, so that our 'fragrance' is smelt by those around us. It brings us back to the fact that our lives should speak, show, and express the life of Jesus living in us. If our lives are centred upon the cross, then to some we will 'smell' of judgment, and that is uncomfortable. Can you think of people you have befriended, and even though you have tried to be as sensitive as possible with them about your faith, yet they have somehow kept you at arm's length? It is as if they do not want you to come too close. There may well be all sorts of other reasons for this, but I wonder whether, at times, the light of Jesus might have repelled them. We are told that *men loved darkness rather than light* (John 3:19), and perhaps it is the light of Jesus Christ that they are reacting to. There are other people who might have said that there is something in you which they wish they had; I would like to suggest that it is the fragrance of life that has attracted them. Jesus must have been the most attractive figure, even though He challenged people hard, and we can only hope and pray that our lives will be attractive and challenging because of His indwelling presence.

How do we smell to God? Sin stinks, and it lingers on until we are washed, just as the smell of pigs must have clung to the rags worn by the prodigal son. No matter how much we try to cover it up with pious words and actions, we cannot pretend to God. He sees and smells through it all. He is preparing a bride who will be fit for a King. Esther had to go through twelve months of beauty treatments, six with oil of myrrh and six with perfumes and cosmetics, before she was ready to be presented to King Xerxes! The church is being prepared to be beautiful and pleasurable to Jesus, the Bridegroom. In Psalm 45:8 we are given a picture of a king and his bride. It is said of him, ...*all your garments are scented with myrrh and aloes and cassia*. And in the Song of Songs again, we are given this beautiful declaration: *"How fair is your love, my sister, my spouse! How much better than wine is your love, and the scent of your perfume than all spices"* (4:10).

Two of the gifts that were brought to Jesus as an act of worship by the wise men were fragrances: myrrh and incense, signifying His death and deity. Perhaps they were the same spices that the women brought to the tomb to anoint His body, although they were not needed at the time as He had already risen. The stories of the prostitute in

Luke 7 and Mary in John 12, anointing Jesus before His death, speak so powerfully of worship as well. In the first of these examples we note, firstly, that it was a costly gift, worth a year's wages in the case of the prostitute, the proceeds of her profession and probably her 'pension'. Being given as a sacrifice, it was seen by Judas as being wasted, yet it shows something of the extravagance of worship that is acceptable to Him. The most precious thing we can bring to Him is our heart, and thus our life. 'What can I bring Him, poor as I am?......give Him my heart.'

Secondly, Jesus commended her for it and accepted it; *"She has done a good work for me"* (Matthew 26:10).

Time spent with Him is pleasing to Him. He welcomes us and loves it when we devote ourselves to loving and listening to Him.

Thirdly, it was an act of intimacy, of which the Pharisees who were there disapproved. She was known to be a sinful woman who was used to another kind of intimacy, possibly even with others in the room, and yet here she is expressing her gratitude to Jesus. She sensed that He accepted her and was prepared to forgive her for her sinful life. She is prepared to throw away whatever dignity she might have had and use the 'glory' of her hair (see I Corinthians 11:15) to wipe Jesus's feet, having already washed them with her tears. If this kind of emotion was shown in your church's worship, would you be embarrassed? Perhaps it is a regular event for many of you, but some I know would be horrified. Yet when there is genuine repentance going on in the heart, tears often accompany it appropriately. It is such a gift to be able to cry and yet, for Anglo-Saxon men, it has been beaten or bullied out of many of us.

In the case of Mary, in John 12, she was a godly person and a friend of Jesus, and she gave her costly gift. Sinner and godly friend, all are welcomed and received by Jesus.

The act was marked by humility. Jesus's feet would have been covered with dust and unmentionable things from the street, and the woman unashamedly washed Him. Jesus Himself washed the disciples' feet, giving this as an example for us to follow. What would be the equivalent today?

John 12:3 says that *the house was filled with the fragrance of the oil,* and the **fragrance of worship** is an expression that sums up much of what I am aiming for, when I seek to help others pour out their hearts to Jesus. Everyone who had been in that place would have left smelling of the perfume. It is the same when one embraces someone who is wearing a strong fragrance: it is transferred to you as well. When we worship from our hearts, using our whole being with every sense, and we 'embrace' Jesus with our adoration, the aroma of Christ will cling to us.

"I pray that as we worship with our hearts and our whole being, using every sense, and as we embrace Jesus with adoration, the aroma of Christ might cling to us. I pray that others might catch His fragrance in and on us, and long to find the life that He offers."

THE AROMA OF CHRIST

May we be a fragrant offering, pleasing unto You
People set apart for Jesus, living out the truth
May we know the full anointing of Your Spirit on us now
May there be a sweet aroma flowing through, as You…
Breathe on us the fragrance of Your life
Breathe on us the sweetness and the spice
Breathe on us the aroma of Christ

May the fragrant life of Jesus spread abroad through us
To a world grown used to nothing but the sickly smell of death
May our lives speak loud and clearly of Your presence here
Standing with a smile of welcome, You are near

Phil Lawson Johnston
Copyright ©2001 IQ Music/1999 Cloud Music

Part Three

Leadership of Worship

11

A SHEPHERD'S HEART —LEADERSHIP QUALITIES

A SHEPHERD'S HEART

We feel Your heart is burning with compassion
For the lonely ones starved of loving care
We know Your heart is reaching out to gather
To lift them up and hold them in Your arms

Give us Your heart Lord, give us Your heart
Give us Your heart Lord, that we may love like You

To feel the pain of a child who's never
Known their father touch them out of love
Their spirit crushed, full of fear and anger
Not allowed to grow up free and strong

So many sheep, broken and unlovely
We could never love them on our own
A Shepherd's heart, burning with compassion
Would give us what we need to bring them home

Proverbs 4:23 has always meant a great deal to me: *Keep your heart with all diligence, for out of it spring the issues of life* [an alternative translation, which I like, is 'wellspring'] —a precept which underlies much of this chapter. Many of the ideas that I express here are opinions I have formed in the light of my own experience. Some of them may only be relevant in a cultural setting similar to my own, and other cultures may require a very different approach. Nonetheless, I feel sure that many of the principles stated here will be common to all leadership situations and I trust that they will be useful.

The leader of worship

The term 'worship leader' as such, does not appear in the Bible, but we can see that there were those who were set apart specifically for the leading of music for the Lord. There were a number who belonged to the priestly tribe of Levites who were appointed by David to ...*minister before the ark of the LORD, to commemorate, to thank, and to praise the LORD God of Israel* (I Chronicles 16:4). Elsewhere, in I Chronicles 6, we read of the appointment of other singers and musicians who were ...*ministering with music before the dwelling place of the tabernacle of meeting....* We are told they *served in their office according to their order.* From these passages we can begin to understand that there was a ministry of spiritual music-leading at the centre of the temple worship, and if we believe that Jesus fulfilled all the priestly ministries of the Old Testament, one can conclude that He Himself is our perfect worship leader. He gave perfect worship to His Father through the fragrant offering of laying down His life willingly for the world, and in Him we are able to do the same through His grace, and the empowering of His Spirit.

Whatever we do, as leaders of God's people in music or any other area of ministry, we do it under the supervision, leadership and blessing of our great High Priest, Christ Jesus, through the Holy Spirit. We lead people to the throne of God, giving them the right opportunity and encouragement to praise, give thanks, and fall down in reverent worship and adoration, but it is the Holy Spirit who enables His people to offer acceptable worship. I was greatly helped by Matt Redman's coining of the title 'lead worshipper' to describe those of us who are given the job of leading the sung worship at our services.

Bill Hybels of Willow Creek speaks of the three qualities of leadership as being character, competence and chemistry, which neatly sums up much of what I want to unpack here. I want to look at some of the qualities of this role of leadership not only to help us in self-assessment of our own ministries but also to help anyone who has the job of choosing and appointing someone to fulfil that role. Many of these qualities are common to any kind of leadership, but with obvious particularities here, which are relevant to music leading. For the sake of convenience I will continue to use the terms 'leader of worship', 'worship leader' and 'leading worship', though they should be considered in the light of what I have mentioned above.

A leader of worship is not just a leader of songs, played to specific instructions and order given by someone else. There are many church music groups who are just there to accompany worship rather than lead it, basically as an alternative to an organist doing it in the time-honoured traditional way. Nor should they be a kind of cheerleader or community singing leader, who bullies reluctant congregations into singing songs that they dislike —even if that is what it may seem like sometimes! They are not to be someone who worships while others watch, rather like someone who has prepared a great feast, invited their friends to come and view the spread, and then sits down at the only place setting and eats while the others watch! Nor are they to be someone who plays while others worship, or a 'warm-up person' before the sermon. It is not a platform for entertainers who want to put on a show and perform so as to be acclaimed, nor for those who want to 'make it'.

There are real dangers for those worship leaders and songwriters who have reached almost cult status through large conference platforms. Great is the temptation to welcome super-stardom and the acclamation of thousands of young people who want to follow you. To be a role model of integrity and godliness takes much grace in that sort of position. The worst scenario is for people to fall into the trap that afflicted the young Corinthian church, where rivalry arose between the followers of different leaders: *each of you says, "I am of Paul"; another, "I am of Apollos..."* (I Corinthians 1:12). Most entertainers or performers have been trained to grab the attention, and basically say, 'Look at me; listen to me!', whereas the essence of leading worship is to help people, through the songs or hymns they sing, to centre their attention on God, not on the leader.

Carl Tuttle

There is an understandable tendency to look for the nearest gifted musician and automatically assume that they are the best to lead the sung worship, but they are not always necessarily the right people to do it. I remember hearing Carl Tuttle speak about the beginnings of the Vineyard movement. It started as a home group made up of burnt-out and beaten-up Christians who wanted to come before the Lord and love Him and be loved by Him. Carl was the guitarist who was chosen to lead them in worship through songs, which helped them express their adoration and longings. On his own admission, he was not the greatest musician in the world, but was the only one available and the Lord equipped him for the role. After a while the group grew into a church, and many other musicians began to join. Carl recognised them and went to John Wimber to suggest that he stand down and let one of the more able musicians take over as worship leader. John said no, because Carl was the one whom God had chosen and that the others needed to become worshippers themselves first, before being involved in leadership. Later, many of them did become worship leaders and wrote a good number of the songs that we have loved, from the Vineyard 'stable'.

Reluctant leadership

Those whom God chose often accepted leadership reluctantly. Moses said to God, *"Who am I that I should go to Pharaoh, and that I should bring the children of Israel out of Egypt?"* when God called him at the burning bush, (Exodus 3:11). Gideon's reaction to being told by the angel that he was to go and save Israel was also typical: *"O my Lord, how can I save Israel? Indeed my clan is the weakest in Manasseh, and I am the least in my father's house"* (Judges 6:15).

Saul reacted similarly, and Jeremiah was worried about his age and inexperience: *Then said I: "Ah, Lord GOD! Behold, I cannot speak, for I am a youth"* (Jeremiah 1:6). The Lord's answer is, *"I am with you."*

Reluctance to lead can be an advantage over too much self-confidence, because of the importance of depending on God's strength instead of one's own. Jesus stressed the priority of humility; *"If anyone desires to be first, he shall be last of all and servant of all"* (Mark 9:35).

Servant leadership

As with all leadership, the leaders of worship need to be servant-hearted, and to be glad to serve. (See Psalm 100:2 [KJV]). They need to be humble enough to be willing to 'decrease' while Jesus 'increases', and in the case of training others, willing to let others increase even to the extent of being eclipsed by them. Jesus's statement in Mark 9:35, regarding the nature of spiritual leadership, sums up our need for humility. The role is one of leading the flock to drink, like a shepherd who leads from the front not shoving from behind. *Shepherd the flock of God which is among you, serving as overseers...* (I Peter 5:2). This verse applies primarily to elders in a church, but insofar as the people are under the care of the leader of worship while they are leading, it is relevant to them, too. We have a list of gifts in Romans 12:6–8, all of which can be relevant to the leadership of worship. *Having then gifts differing according to the grace that is given to us, let us use them: if prophecy, let us prophesy in proportion to our faith; or ministry, let us use it in our ministering; he who teaches, in teaching; he who exhorts, in exhortation; he who gives, with liberality; he who leads, with diligence; he who shows mercy, with cheerfulness.*

As is common to all forms of 'up-front' leadership, one is going to be the focus of people's attention, and that can give one a sense of power and control. People are likely to follow whatever you ask them to do, unless it is too outrageous, embarrassing, or too far outside their comfort zone. I have always been conscious of my own somewhat reserved nature, and have been sometimes surprised at how at ease I feel when faced with large numbers of people. When I took part in one of those assessment schemes which are intended to show you what character and tendencies you have, I was surprised at my results. Everyone was said to fall into three categories: affiliation (good with people), achievement (target orientated) and power (enjoying influence). I scored highly in the area of power, which rather took me aback, until I began to think about it. I realised that when leading people in worship I like having the freedom to lead in whatever way I sense is right at the time, and I enjoy watching people respond.

Sometimes there is quite a thin line between leading and manipulation, particularly when the songs call for a response of intimate adoration, triumphant proclamation or interaction with the

Holy Spirit. I see this particularly when leading worship during a ministry time, when people are being prayed for. I have to ask myself the question: am I choosing this song because I know it is likely to cause people to respond in an emotional way, or because I believe it is a song that God may want to use to speak to someone in a special way? I have to proceed in faith that it is the Spirit leading me, and not my own desire to influence people. When I see the evidence of God's Spirit touching people's lives, and hear how certain songs have been the key to someone's prayer, I rejoice that I can be used in this way. While I am singing I will often watch what is going on, and it sometimes seems like Jesus walking through His garden, pausing by different plants, pruning a little dead wood here and watering a thirsty shrub there, untangling and removing bindweed here, and sowing seeds there. It is one of my most favourite times, and it is always a privilege to see the Lord at work.

Come bless the Lord

Leading worship is similar to being an usher who calmly leads people to a place of face-to-face adoration with the Lord; a conductor who draws the different human instruments that make up a gathering of worshippers into a symphony of praise. There is an element of being an encourager or prompter who guides people towards the throne of God. They are the ones who say or sing: *Behold, bless the LORD, all you servants of the LORD* (Psalm 134:1); and, *Oh come, let us sing to the LORD! Let us shout joyfully to the Rock of our salvation. Let us come before His presence with thanksgiving; Let us shout joyfully to Him with psalms.... Oh come, let us worship and bow down; Let us kneel before the LORD our Maker* (Psalm 95).

Worshippers first

The worship leader needs to be a worshipper first, so that others will follow their example: *...be an example to the believers in word, in conduct, in love, in spirit, in faith, in purity* (ITimothy 4:12).

A good worship leader will be a role model for others. He needs to be able to communicate: *Oh, magnify the LORD with me, and let us exalt His name together* (Psalm 34:3); saying, in effect, 'will you join me in praising God?'

Enablers

Worship leaders are, effectively, enablers; those who enable others to fulfil their roles as priests, now that there is a priesthood of all believers (I Peter 2:9). The worship leader leading a band or music group has a pastoral role: encouraging the members to themselves be worshippers first —worshipping with their instruments, and being sensitive to the Spirit. Worship leaders have a two-fold ministry: a ministry to God, and to people.

A ministry to God

In the midst of the mechanics of trying to get the worship music right, there can be a danger of losing sight of the primary role of *ministering before the Lord*. Sometimes this can get lost, as one gets so caught up in correct keys, intros and outros, and sticking close to the dots on the page. Worrying about the sound or tuning of an instrument, as important as that may be, can so easily distract from having one's heart focussed completely on the Lord. Yet, as we have already seen, this was regarded as a priestly ministry by David. Those responsible were appointed to be *singers accompanied by instruments of music...* (I Chronicles 15:16).

A ministry to people

The leader of worship is there to serve the body of Christ, not to occupy a position of status, although they will be the focus of everyone's attention at certain times when they are out in front. Again we recall the injunction of Jesus to His apostles regarding the need for humility in spiritual leadership.

I believe there is a correct balance between confident leadership and humility. Some would prefer it if the worship leader and group were tucked away behind a pillar and not the focus of attention. I do not think that works very well, because it is a fact of nature that most people like to be led by someone they can see. It takes skill to be able to stand up in front of a crowd and humbly point away from oneself and draw people's attention on to the Lord, so that one is almost forgotten. The tendency to want to draw attention to oneself can be observed in those who talk too much in between songs when the aim is to lead people to the throne of God and then let them dwell there. As soon as you start talking again, it can be a distraction.

Preparation both musically and spiritually is vital. One needs to seek God to know His heart for His people, and to seek to know the people and find out where their hearts are.

Prophetic ministry

It is a prophetic ministry, as we can see in I Chronicles 25:1, where, *David...separated for the service some of the sons of Asaph of Heman and of Jeduthan who should prophesy with harps, stringed instruments, and cymbals.* As Chris Bowater has pointed out, this is worship which is sustained by the reality of God's presence rather than effort on the part of the people.[1] Prophecy is the revealing of God's mind and heart for a particular situation. The sermon can be prophetic, as can a certain song or reading. Whenever someone hears God speaking to them, through whatever means, for them it is prophetic. We are called to judge prophecy, and the plumb line we have for it is the Word of God, the Bible.

Qualities to be looked for in worship leaders

There was always a great significance attached to Hebrew names, as they were meant to describe something of the person's character, and we can learn a lot from the names of those who were appointed by David to minister with music.

Asaph, who wrote a number of the Psalms, means 'one who gathers together and removes reproach'. I find this captures much of what a worship leader is called to do. They gather people together in their thoughts to focus on the attributes and nature of God, one of which is His great mercy towards us. Through the songs one chooses, one can remind people that they are forgiven and that the reproach of sin has been removed. Asaph also means 'collector', which I like to think could refer to the songs that I certainly love to collect in order to have the right one ready for any situation.

Heman, who is described simply as 'the singer' in I Chronicles 6:33, means 'one who is faithful'. The acclamation in Matthew 25:21 comes to mind: "*Well done, good and faithful servant; you were faithful over a few things, I will make you ruler over many things Enter into the joy of your lord.*" Loyalty and faithfulness in character, as well as in practical things such as punctuality and reliability, are vital and sadly cannot always be assumed!

Jeduthan, another of those appointed by David to minister, means, 'one in whom is constant praise', or 'a choir of praise'. Another important characteristic of a worship leader is that they should be someone who has praise at the very centre of their lives. That is not to say that they should constantly go round with a fixed grin on their face, saying 'Praise the Lord' to everyone they meet, or permanently live with their head in the clouds, singing songs! It means that their lifestyle should be a worshipping one, whether they are leading praise or not. It is all too easy to put on a show of proficient song leadership when underneath there is a secret life of sin or selfishness. We are all called to be *for the praise of His glory*.

Chenaniah (or Kenaniah), means 'one who is established by Jehovah'. It is important that one has confidence in one's position and calling in God; to know one's place as a child of God, and a co-heir with Christ of all the promises. We must be sure that we know we are loved because we are His children, not because of what we do, and that our identity comes from our relationship with Him —not from our ministry. It is a sign of our times that people are valued for their occupation or position rather than for who they are. However, it is also vital to know that God has put you in the place of leadership and given you the task of ministry. It is helpful to know that the leadership of the church you are in has that confidence in you as well, and believes in you. It is very undermining when as a leader you do not know for sure that the main leadership believe you are the right person for the job and chosen by God for it. Chenaniah was also chosen because he was skilful. *Chenaniah, leader of the Levites, was instructor in charge of the music, because he was skilful* (I Chronicles 15:22). I would like to think that his skill was not just in music, important as that is, but also in spiritual leadership.

Skill
Skill is important, and we should always strive for excellence, always seeking to improve. Too often we have presented to the world a shoddy, second-rate attempt at musical leadership. In the sacrificial

system, it was the very best sheep or bull that had to be given. God is not happy with second best. So often, though, what we think of as 'best' is not always the same as God's best.

There are two apocryphal stories, which can help our understanding of this. The first of these is of someone from the West visiting an African mud hut church, somewhere in the bush. A man was leading the praise with an old banjo with at least one string missing, and sounding pretty terrible to musical ears. The man said to God in his heart, 'Lord, what do you think of this? It sounds dreadful!' The Lord whispered back to him, 'I've asked the angels to come and listen to this!' The other story is of a monastery with a group of monks who loved to sing and praise the Lord. They used to have wonderful services every day, when they sang their hearts out to the Lord. The only problem was that they had terrible voices; none of them could sing in tune and it troubled them. So they decided to invite the best local choir to come and sing at one of their services. They came and dutifully sang beautifully, and the monks were thrilled, thinking that God would be especially pleased with it. The next day, one of the monks met an angel in the corridor and asked him what he had thought of their service, expecting him to say how wonderful it had been. The angel answered, 'We were wondering what happened yesterday because we couldn't hear your praises like we normally do.' Our best may not be that good, but if it is our best and, more importantly, it comes from our hearts, then that is acceptable. The best fruit comes from a surrendered life rather than natural ability.

On the other hand, we should not be too proud to take criticism or reproof, which is a hard thing for most musicians to accept. We take it all so personally, and often find it really difficult to receive what others say. At the same time we need to be prepared and happy to receive encouragement.

When one is commended for leading well, one is most encouraged, when it has helped someone to engage with God in a new way. The fact remains that one can feel guilty when one gets the praise which one feels should go to God alone. And yet it seems intolerably self-righteous to say, 'Oh, it wasn't me it was God'! John Wimber struggled with this and asked God what he should do, and God apparently replied, 'I'll take the glory, and you can take the encouragement.' That seems to me to be the perfect deal!

David

Chosen to become the greatest of Israel's kings, David was said by God to be *"...a man after My own heart"* (Acts 13:22); and he was also described as the sweet songster of Israel. His name means 'beloved'. To know that the Lord loves one is vitally important, as it gives one great confidence and assurance, and enables one to function properly as a human being. David has so much to teach us about leadership and character.

David —shepherd, poet, king

Though David was one the greatest men in the Old Testament, he came from humble origins. He started off as a shepherd, and ended up as king. He was a poet, a psalm writer, a giant-killer, soldier, and Jesus was of his 'house' or lineage. But he was also a poor father, a betrayer, liar, adulterer, and murderer. The Bible is full of his successes and yet, at the same time, does not hide his failures. He knew the faithfulness and forgiveness of God; he was quick to confess when his sin was revealed. His repentance was genuine, although he accepted he had to bear the consequences of his sin, which was the death of the son from his union with Bathsheba. God still blessed them with another son, Solomon, his successor.

He never took God's blessing for granted, and is listed in the Hebrews 11 'hall of faith'. His life stood in stark contrast to that of his predecessor, Saul, who had started well, full of the Spirit and zealous for God, but allowed his pride and determination to do things his own way to prevail. So God rejected Saul. Samuel breaks the news to Saul: *"You have done foolishly. You have not kept the command of the LORD your God, which He commanded you. For now the LORD would have established your kingdom over Israel forever. But now your kingdom shall not continue. The LORD has sought for Himself a man after His own heart, and the LORD has commanded him to be commander over His people, because you have not kept what the LORD commanded you"* (I Samuel 13:13–14). ...*"you have rejected the word of the LORD, and the LORD has rejected you from being king over Israel!"* (I Samuel 15:26).

David, however, knew that his identity was rooted in his relationship with God, and he learnt to be truthful with Him. *"But as for me, I trust in You, O LORD; I say, "You are my God." My times are in Your hand..."* (Psalm 31:14–15). He went on to do great things for his Lord as well as organising services, choirs, creating instruments, writing approximately seventy three psalms of praise, trust, inner turmoil and lament.

He was free in his own expression of worship, when he danced with all his might before the Lord half naked, and was criticised by his wife Michal for doing so. His reply is instructive: *"...I will play music before the LORD. And I will be even more undignified than this, and will be humble in my own sight...."* (See II Samuel 6:22.) He also sang, cried, clapped, danced, leapt, bowed down, shouted, raised his hands, trembled before God, and remained still before Him.

He learnt on his own

One can imagine David sitting on the hillside watching over the sheep under his care, playing his instrument and worshipping God, writing psalms such as the twenty-third. Though he himself was a good shepherd, he knew that God Himself was his own Shepherd. Perhaps he also wrote the ultra personal Psalm 139 while there, too. He learnt to express himself through his songs, which lasted throughout his life — as we can see from Psalm 51, the deeply repentant prayer following his adultery with Bathsheba. However, as we have already noted, he was free and uninhibited in his expression of worship.

The point is that one needs to learn to worship on one's own first, before beginning to lead others. This personal worship and devotion must be maintained, as one can only really take people where you have been yourself. This is where the relevance of Proverbs 4:23, with which we began this chapter, becomes clear. One's heart must be right with God. And as with David, one needs to learn to be a listener, and realise that one never ceases to be a learner.

He was skilful

David was a skilled harp player as well as shepherd. *So Saul said to his servants, "Provide me now a man who can play well, and bring him to me." Then one of the servants answered and said, "Look, I have seen a son of Jesse the Bethlehemite, who is skilful in playing, a mighty man of valour, a man of war, prudent in speech, and a handsome person; and the LORD is with him"* (I Samuel 16:17–18).

It is a common pattern in the Bible to choose leaders who are capable as well as godly. *"Moreover you shall select from all the people able men, such as fear God, men of truth, hating covetousness"* (Exodus 18:21). *"Therefore, brethren, seek out from among you seven men of good reputation, full of the Holy Spirit and wisdom, whom we may appoint over this business"* (Acts 6:3).

He was chosen for his heart (I Samuel 16:7, 12)

Samuel, like most people, had preconceived ideas of what a king should look like. He was viewing Jesse's family from whom the new king was to be chosen. *He looked at Eliab and said, "Surely the Lord's anointed is before Him!" But the LORD said to Samuel, "Do not look at his appearance or his physical stature, because I have refused him. For the LORD does not see as man sees; for man looks at the outward appearance, but the LORD looks at the heart"* (I Samuel 16:6–7). David had not even been included in the identity parade. *So he sent and brought him in. Now he was ruddy, with bright eyes, and good-looking. And the LORD said, "Arise, anoint him; for this is the one"* (v.12). As I have mentioned before, one can easily get it wrong when choosing someone to lead worship, as one too readily tends to go for the one who has the 'stage presence', or is the most gifted musician. But they may well turn out to be unsatisfactory.

He was anointed with oil (I Samuel 16:13)

Then Samuel took the horn of oil and anointed him in the midst of his brothers; and the Spirit of the LORD came upon David from that day forward (v.13). There was to be another twenty years before David became king, so it seems that God had much more preparation for him. David, for his part, had to learn to be patient and wait for God to fulfil His promise. He did not run after the fulfilment, nor did he try to force the pace of God's timing, but instead waited for the time when he was ready. Meanwhile, he continued to be faithful in what he had to do, attending the sheep and, later, working for Saul.

Anointing

I want to look at the whole issue of anointing in a little more detail before continuing this study of David. One hears the word 'anointed' being used often to describe preachers and worship leaders, as well as songs and 'times of worship' that have been special. I understand what people are trying to say, as I have known talks and 'times of worship' that I would call anointed or special, in that I have felt a particular sense of God's presence, or heard God speak very clearly. It is something like a spiritual 'tingle factor' which one senses. What puzzles me, however, is when two people can be at the same event or service, and for one the speaker or worship leader, or whatever, is 'anointed', while the other is left completely untouched. Is there an anointing or not? Apart from unconfessed sin or a lack of openness to the Holy Spirit, which would dull their spiritual senses, could it be a case of God wanting to speak in a special way to one and not the other? Also, when someone says so-and-so is 'anointed', it can be hard to disagree without seeming to be quenching or grieving the Spirit. The term has a gravity and untouchable authority about it which makes it difficult to argue with. Therefore, I am now not sure that it is the right word to use, having studied it biblically. In the Old Testament, prophets, (I Kings 19:16), priests (Leviticus 4:3) and kings (I Samuel 10:1) were 'anointed' as a form of consecration and being set apart for God's service. There was a holy anointing oil, *an ointment compounded according to the art of the perfumer* (Exodus 30:25), which was used to anoint everything in the tent of meeting to make the articles holy. And the well-known line, *You anoint my head with oil; My cup runs over* (Psalm 23:5), speaks to me of God's blessing being poured out on us. It is a symbol of unity and the blessing it brings, as we read in Psalm 133: *Behold, how good and how pleasant it is for brethren to dwell together in unity! It is like the precious oil upon the head, running down on the beard, the beard of Aaron, running down on the edge of his garments. It is like the dew of Hermon, descending upon the mountains of Zion; For there the LORD commanded the blessing— Life forevermore.*

The term, *The LORD's anointed* (I Samuel 24:6) was used to describe the king chosen by God, and the title *Anointed,* used in Psalm 2:2 and Daniel 9:25–26, points forward to the Messiah or Christ Jesus, a title confirmed by the apostles in Acts 4:26. In the synagogue, shortly after His baptism and temptations in the wilderness, Jesus claimed the messianic anointing for Himself: *"The Spirit of the LORD is upon Me, because He has anointed Me* [literally, 'Christed me'] *to preach the gospel to the poor."* (See Luke 4:18.) And Peter referred to this during his talk at the house of Cornelius (Acts 10:38), when he stated that Jesus had been anointed by God *with the Holy Spirit and with power*. The only two instances when 'anointing' is used in connection with believers other than for healing or burial, are these: *Now He who establishes us with you in Christ and has anointed us is God, who also has sealed us and given us the Spirit in our hearts as a guarantee* (II Corinthians 1:21); and I John 2:20,27, *But you have an anointing from the Holy One, and you know all things.... But the anointing which you have received from Him abides in you, and you do not need that anyone teach you; but as the same anointing teaches you concerning all things, and is true, and is not a lie, and just as it has taught you, you will abide in Him.* Gordon Fee[2] and R.T. Kendall[3] both affirm that the anointing we have is synonymous with the gift and power of the Holy Spirit. The Greek word used in these verses for 'anoint', literally 'to rub', really means 'to Christ'. In other words, we are 'Christed', or 'made Christ's people' by the Spirit.

I think we can learn a lot from the occasion when the early church wanted to choose men who would serve at tables, and they looked for seven who were known to be full of the Spirit and wisdom. One of them was Stephen, described as a man full of faith and the Holy Spirit, and later as a man full of God's grace and power, who did great wonders and miraculous signs among the people. And when the opposition argued with him they could not stand up against his wisdom and the Spirit by whom he spoke, (as we saw in chapter nine). I am sure that if some of us were witnesses to these events, most especially what happened at the death of Stephen, we would have described Stephen as 'anointed'.

In conclusion, I suggest that what we refer to as 'anointing' is really what is happening when there is a special touch of Christ's presence and power, as when *the power of the Lord was present to heal* (Luke 5:17). When we seek to do anything for the Lord, we should aim to do it in His power, and share in the anointing of Jesus, the Anointed One. We maintain our 'anointing' by remaining in Him; *"I am the vine, you are the branches. He who abides in Me, and I in him, bears much fruit; for without Me you can do nothing"* (John 15:5). Our aim is to bear fruit for Him, and we can only do it through being constantly filled with His Spirit, operating in His power and maintaining a close relationship with Him.

Worship leading requires an openness to the Holy Spirit: to listen to Him; to be led by Him; and each time we go out to lead others, we need to surrender our gifts to Him and trust in His power to work through us. Paul describes his ministry in this way: *And my speech and my preaching were not with persuasive words of human wisdom, but in demonstration of the Spirit and of power, that your faith should not be in the wisdom of men but in the power of God* (I Corinthians 2:4–5). All true ministry needs to be like that: more than just natural talent, but gifts and special abilities which flow from a surrendered life; they are given by the Holy Spirit for the fulfilment of His purposes. *For the gifts and the calling of God are irrevocable* (Romans 11:29).

Let us now return to David.

David was called to serve (I Samuel 16:14–20)

King Saul was troubled by an evil spirit and needed someone to come and minister to him. David was sent for, and when he played, *Then Saul would become refreshed and well, and the distressing spirit would depart from him.* Even though David had a servant role at court, through his skill and the power of the Spirit he obviously had a powerful ministry of deliverance. There have been times when I have seen people being set free from the power of Satan through praise, particularly when the name of Jesus is lifted high.

David was a warrior (I Samuel 17:32–51)

He was clearly courageous and not afraid of bears, lions (v.34) —nor the giant, Goliath: *Then David said to the Philistine, "You come to me with a sword, with a spear and with a javelin. But I come to you in the name of the LORD of hosts, the God of the armies of Israel, whom you have defied. This day the LORD will deliver you into my hand, and I will strike you and take your head from you.... ...that all the earth may know that there is a God in Israel. Then all this assembly shall know that the LORD does not save with sword and spear; for the battle is the LORD's and He will give you into our hands."* (See vv. 45–47.) They may have seemed brave but foolhardy words, but they proved to have been the articulation of a sure faith in God's power and victory. How we speak in faith does matter, and that is especially true of those called to be leaders.

Spiritual warfare

There is a battle to be fought, but we know from other passages that the victory, as well as the battle, is indeed the Lord's. When a huge army of Moabites and Ammorites threatened Judah, during the reign of King Jehoshaphat, the prophet Jehaziel spoke, saying; *"You will not need to fight in this battle. Position yourselves, stand still and see the salvation of the LORD, who is with you, O Judah and Jerusalem! Do not fear or be dismayed; tomorrow go out against them, for the LORD is with you"* (II Chronicles 20:17).

Likewise, King Hezekiah was faced with a similar threat and said to the people; *"Be strong and courageous; do not be afraid nor dismayed before the king of Assyria, nor before the multitude that is with him; for there are more with us than with him. With him is an arm of flesh; but with us is the LORD our God, to help us and to fight our battles..."* (II Chronicles 32:7–8).

Now we understand that *...we do not wrestle against flesh and blood, but against the principalities, against powers, against the rulers of the darkness of this age, against spiritual hosts of wickedness in the heavenly places* (Ephesians 6:12); and, as we observed in chapter three, the weapons of our warfare are not carnal. (See II Corinthians 10:4–5).

David later had spears thrown at him by Saul, the equivalent of which are now *the fiery darts of the wicked one* (Ephesians 6:16). One of the weapons we have is the word of God: *For the word of God is living and powerful, and sharper than any two-edged sword, piercing even to the division of soul and spirit, and of joints and marrow, and is a discerner of the thoughts and intents of the heart* (Hebrews 4:12).

We also have praise as a weapon. Interestingly, the tribe of Judah ('Judah' meaning 'praise') always led when the Israelites were on the move, and at the head of the army when it went out to war. Jehoshaphat appointed singers to lead the army against the vast enemy force, and, *Now when they began to sing and to praise, the LORD set ambushes against the people of Ammon, Moab, and Mount Seir, who had come against Judah; and they were defeated* (II Chronicles 20:22).

Can you imagine what it would have been like to be one of those singers or musicians leading the army, with only their instruments to fight with, wondering if, over the next rise, they would be met by the enemy hordes! They did not know that God had already defeated the enemy when they started praising; they had to carry on in faith.

Their faith, though, was not in themselves or their own ability, it was faith in the promise of God that the battle was His. What had happened earlier was that the Spirit had come upon Jahaziel, who had then spoken out the promise— *"Thus says the LORD to you: 'Do not be afraid nor dismayed because of this great multitude, for the battle is not yours, but God's.'"* (See II Chronicles 20:14.)

HIGH PRAISES

Let the high praises of God be in our mouths
And a two-edged sword be in our hands
Let the enemy fear for God is on the move
Let the fire within our hearts begin to burn

High praises to Jesus, His splendour we proclaim
High praises to Jesus for the glories of His name
High praises to Jesus, The King upon His throne
We proclaim the high praises of God

Let the high wind of God blow through our midst
Let it fan the flames of zeal and purify
Let the Spirit proclaim that God is in control
May His kingdom rule be seen in all our lives

Let the high places be where we long to dwell
Let the Most Holy Place become our home
May our praise be mountain high
Our love be ocean deep
Lifting hands, in celebration, to the sky

How many times have we been involved in times of intercession and praise, believing by faith, not by sight, that God was working to bring about victory? Psalm 149:6 brings together the two weapons of praise and the sword of God's word: *Let the high praises of God be in their mouth, and a two-edged sword in their hand.*

That could well serve as a motto for worship leaders. Above all we need to remember that, *If God is for us who, can be against us?* (Romans 8:31); and that, *He who is in you is greater than he who is in the world* (I John 4:4).

Apart from the courage needed to stand up in front of people, as worship leaders we need to be aware that we are often targets because of the high priority God puts on worship. There have been times in my own life when I have been out leading worship somewhere and things have happened at home, which could have been coincidences or attacks of the enemy. The most dramatic occasion was once when I was in the USA, while work was being done on our house in London. We were having a new water tank installed on the roof of our four storey house. Before it was fixed, it was left on the roof over a weekend, and just after one of our children had crossed our terrace, the wind blew the tank off the roof and it landed just where he had been only a few moments before! We were extremely grateful that the Lord had prevented an appalling accident, but wondered if it had been linked spiritually in some way with what I was doing.

The Lord was with him (I Samuel 16:18)
What a simple but profound statement. It is the crux of effective leadership: that the Lord is with us. Without His strength, power and presence, what we do, however skilful, is less than useful. Moses recognised the need for God's presence to accompany the people he was leading. *Then he said to Him, "If Your Presence does not go with us, do not bring us up from here. For how then will it be known that Your people and I have found grace in Your sight, except You go with us?"* (Exodus 33:15).

As I have said elsewhere, the primary aim of a worship leader is to lead others into the presence of God through worship. One test of an effective leader is: do people follow? Another is: do people have a sense of God's presence? And: do they respond? Are they left thinking about Jesus with a sense of having met with Him, or just aware of how wonderful the worship leader is? Skill is nothing if the Lord is not with you, although He still wants the best we can give.

He cared for the flock (Psalm 78:70–72)
He also chose David His servant, and took him from the sheepfolds; From following the ewes that had young He brought him, to shepherd Jacob His people, and Israel His inheritance. So he shepherded them according to the integrity of his heart, and guided them by the skilfulness of his hands. There is a pastoral element to worship leading. It requires a love for the people one is leading; a caring attitude towards the needs that a fellowship has. One is not there just to feed one's own ego and desire to be needed. Peter's call to pastors is as good a piece of instruction as we will find anywhere: *Shepherd the flock of God which is among you, serving as overseers.... ...nor as being lords over those entrusted to you, but being examples to the flock; and when the Chief Shepherd appears, you will receive the crown of glory that does not fade away* (I Peter 5:2).

To sum up
An effective worship leader is one who combines the heart of a servant with their gifts and abilities in the power of the Spirit, to facilitate the heartfelt expression of God's people, helping them to worship God in spirit and in truth and to come to a place of intimate communion with God, the Father, Son and Holy Spirit.

I WILL GUARD MY HEART

I will guard my heart
For it is the wellspring of life
I will turn away from the sin
That so easily ensnares
I will fix my eyes on Jesus
I will fix my eyes only on Him
For He alone can keep me from falling
He's the guardian of my soul

Phil Lawson Johnston
Copyright ©2001 I Q Music

Notes

[1] See *The Believer's Guide to Worship*, Kingsway, 1993, p.72.
[2] See Gordon Fee, *God's Empowering Presence*, Hendrickson/Paternoster pp.291–2.
[3] See R. T. Kendall, *The Anointing*, Hodder & Stoughton, 1998.

12

WE WILL MAGNIFY
—LEADING TO THE THRONE

WE WILL MAGNIFY

O Lord, our God, how majestic is Your name,
The earth is filled with Your glory.
O Lord, our God, You are robed in majesty,
You've set Your glory above the heavens.

We will magnify, we will magnify
The Lord enthroned in Zion.

O Lord, our God, You have established a throne,
You reign in righteousness and splendour.
O Lord, our God, the skies are ringing with your praise,
Soon those on earth will come to worship.

O Lord, our God, the world was made at Your command,
In You all things now hold together.
Now to Him who sits on the throne and to the Lamb,
Be praise and glory and power for ever.

People's expectations of church are so often governed by their experiences of very little happening of a really spiritual nature. But the very thought of anything supernatural taking place can fill people with discomfort or fear. 'We don't want anything of that sort happening here!' they might say. There was once a church notice which said, 'This is the house of God, the gateway to heaven. This door will be closed during winter months' —such promise, and yet no sense of real expectation! I do not want to be unfair to all those devout churchgoers whose faith plays an important part in their lives and whose worship of God is genuinely real. But in the average church service there is so little sense of the possibility of actually encountering the living God, that it is not surprising that many people find it a waste of time going. Personally, I have always disliked the trappings of religion. I have little time for the formality of ritual, and over serious intensity of ceremony for ceremony's sake. Ravi Zacharias has written wisely of the emptiness of the ceremonial, pointing out that whilst it may 'soothe and mollify the conscience', it no more alters reality than outward behaviour guarantees love. He reminds us that 'religion' may lose contact with the real meaning of salvation and the power of God.[1]

Without the centrality of a relationship with Jesus I see no point in going through the motions of religion. Talking to young people today, I am often struck by their lack of interest in anything that is not 'real'. 'Church without reality' has little to offer them. What seems to happen to those of us who are older is that we can lose our cutting edge and become more prepared to settle for less. There is research which suggests that many people go to church having a desire to meet with God, who end up disappointed. Their sense of expectancy diminishes and they make do with a pleasant but perhaps rather unexciting experience.

There are a number of different reasons for the decline in church attendance in Britain over the last decade or so. The most important of these is the lack of certainty and adherence to the truth of God's Word: the church trying too much to emulate secular society, pandering to its liberal morals, thereby weakening the power of the gospel. Boredom and irrelevance also has played a large part in the fall-off in the numbers of young wanting to be a part of the church. That is not to say that the answer is in being 'modern' and copying the latest trends in music or fashion, and in the process, losing sight of the eternal truth of the gospel, but there is a need to speak (and sing) in a language which is relevant to the world in which we live. Jesus spoke everyday Aramaic, the common language, as opposed to Hebrew, the religious language. When the Spirit fell on the disciples at Pentecost, they spoke supernaturally in the languages of many nationalities which were represented in Jerusalem at the time.

There is a need to present the unchangeable Truth in packaging that is relevant to the twenty first century, i.e. worship that connects. This applies to the songs that we sing as well as the way in which we lead, and I want to now look at the whole area of leading worship in a contemporary style but within an established church setting. The views that I express and the suggestions I make will inevitably be derived mostly from the experience I have had over the last thirty years. I recognise that I am now older than I was, and that there is a need for new packaging all over again. This is true of every new generation, but I hope that some of the principles that I have discovered to be helpful will be relevant to those who are setting out to be creative in the way that they lead people to the throne of God.

Leading worship

Leading worship is more than just accompanying songs or enthusiastic cheerleading although there are those who regard it as such, and some who are downright scornful of what we are trying to do. Ezekiel faced those whose hearts were cold and therefore did not respond to the word of God: *"So they come to you as people do, they sit before you as My people, and they hear your words, but they do not do them; for with their mouth they show much love, but their hearts pursue their own gain. Indeed you are to them as a very lovely song of one who has a pleasant voice and can play well on an instrument; for they hear your words, but they do not do them."* (Ezekiel 33:31–32).

The verse that sums up leading worship for me is from Psalm 34:3, *Oh, magnify the LORD with me, and let us exalt His name together.* David is in effect saying: I am going to worship the Lord; will you join me? And that, by and large, is what we are doing when we lead others to the throne to respond to all that God is, and all that He has done for us. To magnify the Lord is not to make Him any greater, of course; just as a magnifying glass does not make the object you are observing any bigger, but enlarges and clarifies our view of it, so our understanding of God is expanded when we worship Him.

Needless to say, we do not praise God to make Him feel better or more appreciated. He does not *need* our praise, but He has *commanded* us to praise Him; and as we do so, our vision of Him is enlarged, and our faith in Him rises. *Bless the LORD, O my soul; and all that is within me, bless His holy name! Bless the LORD, O my soul, and forget not all His benefits: Who forgives all your iniquities, who heals all your diseases, who redeems your life from destruction, who crowns you with lovingkindness and tender mercies, who satisfies your mouth with good things, so that your youth is renewed like the eagle's* (Psalm 103:1–5). In another translation, 'bless' is rendered 'praise'.

C.S Lewis described praise as inner health made audible. He also observed that in commanding us to glorify Him, God is in fact inviting us to enjoy Him.[2] Enjoyment of God is perhaps alien to those of us who have been schooled in the attitude that we have a duty to worship God whilst expecting nothing in return. While it is true that we are commanded to worship Him, it is also vital that we know He wants to bless us as we do. Hebrews 11:6 tells us that those who come to God must not only believe that He exists, but that He rewards those who seek Him wholeheartedly. This will make a huge difference to how people respond when one leads them in worship. We need to come to God expectantly. If we think that we should not expect anything from Him, we make ourselves the giver(s) and Him the receiver —which can almost border on blasphemy. He is the Giver of all good things, and we show a deep disrespect for Him if we shun His desire to bless and give to us.

In Psalm 16:8–11, David tells us of the joy we can experience in God's presence:

"I have set the LORD always before me; Because He is at my right hand I shall not be moved. Therefore my heart is glad, and my glory rejoices; My flesh also will rest in hope.... You will show me the path of life; In Your presence is fullness of joy; At Your right hand are pleasures forevermore."

A hunger and thirst for the living God is what the Holy Spirit is looking for. What will give God more pleasure —a false piety, which does not ask anything of Him, or a cry coming from our hearts, like that of David, *When shall I come and appear before God?* (See Psalm 42:2; and, as we noted in chapter eight above, see also Psalm 63:1,5)?

There is a world of difference between leading worship for a group of reluctant people or for a group of expectant people who really long to engage with God, knowing that His desire is to meet with them. And yet, that is what one is faced with quite often, and I am constantly looking for ways to encourage others to turn from being reluctant to being expectant, without bullying them. (That never works anyway!) People generally feel confident when they can sense they are being led by a safe pair of hands. Very few people want to be made to do anything that makes them feel uncomfortable or embarrassed.

Embarrassment

I remember making a classic mistake after Cloud had been to help lead worship at a conference in Ipswich. We had learnt a song which said, 'I love you with the love of the Lord', and we were all encouraged to go round and sing it to people, face to face. We found it incredibly difficult and embarrassing, but as we were part of the team we did not have much choice! But as we began, rather sheepishly, to do it, we found that the Lord used it to break down many barriers, and many people ended up being prayed for. We went home thinking that this was a good thing and decided to introduce it to Holy Trinity Brompton (HTB). We did, and it caused the same kind of embarrassment without the desired effect of melting people's hearts. In fact there was quite a backlash and there were questions raised in the church council, and it was never done again!

Change

It is one thing to challenge people to move forward in their worship, but another to take them so far out of their comfort zone as to alienate them completely. However, there are times when God wants to move us out of our complacency and will shake us out of self-interest by challenging us or convicting us of sin. The skill of a worship leader is to be sensitive and know when this is the case. Moses had continual trouble with the complaining Israelites after they had left the relative, if meagre, comfort of Egypt, to head out into the desert. There were many times when they wanted to return to what they had become accustomed to. Sheep often tend to stay munching at a scrap of grass that is comfortably close to them, not realising that there is a fresh meadow just over the hill. Similarly, people nearly always seem to veer towards the familiar, particularly when it comes to music. They feel safer on familiar ground and are generally reluctant to change. Someone once said that the only person who is keen to change is a baby with a wet nappy! However, it is true that the only things that do not change are dead; everything alive changes.

Churchgoers fall into four different categories when it comes to change. There are those who resist change at all cost. They are very possessive over 'their' church, and will say, 'over my dead body', to any new ideas. Secondly, there are those who like things the way they are, but would probably follow reluctantly after some persuasion, if they can see the benefits of change. Thirdly, there are those who are keen to please God, are prepared to listen and will accept change if they can see that God is in it. Fourthly, there always seem to be some who want constant change, and will leave unless there is always something new happening. The second and third types are generally the largest group in any church, and they are the ones to concentrate on.

In many churches where there are falling numbers and survival is the name of the game, there is always a tendency to hang on to as many members as possible, and, therefore, try to please everyone. This can become a nightmare for most leaders, as it is virtually impossible to do so. The situation is somewhat different if you are in a city as opposed to being in a village. In a city there is much more choice and if people disagree with what you are doing, then there is always another church to go to, whereas in a village that choice is not normally available. Most villagers are very reluctant to go to a neighbouring church, and so it is harder and takes longer for a village vicar to bring about any change. Most have to look after anything from three to ten different churches anyway, which only compounds the problem for them.

Ancient and modern
There are many churches which have been trying to create a blend of the old and the new in their worship; to have a service which serves the preferences of as many as possible. The danger of this

is that often no one will end up with enough of what they prefer. I remember we tried this at HTB, when we had a paid choir who sang introits and anthems in the morning service, and yet there was an increasing number of people who wanted more informal worship. We (Cloud) came in to lead children's praise and some worship songs during communion, while the choir would lead the other parts. What happened during the children's songs, particularly the ones with actions, was that we would be in front leading and behind there would be some choir members who would join in singing and with actions, and others who sat stony-faced with their arms folded. Because the choir stalls were higher, they were visible to the whole church, and a clear presentation of disunity was being displayed in full view! It was totally unsatisfactory and could not last. After I had left, I am glad to say it was changed dramatically.

There is a danger of having too much of a consumer approach to worship music, being more concerned about what suits us rather than what God really wants. We can make it something that has to be critiqued afterwards —not for its quality or spiritual content, but purely on the level of whether it meets our preferences. Imagine the Israelites just after the crossing of the Red Sea saying, 'Miriam's dance was far too irreverent, and as for that awful tambourine...!' or later, 'I don't like the way Moses leads worship; I much prefer Aaron. He's far more sensitive, and isn't his voice lovely.'

For some churches, even the introduction of 'the Peace' is still contentious, and the new song from Mission Praise or Songs of Fellowship is suspiciously regarded as the thin end of the wedge. The other extreme, of course, which can be just as bad, is when everything traditional is thrown out, and one loses the richness of the older hymns. Lyndon Bowring, Chairman of CARE, believes that, 'We need the old hymnbooks searched and plundered to rediscover the beauty and profundity of the old songs which, together with new music and tempo, would reap huge rewards.'

One of the challenges for me is to be able to blend in traditional hymns as part of the worship I lead without them sticking out as being something different from, or alien to, the more contemporary material I use. Which really brings me now to the point of looking in detail at what I am trying to do, and how I construct a 'worship set'.

Repetition and length

Two of the common criticisms of contemporary worship music are: too much repetition; and too long spent singing similar songs.

The only worship joke I know of that pokes fun at the way we sing songs and hymns is too long to print here in full, but the description in it of a typical praise chorus sums up what many feel about them:

"If I were to say to you: 'Martha, Martha, Martha, Oh Martha, MARTHA, MARTHA, the cows, the big cows, the brown cows, the black cows, the white cows, the black-and-white cows, the COWS, COWS, COWS are in the corn, are in the corn, are in the corn, the CORN, CORN, CORN.' Then, if I were to repeat the whole thing two or three times, well that would be a praise chorus." (Anon.)

Lyndon Bowring has observed that the repetition in many worship songs is wearisome for many people. He points to the 'need' to sing the last verse twice, the last chorus twice more, and the final line twice again to make the song worthwhile. I know I have fallen into this trap all too often, and have failed to realize that others do not always share the same enthusiasm I have for certain songs. The desire for creating an effect can easily have the opposite response.

Length of time spent singing is also a concern. Although I am all for a decently unhurried time spent in God's presence, I know that one can just sing song after song for the sake of it, and think that one has been genuinely worshipping Him, when it has just been 'singing the songs'. Space and silence is needed as well as loud high praise. It may sometimes be appropriate, as some have suggested, to have shorter worship times early in a service, early biblical teaching and more extended worship after that, to enable the congregation to respond to the Word. Though there are times when praise should continue until there is a 'breakthrough'. But I have often found that one reaches a deeper sense of worship in God's presence in response to His Word, and people have frequently found Him continuing to speak to them during this time.

A progression

However long I am given to lead worship at a service or gathering, I see it very much in terms of a progression, taking people from one place to another through a series of songs and hymns. I consider it sometimes rather like Psalms 95 or 100, both of which start with an invitation to 'come': *Oh come, let us sing to the LORD! Let us shout joyfully to the Rock of our salvation. Let us come before His presence with thanksgiving...* and, *Make a joyful shout to the LORD, all you lands! Serve the LORD with gladness; Come before His presence with singing...,* leading to statements about God: *For the LORD is the great God, and the great King above all gods...* and, *For the LORD is good; And His truth endures to all generations.*

I tend to start with something that gives an invitation to draw near, then songs or hymns that are objective in content, reminding us of who God is and what He has done. Starting this way helps people to lift their sights off their circumstances or the 'baggage' they have come with, and onto the Lord, so that they might begin to view things from His perspective. It is like building a platform of praise; taking people from where they are, perhaps low in faith, to a place of expectation where they remember God's mercy and can bathe again in His grace. Psalm 95 moves us on to a further invitation: *Oh come, let us worship and bow down; Let us kneel before the LORD our Maker. For He is our God....* We move from the objective to the more subjective elements of how we relate to Him and what He wants from us. Also, we move from singing 'about' Him to singing 'to' Him. *Oh, sing to the LORD a new song! Sing to the LORD, all the earth* (Psalm 96:1). One can use an illustration of the Queen to help us understand the difference between praise and adoration. Suppose you were in the crowd in the Mall, and the Queen was passing by in a procession, perhaps during the Jubilee celebrations. You might be cheering at the top of your voice and waving your flag. That would be rather like praise and exultation. Then, suppose a royal courtier came down into the crowd and gave you an invitation to come and have an audience with the Queen herself. You would be led off through the gates into the palace, and into the very throne room to meet her. To continue waving your flag and cheering would be considered rather inappropriate, would it not? You would be more likely to stand in silence and wait to be addressed. Suppose one step further and you happened to be adopted as her son or daughter. She would still be your queen, but also your mother. That would be more analogous to intimate worship before the throne of God, and being a child and co-heir with Christ. (See Romans 8:17).

It is hard to get this feel of a progression when you only have one song or hymn in which to achieve it. You can just do it with three but, ideally, I like to have at least four or five songs or more, and then I have time to take people on this journey from being a bit distant to coming really close and experiencing a loving intimacy with Jesus and our heavenly Father. Many of the shorter songs have been written with the intention of being put into a progression, where a theme is developed with a sense of drawing closer, song by song, until one is left before the throne, maybe even in silence. There is a regrettable tendency in many services to want to get on to the next item, without any awareness of dwelling in God's presence and, as someone has put it, just 'wasting time' with Him.

Patterns of worship

There are scriptural patterns that one can follow loosely to help create something of a progression. I have already mentioned using the pattern in Psalm 100, which follows the shape of the biblical tabernacle or temple; entering the gates and going into the courts and then approaching and entering the holy of holies, which of course is the privilege and freedom we have under the new covenant. The dramatic tearing apart of the curtain in the temple, depicted in Mel Gibson's *The Passion of the Christ*, brings this home powerfully.

One can use the account of the transfiguration of Jesus (see Matthew 17 and Luke 9) as a pattern for worship, with some creative use of one's imagination. It starts with Jesus leading His closest apostles up and away to pray on a mountain. This matches the invitation to come and meet with Him. Then Jesus is transformed, and His glory is revealed. *His face shone like the sun.* This suggests the idea of having our view of God magnified and expanded as we lift our eyes to Him through praise. Elijah representing the prophets, and Moses representing the law, then appear —both acknowledging the supremacy of Jesus, the Word. They are heard speaking with Him about His departure, referring to His death, resurrection and ascension. This reminds us of the centrality of the Bible and the cross to our worship. Peter, out of nervousness (*not knowing what he said*), suggests that they build shelters for Jesus, Elijah and Moses. This is so like us when we want to encapsulate or repeat an experience, or when we think we have found the key to worship and want to hang on to it. This is quickly forgotten when the bright cloud envelops them and they are filled with fear. This is sometimes called the 'shekinah' of God, or the glory of His presence, which reminds us of the occasion when the cloud of His glory broke into the worship and filled Solomon's new temple (see II Chronicles 5). God then speaks: *"This is My beloved Son, in whom I am well pleased. Hear Him!"* Here the Father affirms His love for Jesus, and we who are in Christ can share in that love and affirmation as we hear Him speak to our hearts through His word. Jesus finally reassures them, saying, *"Arise, and do not be afraid."* Then He returns to 'normal' as it were, and leads them back to the world and the needs of people. Having met with Jesus in our worship service, it is good when we are sent out from there to serve Him in the community.

John Wimber used to suggest a pattern, which is I suppose similar to the one I have adopted. He starts with **the call to worship**, the invitation to come and worship now. Then follows **the engagement**, the meeting with God expressing praise, joy and adoration. **Intimacy** follows, when we draw ever closer, meditating on our relationship with Him. Then comes **the visitation**, the presence of God coming down and working among us. Finally, there is **giving away** what we have received, through our energy, time and resources.

These patterns are only intended to be useful as a starting point to help us construct an act of worship. We should not get tied up with trying to stick too rigidly to them; otherwise one can fall into empty ritualism if one is not careful.

Too much talk

There is an inclination for some worship leaders or service leaders to talk too much between the songs. They have to give an introduction, which often borders on being a little 'sermonette' each time. Firstly, this is usually unnecessary as most songs speak for themselves and do not need any introduction. Secondly, it can waste time, and without it one could probably have included another song. Thirdly and, I think, more importantly, it constantly draws people's attention back to the speaker, when what one is trying to do is to have people concentrate on the Lord not on you! Half the job of a worship leader is to lead without people even realizing it, to the point where they are not aware of the leader because they are caught up in adoration of their Lord.

I, BY YOUR GREAT MERCY

I, by Your great mercy, will come into Your house
In reverence and awe will I bow down
I, by Your great mercy, will wait before Your throne
Feasting my eyes on You

I love the house where You live, O Lord
The place where Your glory dwells
To gaze upon Your beauty, Lord
This is my one desire

I, by Your great mercy, with confidence will say
'O Lord, how lovely is Your dwelling place'
Now but a reflection of what will be revealed
When I see You face to face

(See Psalm 27:4)

Phil Lawson Johnston Copyright ©2001 IQ Music/1995 Cloud Music

Creating a flow

As well as being concerned with following a progression in worship, I am passionate about creating a flow within it. What I mean by that is letting the songs almost run into each other without much of a gap between them. That is not to say that I want to rush from song to song because, at the same time, I look for there to be musical space within and between the songs, to give time to breathe and dwell in the Lord's presence. Extended times of singing can allow for this most effectively, but it requires skill and sensitivity to prevent it becoming just a string or medley of songs thrown together, however proficiently the music is executed.

I love it when the music develops and grows with a variety of dynamics, which cause a swell and fall, and then almost leaves us hanging in space, and then at other times creating a tidal surge of passion which flows forth from people's hearts. I seek to keep people in a place of adoration without interruption, and allow space for the Holy Spirit's creativity and ministry to the people. Even out of the singing of a known song or hymn, a spontaneous outpouring of praise and joy can come (and this is not just a modern phenomenon). The rigid structure of the music can sometimes restrict us, and we need to learn to find freedom from the confines of the dots on the page; to step out and allow the Spirit to enable us to prophesy in song, to intercede in song, to bless and minister in song. Courage is needed especially for instrumentalists who are not used to improvisation. Anyone who has been trained in music will not easily allow themselves to risk making a mistake. When fear is overcome and they yield themselves to the Spirit, allowing Him to lead, inspire and 'fill their sails', they start to worship with their instrument and find a new freedom in their playing. Even through instrumental passages, God can speak to people, minister to them and release gifts of the Spirit in their lives. I have seen this happen many times with different musicians. A flautist I used to play a lot with, Mike Chase, sometimes used to walk away from the band and start playing over people in the congregation. Time and again, the Lord would bless people through him, and I even remember one person becoming a Christian through his playing.

Different sized groups

Over the thirty-two years I have been involved in leading worship, I have been in every conceivable shape and size of group and band. Cloud varied widely in size and make-up, from 6 to 21 at any one time, with every possible instrument. Since the end of Cloud, I have worked on my own; with one other singer, or pianist; sometimes a singer, pianist and flautist; sometimes pianist, singers, violin, flute, bass and drums. The size of meeting will usually dictate how many I work with, although one feature of the Alpha conferences I have led at in the USA is that I have always worked on my own. The main reason for this is to show that one does not necessarily always need extensive resources to lead worship effectively. It is undoubtedly much simpler working on my own; I only have myself to organize! However, it is a joy to have good musicians around me, enabling a much greater musical scope. I am not very good at directing a group, and tend to let them all decide how and when they play. I know some find this hard and would prefer a more directive approach, but when it works it does give each one the chance to feel that they are contributing spiritually as well as musically.

During the Cloud years, we used to meet every Thursday to

practice. This enabled us to get to know one another, have fellowship, pray and minister to each other, as well have time to learn the songs. When introducing a new song I would usually suggest that no one played their instrument but just sang it first, in order to make it their own worship song. Then they would pick up their instruments and begin to experiment musically. I did not often give them music to play from, but just the words with guitar chords. Although this was daunting for those new members who were not used to improvisation, it did bring a greater freedom into what they played. There were very skilled musicians who were horrified at the idea of no music, and insisted that they could not improvise. Invariably, I found that they could, once they had got over the fear of making a mistake and began to find the freedom to play without music, and it often seemed to coincide with a new spiritual release in their lives.

In the two churches I have been in while living in Oxford, St. Aldate's and St. Andrew's, the system has been very different. In recent years there have been no set bands, with no weekday practices, and every time I have led worship at services, it has been a little like starting all over again. However, as the same people have come round in rota there has been some opportunity to get to know each other musically, although it does not give much scope for risk-taking or experimentation. One advantage of doing things this way is that more people have a chance to be involved and there is less time commitment for each person. But on balance I prefer working with the same people consistently for the reasons I have mentioned before, but it does require much greater commitment, especially if there is a weekday practice.

Small group worship

Different sized meetings have different dynamics and require different approaches to worship leading. Generally speaking, the larger the meeting the stronger the leadership needed. The small meeting needs less hands-on leadership, but that does not necessarily make it any easier. In fact, those who are used to leading a large gathering can sometimes forget to change their approach and start leading in a home group in the same way. One cannot expect people's response to be the same as in a larger group, just as one cannot always expect the same level of engagement and expectation at a regular weekly service as at, say, *New Wine* or *Soul Survivor*.

Many churches have recognised the value of the small house group, and in some cases the cell church, providing worship, fellowship, teaching and outreach. There is plenty of biblical precedent for this. Paul mentions 'the church that meets' in the houses of Priscilla, Aquila, Nympha and Archippus. Archaeology has shown that these houses were likely to be in the Roman atrium style, with a central area where up to fifty people could gather. Jesus spoke of the smallest group when He said, *"For where two or three are gathered together in My name, I am there in the midst of them"* (Matthew 18:20).

Throughout history Christians have realised the importance of the church in the home, John Wesley, the founder of Methodism, being one. I found a picture of Martin Luther and his family at worship in his home, even with 'guitar' and song sheets!

When creating the series of albums *Worship in the Room*, especially for small group worship, I had to think through what might be the most effective approach, and I came up with a few particular elements that I thought would be helpful. One was the keys that the songs were in. In the songbooks, I find they tend to be quite high, and in recording for small groups I lowered many of them, to make them more comfortable to sing. People can feel more exposed and vulnerable in a smaller group and therefore can be more inhibited, particularly if they have to sing high. Sensitivity to this is needed, and generally speaking a gentler choice of songs is also more appropriate. I used a mixture of older familiar songs and traditional hymns as well as a selection of newer ones, ordered so as to suggest the type of progression discussed above.

In a small group, I find that there is more scope for prayer and contributions from others, and less need for a worship leader to be upfront with their leading, and certainly not domineering, although a confident approach is still important. People can be encouraged to be more relaxed in a small group (though watch out for sleepiness!) and there are more opportunities for personal ministry. One can afford to have longer, unhurried times for worship. It is like a leisurely meal contrasted with a working lunch with a tight agenda; more like Mary sitting at Jesus' feet, listening, than Martha rushing about being busy.

I DELIGHT TO SIT AT YOUR FEET

I delight to sit at Your feet, Lord
I love to see Your face
To rest in the shade of eternal love
Is a fruit so sweet to taste

There is no other place I'd rather be
Than here at Your side
There is no greater lesson I can learn
Than to rest and abide

I delight to gaze at Your beauty
No other can compare
I'd sooner spend a single hour here with You
Than a thousand days elsewhere

The use of Scripture, particularly the Psalms, read during worship can really enhance such times. Others, I know, like to use various symbols, such as candles, to help focus their hearts on the Lord.

By and large, a guitar is the most suitable, intimate and sensitive instrument to use in a home group. Errors are smaller and more correctable. People are generally more forgiving, and therefore it can be a good training ground for emerging worship leaders. Also, it is usually more practical to use books or sheets (rather than an OHP or computer-projected view of the words, both of which are less usable in a small space.) There are different categories of small group, some of which are more specialised in their purpose, and they therefore need appropriate approaches when it comes to leading worship in them —for example, the group doing an Alpha course.

Worship at Alpha

There are good reasons for having some worship at Alpha, the main one being that you are giving people a taste of all that the Christian life can offer — fellowship, the Bible, prayer, guidance, God's power to heal, etc. — and if worship is the believer's priority, it would be strange to miss it out. But great sensitivity is needed in the way you do it as (hopefully) a large proportion of those attending are not likely to be believers at all. The choice of songs is crucial, and one tends to encourage more objective hymns and songs at the early stages of the course: statements of truth that reinforce what is being said during the talks, rather than intimate love songs to the Lord, which can be inappropriate or embarrassing at this stage. You cannot expect the visitors to sing much, and you and the team have to be prepared to be the only ones participating. It is not helpful to have lengthy times of singing, and I would recommend a maximum of two songs to start with, one of which could be a well known hymn, until the weekend or day away, when you can safely sing for longer. Sensitivity is also needed in the way the believers express their worship.

One Alpha group that I had in our home was for men only, and I felt that it was not right to even try to have worship. To save embarrassment, I decided to sing one song or hymn to them, following the theme of the evening. I was never quite sure how well this was being received, until the evening when I did not sing anything at all —and got a disappointed reaction! Having not encouraged any participation other than listening, I sang Amazing Grace one evening, and found nearly everyone spontaneously joining in.

Prison Alpha

Leading worship at a prison Alpha course has its own characteristics, as in many ways there is a greater freedom amongst the inmates to express themselves. My experience is that they seem to love singing, or at least listening to you sing, whether they believe or not. I have found that one can sing much more lively songs and hymns (they always love Amazing Grace!) and be much more 'upfront' about one's beliefs.

The prayer group

Leading worship in a prayer group can be an exciting experience, although my own early memories are permeated with heaviness and boredom, as one ploughed through endless shopping-lists of requests. It is hard work to intercede, but with worship at the beginning and dotted throughout the prayer time, it can become very uplifting. Praising and lifting Jesus up, is like stoking the fire of faith and intercession. When people are beginning to flag, to then sing and lift one's eyes up to the heavens can give a new impetus to the prayer. It also creates the opportunity to use a different type of song from the mainstream praise and worship repertoire. Songs and hymns that express God's victory and power can add a sense of doing battle with the spiritual enemies of God, spiritual warfare playing an integral part in intercession. Songs that express concern and compassion for particular situations or people can be used as intercession themselves; for example a lament for the unborn who are being aborted:

LAMENT FOR WASTED LIVES

Can you hear the sheep crying?
Can you see the lambs dying?
Denied the light of day
They will never see the sun

Four million[3] petals falling
Four million babies calling
Their silent screams fill the sky
They will never see the sun
They will never see the sun

Their angels cry out before the face of God
"How long will our precious ones be sacrificed
to the gods of convenience and pride?"
Bodies torn apart
Wasted lives
Bodies torn apart
Wasted lives

Their blood cries from the earth
Denied the right of birth
Refused the light of life
We try to hide them from our sight

Can we push the guilt away
And ignore the bloody stains
On our nation's hands?
God have mercy on our land
God have mercy on our land

Their angels cry out before their Father's throne
"Who will stand up for them
And keep for them a home that is safe
Where they're wanted and prized?"
Bodies torn apart
Wasted lives
Bodies torn apart
Wasted lives
Can you hear the sheep crying?
Can you hear the lambs dying?

**Extract taken from the song "Lament for Wasted Lives" by
Phil Lawson Johnston.
Copyright ©1989 Thankyou Music***

Ministry songs

I am sure most people would agree that music has extraordinary power
to touch and stir the emotions in ways that words alone cannot. Dame
Janet Baker said, 'At the inner core of music is the possibility that
performing can touch and change the human heart.'[4] I recognise there
are dangers of inadvertent manipulation, or inappropriate 'tugging
at the heart strings', by the choice of songs or music that one might
use, even to the extent of making people do things that they would
not normally be comfortable with. However, I firmly believe that

God can and does use music and song to reach people's hearts and release His healing and delivering power. I have witnessed occasions when people have been healed and set free from things that have held them bound, during worship and songs that speak of how much God loves and values them. There have been other occasions when people who are dying have listened to worship music, which brought them great comfort. For example, I remember one man who died while repeatedly listening to one of Cloud's early albums, *Watered Garden*. Others have been brought through very dark periods almost entirely by listening to the album *Value Me*.[5]

Over the years there have been many times when I have been at meetings and services during which there have been opportunities for people to be prayed for individually by a ministry team. While this has been happening I have sung quietly in the background. This helps create a backdrop of sound to give people more privacy, but also I have regarded it as an opportunity to sing songs that minister as well. One needs to be loud enough to be just heard, but not too loud so as to disturb or distract. It is not the occasion to be singing loud up-tempo songs, but more meditative, devotional ones that speak of God's love for the individual. Personally, I think I enjoy these times almost more than any other time. I love watching what is going on and often see how God is touching people and releasing, blessing, and healing them. I have been so encouraged to hear later how the words of songs I have sung have permeated the prayers that have been prayed. Sometimes a certain song will have been heard when prayer has come to a 'brick wall', and it has provided a fresh train of thought to enable the prayer to move on again. Once there was a couple that were praying for someone and had ground to a halt, not knowing how to continue. They did not seem to be getting anywhere, and were sitting in silence. The words of a song about the river of God washing over us then penetrated the person's heart and he or she broke down in tears, and the couple ministering were able to pray more effectively again. It was as if a floodgate had opened or a key had opened a locked door.

On another occasion when I saw the power of God released through a worship song, I was not leading worship but was attending a conference in Brighton on spiritual warfare. We were worshipping, and singing a song about the Father's love for each of us, and I was standing behind a girl I did not know particularly well. I noticed that she was trembling, and that the two girls next to her were praying for her. I had a strong sense that the song we were singing was really what God wanted to say to her, and I leant forward and whispered in her ear, "This one's for you." I don't know whether she heard it or not as the music was loud, but I felt God was touching her in a special way, so I continued to pray for her by just reaching out my hand towards her and asking God to bless her. I had one of those nudges in my heart, which I am never quite sure are from God, but are sufficiently strong for me to step out in faith. I sensed that He wanted me to stop waving my hand in her direction and to lay my hands on her shoulders and pray for her that way, so I did. Soon afterwards, there was a break in the proceedings and she rushed off. The girls turned to me and said that I ought to go and have a word with her. They had seen me lay my hands on her and thought that she would flip out as she had a fear of men, and would never let them pray for her. I had not a clue about this and had just gone with my instincts, but she had not flipped, and so I went to find her. She was in the corridor, and we sat down to talk. She explained that she had been sexually abused as a child by her stepfather from the age of six, and was forced to steal for him and his friends, and was regularly beaten by him and her mother. When she was thirteen, she told her mother about the abuse. She did not believe her, and called her a 'slut'. This continued until she was eighteen, when she finally left home. Having been through many other traumas and drug related experiences, she had recently given her life to Jesus and was receiving much prayer for her messed-up past. She had received healing in many areas, but had not opened her heart fully to God's love. She would not allow any man to come near her to pray, and would normally run from the room if they did. She had known that a man had laid his hands on her during the worship, and yet had been surprised herself at not reacting in her usual way. In fact, she found herself opening her heart for the first time to allow God's love in to bring healing. I felt incredibly privileged to have played a small part in the process of her restoration. I know she went on to have more ministry, but have since lost touch with her.

I tell you this story not just to illustrate how God can use a seemingly small step of obedience to perform His wonders, but also because it led me to write a song about her in the form of a prayer for anyone who has known abuse. I sent it to her to ask whether it came close to her experience, and she wrote back to tell me it did. I have used it guardedly in prayer ministry situations and found it causing a profound response in those who have been through similar abuse. It is not a song I would use lightly or too often, for the very reasons I mentioned at the beginning of this section; it could easily fall into the category of emotional manipulation if used unscrupulously. I would only sing it in a safe environment, when there were others nearby to step in to comfort and pray for those whose deep feelings it had stirred up.

In passing, I would stress that any local church pastoral rules and guidelines concerning the 'laying on of hands' as in that example, or indeed any physical contact, are to be observed. Worship leaders are often accorded a somewhat privileged position in these matters, and this must be exercised within a framework of wise pastoral oversight. In the personal example above, I was not a complete stranger, as I had seen the person at my church and she, and others who had been praying with her at the time, would have known who I was. It should perhaps also be pointed out here that the onus is upon us all to accept such ministrations ourselves only when we feel it right to do so. The climate in a church should be to offer appropriate ministry, but never in a manipulative way that makes people feel obligated to accept. Worship leaders, like all in positions of responsibility, have to remember that ministry is not about doing anything against anyone's will or better judgment; and even Jesus gave people the option of saying 'no' to Him. Many will feel that it is unwise to accept ministry involving physical contact, unless they are confident that those ministering have been authorised or trained by the church leadership, and/or they personally know them to be born again, Spirit-filled, Bible-believing Christians who are walking in obedience. At large events, where people from many churches may be present, those authorised to minister are often trained as a team beforehand, and may be identified by special badges. HTB produces excellent training resources, incorporating helpful guidelines, for those who will be involved in such kinds of prayer ministry.

MAKE UP THE YEARS

The child never knew what it was to be
An object of love and affection
The child only knew what it was to be
An object of scorn and rejection
What a tragedy!
They were never free
To be what God intended

The child never knew what it was to be
Adored and held in arms of safety
The child only knew what it was to be
Abused and torn by hands of hatred
What a tragedy!
They were never free
To be what God intended

Father, make up the years
Come soak up all of the tears
Make up for the love that was denied them
Father, make up the years
Take all the shame and the fear
Lead them by Your hand
To wholeness and freedom

The child never knew what it was to be
Someone of value to be respected
The child only knew what it was to be
A captive to fear always subjected
What a tragedy!
They could never see
It's not what God intended

If the child only knew that nothing's hid from view
All is seen by God in heaven
He can restore the years and wipe away the tears

With healing love so freely given
How He longs to see
Every child set free
As He intended

Extract taken from the song "Make up the Years"
by Phil Lawson Johnston
Copyright ©1993 Thankyou Music*

Leading to the throne

The goal of all worship leading is to bring people to the throne of God where they can meet Him, listen to Him, love Him and be loved by Him. My aim is always to help people to engage with the Lord, and to do this I desperately need the help of the Holy Spirit. I need to be sufficiently open to Him to be able to recognise what He is doing, and following Him, rather as Moses and the Israelites were led by the pillar of fire and cloud, moving when it moved and staying when it was still. We need to have our hearts focussed on God's direction through the Spirit. We need to have the same attitude as Jesus had when He said that He only did what He saw His Father doing. I may have given the impression that I always know what I am doing and get it right all the time, which could not be further from the truth; so much has to be done in faith, and God, in His mercy, so often is gracious and rectifies the mistakes I make.

Even after all this time, I still get apprehensive before events. Often, when I am driving off to some service or other, I have an overwhelming desire to turn round and return to the safety of home! Sometimes I dream about leading worship, and in the dream all manner of disasters happen: I leave my guitar behind or forget the words, or I arrive and find someone else already doing it; there are always people present whom I want to impress, and I show myself up as a completely incompetent fool! I wake up wishing that I had never accepted the next invitation. I am never quite sure whether this is just a product of my own imagination, an enemy attack, or that I am being taught to be completely dependent on the Lord.

In any event, it has the desired effect of sending me to my knees and crying out to God for help.

"Father, I pray that those who are seeking to become more effective worship leaders would learn how to trust in You for their strength; that they would keep their hearts soft towards You, and that You will lead them as they seek to lead others; in Jesus name. Amen."

ASCRIBE TO THE LORD

Ascribe to the Lord, O family of nations
Ascribe to the Lord glory and strength
Ascribe to the Lord the glory due His name
Bring an offering and enter His courts

Worship, worship, Oh worship the Lord
In the splendour of His holiness
Worship, worship, stand in awe of Him
All the earth

The fear of the Lord is the beginning of wisdom
Let all upon earth fear His holy name
The voice of the Lord is powerful and mighty
Let all in His temple cry, 'Glory'

Worship, worship, Oh worship the Lord
In the beauty of His holiness
Worship, worship, stand in awe of Him
All the earth

Extract taken from the song "Ascribe to the Lord"
by Phil Lawson Johnston
Copyright ©1985 Thankyou Music*

Notes

[1] See Ravi Zacharias, *Recapture the Wonder*, Integrity Publishers.

[2] See C.S. Lewis, *Reflections on the Psalms*.

[3] This refers to an Albert Hall meeting organised by CARE (Christian Action, Research and Education) on behalf of the unborn child, when four million petals were dropped from the ceiling, each representing a child aborted since 1967 when the Abortion Act was passed. Now it would need to be six million petals!

[4] Janet Baker, *Spirituality and Music*, the Eric Abbott Memorial Lecture 1988.

[5] By Phil Lawson Johnston and Helen Kucharek, originally released by Bible Reading Fellowship, re-released as *You Value Me*, Worship in the Room No. 4, Cloud Trust.

Part Four

The Fruit of Worship

13

CHANGED
—A GLORIOUS REFLECTION

CHANGED

We don't know what we will be
But we know that when we see His face
We shall be changed
We don't know when that will come
But we know that in His Son
We shall, we shall be changed
So let grace increase, pray He will release
His power to change

We're the workmanship of God
As He writes upon our hearts
His law and purposes
We're created for His praise
To live for all our days
According to His will
So let grace increase, pray He will release
His power to change

THE SONG OF THE FATHER'S HEART

We are a new creation
The old has passed away
The new life of Jesus is here to stay
He'll bring to completion
The work that He began
We shall be changed, we shall be changed

He began a work in me
That one day will be complete
And I'll know as I am known
As I stand with open face
And reflect His glorious grace
The seeds of change are sown
So let grace increase, pray He will release
His power to change

We go from strength to strength
As we tread the narrow way
Our lives shining brighter until that day
In a radiant flash of light
In the twinkling of an eye
We shall be changed, we shall be changed

On that final perfect day
When all things have passed away
His word will be fulfilled
'Behold I make all things new'
All My promises are true
You shall, you shall be changed

Phil Lawson Johnston
Copyright ©2002 IQ Music

They looked to Him and were radiant, and their faces were not ashamed (Psalm 34:5).

It is such an easy thing to fall into the trap of forgetting that Jesus is looking for our lives to reflect the words we sing or say. His strongest remarks to some religious people concerned the fact that what was in their hearts did not match what they said. We can observe the Pharisee 'baddies' and say how evil they were, and fail to see how we as Bible-believing Christians can act just as hypocritically. We are good at singing the latest song or attending the current popular Christian event and then walking away and behaving no better than anyone else. *But be doers of the word, and not hearers only, deceiving yourselves. For if anyone is a hearer of the word and not a doer, he is like a man observing his natural face in a mirror; for he observes himself, goes away, and immediately forgets what kind of man he was. But he who looks into the perfect law of liberty and continues in it, and is not a forgetful hearer but a doer of the work, this one will be blessed in what he does* (James 1:22–25).

We are called to be different, to swim against the world's current and to take a stand against ungodliness, not just by shouting louder but by the way we live. Do people look at us and see the fruit of the Spirit, the characteristics of Jesus, shining through our alternative lifestyle? If we belong to Christ and have been truly born from above, we are part of a new creation: *Therefore, if anyone is in Christ, he is a new creation; old things have passed away; behold, all things have become new* (II Corinthians 5:17). For this to show in us we need to allow the word of Christ to dwell in us richly (see Colossians 3:16) and be filled with the Spirit every day, living as branches that are connected to Jesus, the vine, as we have already seen. (John 15).

I think that too often I carry on life thinking that I am basically OK and not too bad at what I do, and hoping that my life is on the whole quite pleasing to Jesus. But, if I am honest, I am probably living most of the time in my own strength, relying on my abilities rather than His. I forget that He might be looking for more from me.

AS SURELY AS THE LORD LIVES

As surely as the Lord lives
You perceive the thoughts of my heart
As surely as the Lord lives
You have known me right from the start
You have known me right from the start

THE SONG OF THE FATHER'S HEART

As surely as the Lord lives
There is no way I can pretend
As surely as the Lord lives
You want truth from beginning to end
You want truth from beginning to end

Your eyes look for fruit in me
Your eyes look for righteousness
What do You see
When searching through me?
Do You see the truth in my heart?

As surely as the Lord lives
You want Your image growing in me
As surely as the Lord lives
You want love and humility
You want love and humility

As surely as the Lord lives
There is only one way this can be
As surely as the Lord lives
It's Your Spirit living in me
It's Your Spirit living in me

Your eyes look for fruit in me
Your eyes look for righteousness
What do You see
When searching though me?
Do You see the truth in my heart?

As surely as the Lord lives
You will purify my heart with fire
As surely as the Lord lives
You are truly my only desire
You are truly my only desire
Truly, truly my only desire

Phil Lawson Johnston Copyright ©2003 IQ Music

I am sure you can see many signs of God's life at work in you, and look back at how much He has changed you; but there are sometimes frightening inconsistencies in the way we conduct ourselves: now praising Him, next minute cutting up another driver, or demanding our place in the queue. James puts it this way: *But no man can tame the tongue. It is an unruly evil, full of deadly poison. With it we bless our God and Father, and with it we curse men, who have been made in the similitude of God. Out of the same mouth proceed blessing and cursing. My brethren, these things ought not to be so. Does a spring send forth fresh water and bitter from the same opening?* (James 3:8–11).

Paul describes a similar struggle: *For the good that I will to do, I do not do.... Who will deliver me from this body of death?* (See Romans 7:21–24).

Transformation

I believe God is looking for there to be change and growth in us, which can only really come from His own hand, and which will be complete when we see Him face to face. It is no good trying to change ourselves; a transformation has to take place. Someone illustrated this by comparing us to salt that has been mixed with pepper. We may think that by shaking ourselves up, or rearranging ourselves, the salt will separate from the pepper. Rearranged pepper will still be pepper and never become pure salt. Only God can make us into the salt of the earth, by our being born again from above. Only He can bring about a transformation of our old nature and, day by day, we need to co-operate with His Spirit, to allow the process to take place. *Therefore we do not lose heart. Even though our outward man is perishing, yet the inward man is being renewed day by day* (II Corinthians 4:16).

There are certain ways in which we can facilitate this. Firstly, it helps for our focus to be directed aright. *If then you were raised with Christ, seek those things which are above, where Christ is, sitting at the right hand of God. Set your mind on things above, not on things on the earth. For you died, and your life is hidden with Christ in God* (Colossians 3:1–3). By an act of our will we can have our attitudes changed: *And do not be conformed to this world, but be transformed by the renewing of your mind...* (Romans 12:2); and turn away from ungodly behaviour, which is described as putting off our old selves and putting on the new: *But now you yourselves are to put off all these: anger, wrath, malice, blasphemy, filthy language out of your mouth. Do not lie to one other, since you have put off the old man with his deeds, and have put on the new man who is renewed in knowledge according to the image of Him who created him* (Colossians 3:8–10). *...that you put off, concerning your former conduct, the old man which grows corrupt according to the deceitful lusts, and be renewed in the spirit of your mind, and that you put on the new man which was created according to God, in true righteousness and holiness* (Ephesians 4:22ff).

It is the Lord Himself who does the work in us; *...for it is God who works in you both to will and to do for His good pleasure* (Philippians 2:13). Ultimately, the transformation will be complete: *For our citizenship is in heaven, from which we also eagerly wait for the Saviour, the Lord Jesus Christ, who will transform our lowly body that it may be conformed to His glorious body...* (Philippians 3:20–21). *For this corruptible must put on incorruption, and this mortal must put on immortality.* (I Corinthians 15:53).

I believe that as we seek to worship the Lord in spirit and truth, with our hearts, souls, minds and bodies, and aim to serve Him with all our strength, allowing His Spirit to fill us so that we produce His fruit in our lives, we will glorify Him. When we come to worship Him, together or on our own, standing before Him and looking up into His face, in our hearts a transformation will take place. (See, again, II Corinthians 3:16, which we considered in chapter nine). It would seem that as we worship and contemplate His glory, then we begin to reflect His likeness, and the more we spend time before Him, the more we will become like Him. When I expose myself to the sun I go a certain shade of pink, others a glorious tan! How wonderful for people to look at us and somehow know that we have been with Jesus, because they see something of His image in us. The authorities saw the courage of Peter and John and yet that they were 'ordinary' men; and, we are told, they took note that they had been with Jesus. Oh that others would see the family likeness in us. Jesus said that he was the Light of the world, and at another time that we were the light of the world. We can begin to reflect something of His light.

Moses reflected the glory of God, having spent much time in His presence; his face glowed, and yet faded after a while. With him it was on the outside, whereas with us the Holy Spirit produces it on the inside. Metamorphosis is being changed into another form from within, like a butterfly emerging from a chrysalis, whereas a masquerade is fashioned from the outside. When the outward image does not tally with the inside, it becomes pretence or worse —hypocrisy. From I John 3:2, we learn that we will ultimately become like Jesus when we see Him fully. The glorious reflection will then be complete. In the meantime, the image grows and we are changed gradually as we expose ourselves more and more to His presence, looking into His face in worship and prayer. As we surrender ourselves to Him in mind, spirit, and body, we will be changed. (See Romans 12:1) As I have said elsewhere, we become like the one we worship. (Psalm115:8). In one sense we have been made 'perfect' or holy, but in another we are still being made holy, *...For by one offering He has perfected forever those who are being sanctified* (Hebrews 10:14).

Jesus is committed to seeing His church become a perfect bride.

...Christ also loved the church and gave Himself for her, that He might sanctify and cleanse her with the washing of water by the word, that He might present her to Himself a glorious church, not having spot or wrinkle or any such thing, but that she should be holy and without blemish. (See Ephesians 5:25ff).

Christlikeness in our character and conduct should begin to flow as we worship. Someone has said, 'A little reflection on God's perfection leads to the correction of my direction.' If we are in Christ, then we will change and grow to be more like Him. We will show the 'family likeness'. The Bible uses a number of different illustrations to describe God's people, all of which involve growth or being built together, a few of which might be helpful to look at as we explore this subject of how God wants to change us into His image. We are described variously as the family of God, the bride of Christ, the army of God, the household of faith, God's field, various kinds of trees, a well-watered garden, a building and temple and God's work of art. I want to take just some of these to illustrate the process of growth: His field or garden, His building, and His workmanship.

God's field

Paul saw God's people as a field to be cultivated. *I planted, Apollos watered, but God gave the increase. So then neither he who plants is anything, nor he who waters, but God who gives the increase. Now he who plants and he who waters are one, and each one will receive his own reward according to his own labour. For we are God's fellow-workers; you are God's field, you are God's building.* (See I Corinthians 3:6ff). There are plenty of references in the Old Testament to God's people being sown, and growing as plants, trees or gardens. *Also your people shall all be righteous; They shall inherit the land forever. The branch of My planting, the work of My hands, that I may be glorified* (Isaiah 60:21). *...That they may be called trees of righteousness, the planting of the LORD, that He may be glorified* (Isaiah 61:3b).

The purpose is always to bear fruit that will glorify God, and when the plant is fruitless it is a cause of disappointment to Him. One of the strongest images used throughout the Bible to portray God's people is the vineyard. It is an image of fruitfulness bringing glory to God. As with all fruit trees, for there to be greater fruitfulness, pruning is required, and this can be painful. It can happen in our lives individually, or in churches and Christian organisations when we have been fruitful in ministry. God sometimes wants to cut back or redirect our activity, in order to make us even more effective. We often do not understand at the time what God is doing, and only in retrospect can we see the effect of His restraining or directive hand. We can get very possessive of the ministry to which He calls us, and any restriction, or even cessation, feels like a part of us is being taken away. There were times in the history of my worship group 'Cloud' when I had to offer it all back to God because I was in danger of being too dependent on it, or getting too much of my identity from it. I found the prospect of losing what I had become so fond of doing, very painful and hard to bear; it was as if I had to give up 'my baby'. But He allowed me to continue until there was an obvious moment for it to come to an end, and then it seemed so right.

In Isaiah chapter five, the Lord laments over the vineyard that He has planted when it yields only bad fruit. In despair He cries, *"What more could have been done to My vineyard that I have not done in it?"* (v.4). We can see His care and concern there, as well as His delight at fruit from the same vineyard in Isaiah 27. *"In that day sing to her, a vineyard of red wine! I, the LORD, keep it, I water it every moment; Lest any hurt it, I keep it night and day. Fury is not in Me. Who would set briers and thorns against Me in battle? I would go through them, I would burn them together. Or let him take hold of My strength, that he may make peace with Me; and he shall make peace with Me."* Then follows a promise: *Those who come He shall cause to take root in Jacob; Israel shall blossom and bud, and fill the face of the world with fruit."* Perhaps one can see this fruitfulness being fulfilled literally by Israel's supply of oranges and other fruit to the world; in spiritual terms, we cannot but think of the promise of Jesus, recorded in John chapter fifteen, that *"He who abides in Me, and I in him, bears much fruit...."* We have to be planted by the Lord and then remain connected to Him, in order to please Him and bear fruit that honours the Father. *"...Every plant which My heavenly Father has not planted will be uprooted"* (Matthew 15:13).

As I am writing this, I am sitting surrounded by a vineyard in France, and I can see the great care and attention that is needed to make the vine be as fruitful as possible. The combination of pruning, watering, sunshine and soil works together to give it the best chance of producing what is expected of it. The vines are neat and uniform, laid out in long lines that run across the countryside, and yet each one is individual and needs special care. The Lord is undoubtedly looking for a harvest from us, which will not only please Him, but also provide for others the life they are hungry for.

God's garden

Another repeated (and not wholly dissimilar) scriptural picture is that of the garden. *The Lord will guide you continually, and satisfy your soul in drought, and strengthen your bones; You shall be like a watered garden, and like a spring of water, whose waters do not fail* (Isaiah 58:11). *Therefore they shall come and sing in the height of Zion, streaming to the goodness of the LORD— for wheat and new wine and oil, for the young of the flock and the herd; Their souls shall be like a well-watered garden, and they shall sorrow no more at all* (Jeremiah 31:12). We generally think of the main purpose of a garden as bringing pleasure and peace to those who are able to enjoy it. Gardens are places of colour, smell and interest. It was a garden that God created as the first environment for man and woman to live in. There is something in every human being that needs to find the way 'back to the garden'. We human beings have a desire for the peace, contentment and creativity which is aptly symbolised by the picture of a garden. A garden is meant to be a place to excite curiosity. I recently visited a garden which, in overall size, was relatively small, but it had so many hidden corners, with arches and paths, that it felt as if one was in a much larger space. True, those who have enough space today have kitchen gardens where produce is grown, and gardens in the time and place of Jesus's earthly ministry are unlikely to have been purely ornamental. But the garden image in Scripture does focus on beauty and fragrance, not just the utilitarian. (Consider the Song of Solomon, quoted below.) In the same way, it would be a mistake to think that the only purpose of our lives was to be productive, important as that is. There is also a place for beauty for the sake of beauty. God did not look at each stage of His creation and say, 'That will be useful for....' He looked at it and saw that 'it was good'. I think we too often try and find a productive purpose in everything, while forgetting that some things are for pleasure and enjoyment. It has been observed that a wise worshipper would say that God made the flowers beautiful, and the birds to sing, so that we might enjoy them, whereas a sceptical scientist might say that the bird sings just to attract the female or stake their territory, and that this is purely a biological instinct. Tozer's answer to this attitude was to point to the fact that God *created* the creature in such a way that he would sing —rather than make horrible noises! He goes on to use of God metaphors such as 'chief musician' or 'composer'.[1]

When a gardener plans a garden, he has a picture in his mind of what he wants. He starts by sowing and planting, knowing that much of it will not appear until later, perhaps even after some years have elapsed. It takes time to create and nurture. My father was a mad-keen gardener (strangely, a characteristic I have not inherited!) and he took an overgrown field and painstakingly, over the years, created what became a beautiful garden, which was enjoyed by many. God takes what seems to be the most unpromising group of people, shaping and nurturing them into something that reflects His beauty and character. Paul puts it like this in Romans 8:29, *For whom He foreknew, He also predestined to be conformed to the image of His Son....*

The delight that the lover has for his beloved in the Song of Solomon is shown when he eulogises over her and compares her to a garden of choice fruits: *"A garden enclosed is my sister, my spouse; a spring shut up, a fountain sealed. Your plants are an orchard of pomegranates with pleasant fruits, fragrant henna with spikenard, spikenard and saffron, calamus and cinnamon, with all trees of frankincense, myrrh and aloes, with all the chief spices— a fountain of gardens, a well of living waters, and streams from Lebanon. Awake O north wind, and come, O south! Blow upon my garden, that its spices may flow out. Let my beloved come to his garden and eat its pleasant fruits. I have come to my garden, my sister, my spouse..."* (Song of Solomon 4:12ff).

A productive garden is depicted in that passage, of course—the spices and fruits are all useful in their various ways—but the vivid language also conveys a picture of great aesthetic beauty. This is not an image of factory farming and pesticides! It is a place where God's loving, passionate cultivation yields an almost tangible sense of delight —the multitude of smells that one gets in a garden can be a great delight; there is the freshness that fills one's senses just after rain; the waft of different scents, as one walks through fragrant plants. I liken it to the fragrance of God's presence, which so often comes when we worship.

As we think about the sheer beauty and fragrance of a well-tended garden, which goes so far beyond its 'utility', we are reminded as worshippers of the sheer delight we can have in our own hearts as we praise and worship God with our instruments and voices.

The beauty of true praise and worship is like that garden in the Song of Solomon, when love and delight are present. Worship is our opportunity to delight ourselves in the Lord together.

WELL-WATERED GARDEN

The poor and needy search for water
Their tongues are parched with thirst
The Lord will answer them
He will make rivers flow

THE SONG OF THE FATHER'S HEART

Turning deserts into springs
So, come all you thirsty ones
Come to the waters
Come to the Fountain of Life
Come with your empty cup
Stand at the waterfall
Jesus will satisfy

You will be like a well-watered garden
Like a spring whose waters never fail
Like a pool in the desert
Bursting forth in the desert
Like the garden of the Lord
You will be like a well-watered garden
Like a spring whose waters never fail
Spring up, O well
Spring up, O well

The Lord is your Shepherd
You will lack nothing
You will lie down in peace
There, in green pastures
And by still waters
He will restore your soul

So, come all you weary ones
And heavy-laden
Come now and be refreshed
Come with your weariness
Lay down your burden
And Jesus will give you rest

God's building

Just as God's field and garden are constant themes throughout Scripture, so is the image of a building: it is planned; foundations are laid, and it rises to become a temple, or dwelling, for God. This is both a corporate and an individual illustration. We see it appearing repeatedly in Paul's epistles: *Do you not know that you are the temple of God and that the Spirit of God dwells in you?* (I Corinthians 3:16; also, see again I Corinthians 6:19). Like any building it needs to have firm foundations (as we observed above; see I Peter 2:4, I Corinthians 3:10 and Ephesians 2:18ff).

It is a building that is created by God Himself. *For every house is built by someone, but He who built all things is God. And Moses indeed was faithful in all His house as a servant, for a testimony of those things which would be spoken afterward, but Christ as a Son over His own house, whose house we are if we hold fast the confidence and the rejoicing of the hope firm to the end* (Hebrews 3:4ff). *For we know that if our earthly house, this tent, is destroyed, we have a building from God, a house not made with hands, eternal in the heavens* (II Corinthians 5:1).

Just as a gardener has a mental picture of what his garden is to look like, so the architect has to make meticulous plans before the building can be started. God had a blueprint in mind when He planned and set creation in motion.

A building is, in a sense, incomplete until it is occupied. A house is not a home until the people who will live there are in place. We can apply this picture of a building to the people of God. Buildings can fall into disrepair and end up unoccupied and derelict. Similarly, the church in every age has fallen into unbelief or corruption, so rebuilding is needed:

Those from among you shall build the old waste places; You shall raise up the foundations of many generations; And you shall be called the Repairer of the Breach, The Restorer of Streets to dwell in. (Isaiah 58:12).

The LORD has appeared of old to me, saying, "Yes, I have loved you with an everlasting love; Therefore with lovingkindness I have drawn you. Again I will rebuild you, and you shall be rebuilt" (Jeremiah 31:3f).

God's workmanship

The final image that I want to look at is that of God's workmanship, or work of art. *For we are His workmanship, created in Christ Jesus for good works, which God prepared beforehand that we should walk in them* (Ephesians 2:10).

The word normally translated 'workmanship', (Greek *poema*, from which we presumably get our word poem) literally means, 'work of art'. We are God's work of art, the work of his hands, His masterpiece. Again, as with the gardener and the architect, the artist envisages the finished piece or design and goes through the various stages seeing how it develops, sometimes exactly as he thought, sometimes evolving into something different. Sometimes, the initial groundwork takes a long time and the final stage can be quite quick. The picture comes to mind of Michaelangelo 'freeing' the slaves from the blocks of marble as he chipped away.

The illustration of God the potter working on His people, the clay pot, is a recurring one in Scripture. *The word which came to Jeremiah from the LORD, saying: "Arise and go down to the potter's house, and there I will cause you to hear My words." Then I went down to the potter's house, and there he was, making something at the wheel. And the vessel that he made of clay was marred in the hand of the potter; so he made it again into another vessel, as it seemed good to the potter to make. Then the word of the LORD came to me, saying: "O house of Israel, can I not do with you as this potter?" says the LORD. "Look, as the clay is in the potter's hand, so are you in My hand, O house of Israel!"* (Jeremiah 18:1ff).

But indeed, O man, who are you to reply against God? Will the thing formed say to him who formed it, "Why have you made me like this?" Does not the potter have power over the clay, from the same lump to make one vessel for for honour and another for dishonour? (Romans 9:20–21).

Paul also speaks of people as letters that are being written by the Spirit, to communicate the gospel to others: *You are our epistle written in our hearts, known and read by all men; clearly you are an epistle of Christ, ministered by us, written not with ink but by the Spirit of the living God, not on tablets of stone but on tablets of flesh, that is, of the heart* (II Corinthians 3:2–3).

Others, such as Don McMinn, have described us as instruments of praise, on which God wants to play His tune, suggesting that we are designed for that very purpose.

As an artist/craftsman and singer/songwriter/guitarist, I suppose the illustration of us as God's work of art, or instrument of beauty, is the one which means most to me personally. When I set out to engrave a piece of glass, too, I have in my mind the intention of creating something that in some way reflects God's creativity, His beauty, and His care and attention to detail. My more-or-less subconscious prayer each time is: *And let the beauty of the LORD our God be upon us, and establish the work of our hands for us; Yes, establish the work of our hands* (Psalm 90:17). I expand on my own view of creativity in chapter fifteen.

A field needs to be productive; the plants need to multiply and yield nourishment. This is a powerful image of the creative, fulfilling work that worship ministry involves, and the blessing it brings to others.

A garden needs to be enjoyed, to be visited and experienced, and the keys to success are good soil, water, sunlight and a loving gardener. The key to being a successful planting of the Lord is to remain in Jesus as He remains in us. (See John 15.) This is a picture of beauty and fragrance, which marks true worship, as we express our love for Him, and we begin to be more aware of His love for us, as He 'inhabits the praises of His people'.

A building is a place for people to come and find welcome and shelter, and the key elements are that it needs to be occupied for it to be a true home or temple, the occupant being the Holy Spirit. At every moment as we join in worship, and sometimes lead it, we must keep in sight the ongoing work of the Spirit as we minister to the Lord.

Works of art need to be seen and enjoyed. This picture speaks of a message of love, beauty and care, and the key is for it to be submitted to the artist, in other words, the potter, or Father God, our perfect, holy Creator, whose new creation we are.

Whether we see ourselves most readily as a garden being nurtured and cultivated, a building that is under construction, or a work of art in progress —as we submit ourselves to His almighty hand, the beauty of His creativity will be shown, as He transforms us from one degree of glory to another, until that Day when we shall all stand before Him.

Every worship leader, and indeed every worshipper, would do well to reflect on these scriptural images frequently and deeply. Take time to allow the scriptures I have quoted in the chapter to take root, to go on shaping what the Lord is saying to you about your own calling as a worshipper and, if appropriate, a worship leader. Learn more about the Father's heart for you and for His people. Above all, go on being filled with the Holy Spirit, and be open to the transforming work He has begun in you.

"Make us like You, Lord."

Note

[1] See A.W. Tozer *Whatever Happened to Worship?* Christian Publications

Part Five

Creative Worship

14

A NOBLE THEME
—WORSHIP SONGWRITING

A NOBLE THEME

My heart is stirred by a noble theme
Reciting verses for my King
My heart will sing to You
My heart is full of love for You
And so my heart will speak

My heart is stirred by a noble theme
Reciting verses for my King
My mouth will make You known
My mouth will sing of Your renown
And so my heart will speak

My tongue will be the pen of a ready writer
Composing songs for You, my Master
And so my heart will speak
And so my heart will speak

THE SONG OF THE FATHER'S HEART

My heart is stirred by a noble theme
Reciting verses for my King
My heart will overflow
Expressing all the love I know
And so my heart will speak
And so my heart will speak

Phil Lawson Johnston Copyright ©2004 Cloud Music

My heart is overflowing with a good* theme; I recite my composition concerning the King; My tongue is the pen of a ready writer (Psalm 45:1). [*The word rendered here as 'good' may also be translated as 'noble'.]

I sometimes imagine asking God what His favourite song might be. I think of music by Bach, Handel, Isaac Watts, Charles Wesley, Graham Kendrick, Matt Redman and many others, including my own. In my imagination there is the big build-up to the moment of truth and, instead of a dramatic pronouncement, He looks over our heads towards an old lady sweeping the floor with a smile on her face. 'Her song', He answers. 'She's no singer, musician or composer, but she sings with a melody in her heart to Me. That is My favourite song.'

Paul encourages us to be filled with the Spirit, *speaking to one another in psalms and hymns and spiritual songs, singing and making melody in your heart to the Lord, giving thanks always for all things to God the Father in the name of our Lord Jesus Christ.* (See Ephesians 5:19f.)

With the commercialisation of praise and worship music throughout the world, there is a great danger for songwriters: to seek to write more for the market rather than to express the heart of God. One sees the success of certain songs, which have been catapulted to the heights of popularity via conference and album exposure, and one is tempted to write in order to try to follow in the same steps by copying them.

We live in a disposable and instant society, and it is inevitable that songs can suffer the same fate. Observing the fluctuating nature of the song repertoire over the last thirty years, I see that there are some great songs that pass the test of time, whereas the vast majority last but a short while. There are others (including some of my own) that probably should not have seen the light of day at all! It is the nature of the type of worship song that we have been using to be fairly short-lived, and sometimes we run the danger of overkill by pushing some way beyond their sell-by date. However, there are some classics, which will last for years, expressing themes in a style that has a timeless value. It is easy to forget that writers like Charles Wesley wrote many hymns, and that the ones we sing now are only a small selection of the best.

I have often heard people criticising the quality of many of the current songs, comparing them to the great hymns of the past, when they are not really comparing like with like. To compare a song which does not say much more than 'I love You, Lord' to one of the doctrinally rich hymns is like comparing the content of a good discussion with one's wife or husband with the words, 'I love you!' If those words are said from the heart, then there is just as much content and depth; they just have a different purpose. Just as in a marriage one needs both, one also needs both the rich doctrinal content in what we sing as well as the heartfelt, 'I love You, and thank You for all You've done in my life.' One has to be able to express in heart and mind both the truth about God and our response to that truth. Many contemporary songs have been written with a simple theme or thought, and work well in a flowing progression that gradually develops that theme. They are not meant to replace hymns but to complement them.

Most of what I want to say about songwriting will come from my own experience. Some of it will be obvious, some of it subjective. Most of it will be informative rather than instructive, but I hope it will provide some foundational thought for those who are setting out on their songwriting journey.

Who is it for?

One of the first things to consider is: who are you writing for? First of all, one is writing for an audience of one, the Lord Himself, but because we can get rather dazzled by the prospect of a song that might become successful (and earn us a lot of royalties!), we can forget that sometimes a song is just for you and God alone. Likewise, it may be only for your friends, home group or church to enjoy, not necessarily for universal usage or acclaim. This can be hard to accept sometimes, and I know from my own feelings that there are songs of mine that I think are as good, if not better than, some that are widely used, and I have to watch my pride. It is like the way that one thinks one's own baby is the most beautiful in the world, and cannot understand why others fail to show the same degree of enthusiasm!

What the Spirit is saying

One has to think not so much about what 'I' want to write about, but perhaps what God is wanting to say to the church. *"He who has an ear, let him hear what the Spirit says to the churches"* (Revelation 2:7), or what the feelings of the people are, that you could put into song. One needs to pray, therefore, that one's writing would be priestly, expressing the heart of the people, as well as prophetic, expressing the mind and heart of the Lord. Thus, listening to God plays a significant role in the process. Being well versed in the word of God is also essential. (See Colossians 3:16). As that word dwells richly in us, and we pray continually to be filled with the Spirit, then what one writes will be guarded from being unscriptural, and will become a means of teaching the truth to people. It even can become an effective way of memorising Scripture. *My mouth shall speak wisdom, and the meditation of my heart shall give understanding. I will incline my ear to a proverb; I will disclose my dark saying on the harp* (Psalm 49:3–4).

To learn

What then, is the correct formula for a good song? What are the rules? I certainly evaluate songs much more according to my own subjective opinions than any songwriting rules, if there are any. However, I do know it is a skill to be learned, developed and improved, and there have been times when important changes have taken place in my own writing. One of the most significant was when I was preparing to record the seventh album with Cloud. I wanted an outside objective ear to listen to the songs and help produce them as effectively as possible. I asked Andy Piercy, whom I did not know well at the time, but who I knew had experience in writing and recording, albeit in a very different style to my own. He took me through a painful but highly rewarding process of rearranging, pruning and rewriting the songs I had selected to record. He did not impose his own style on them, but got me to work the songs into shape in a way that brought the best out of them. He would ask me why I was repeating lines; why I was going into the minor when the words suggested the major. He helped cut out masses of dead wood from the songs. One went through about five rewrites before he would let us even consider rehearsing it!

He has subsequently become a great friend, but I am eternally grateful for his tough but loving approach, and I still imagine him standing at my shoulder when I am writing, saying, 'Uh, uh, why are you doing that?!' I would highly recommend this to anyone trying to write songs: find a person you respect and trust, who will be prepared to tell you the truth about your songs! We get very possessive over what we write, and sensitive to criticism of it, but I only wish I had had Andy or someone like him around when I started out, and I could have avoided many mistakes and produced far better songs. I think I had the impression that because I thought the songs had been 'given' to me by God, nothing could be done to them; they were sacred and not to be touched. This was a fairly common attitude then, and God got the blame for many poor songs and albums. I remember early contemporary Christian records that were fairly rough and ready and yet had, 'Produced by the Holy Spirit' written as part of the credits!

Aim high

It is important to aim high, to go for excellence and not be prepared to put up with second best. Sometimes one runs the danger of reproducing the same old song in a slightly different guise, and although it is normal for songs written by the same person to have a similarity about them, we all need to stretch our creativity and aim to produce something fresh each time. If one is writing for congregational use, one has to take into account the limits that the average person has in terms of their singing ability. It is good to stretch congregations creatively, but not to the extent of complete discomfort, and if a song is too complex, or has too wide a range of notes, most will give up singing and just listen.

Church poets

It has been said that the songs of a nation have more influence than its laws. What we sing about is important, as it reflects our thinking and beliefs. One can learn much about a church's theology by listening to the songs they sing, just as one can learn a lot about a society by studying their music. However, there can be a danger of allowing one's theology to be shaped by the songs, rather than letting theology mould the songs. There is a need, however, for songs to express what a church might be going through; what God is saying and doing in their midst. That is where the songwriters come in. Someone has described us as 'the church's poets', and although many of the songs and hymns we sing are general in content, there is a place for the song that expresses what God is doing locally. The psalmist so often sings from the heart of human experience —in the light of faith; and that must be one of our primary models.

As I recounted in chapter two of this book, beginning to write songs for the Lord coincided very much with being filled with the Holy Spirit, and I can say that, ever since then, *The LORD is my strength and song, and He has become my salvation* (Exodus 15:2a). Jesus, indeed, became the message of my song.

The message

Good melody is obviously important, but in my opinion it takes second place to content. Birdsong provides a useful illustration, in that birds communicate with each other through song. I do not believe that they are particularly concerned with the beauty of the tune they sing, but the message they are seeking to convey is all important, whether it is establishing territory or attracting a mate! Many people respond to God's truth through songs far more readily than by listening to spoken words alone. *Your statutes have been my songs in the house of my pilgrimage* (Psalm 119:54). Although music itself may be neutral, all songs give a message of some sort. It can be used by God or by the devil. I do not believe that any style is godlier than another, but the lyrics show what the underlying message is. And we have a message to communicate and proclaim: the truth about God. It is important that the message is scriptural; not necessarily always straight Scripture itself, although when it works it is very powerful. The Word is eternal, and, as I have already mentioned, singing it can be a good way of memorising Scripture in an age when it is unfashionable to memorize anything important. Many have tried to put Scripture verses to music, and only ended up squeezing them into a tune that does not really work; but a song which is shaped and adapted from Scripture can often be effective.

Literal and perceptual

One thing to look out for is the difference between literal and perceptual language. For example, when one says, 'The sun rises', one is using perceptual rather than literal imagery. The sun does not literally rise; as we know it stays still and the earth turns, but we perceive that it rises, so we use that kind of language to describe it. The same thing applies with some worship lyrics. We simply need to be aware of this distinction as we compose, and ensure that the imagery we employ is consonant with biblical usage.

Objective and subjective

Another area of contention can be the pendulum swing between objectivity and subjectivity in what we sing. One needs to be aware of the fact that throughout history there has been a battle between the two. It is said that the Arian heresy was spread through the singing of songs, which led to a ban on any hymns that did not specifically state objective biblical truths. Nothing subjective was allowed. I have heard similar objections to us singing too many songs that express our relationship with God in love language, rather than straightforward objective truths. I thought I would check the Bible's hymnbook, the Psalms to see what balance there was there. On a quick scan I could see that they were roughly 50% objective truths about God and 50% personal feelings and responses; everything from triumphant victory, hope and faith, to 'I'm in a mess, please help me!' Sometimes the psalmist would go from the objective to the subjective within a single psalm. I would deduce from this, therefore (unsurprisingly), that a balanced approach would be best.

I am concerned with trying to create songs that have poetry in them, even allegorical language, language of the eye and heart as well as the ear and mind, using both sides of the brain. It is all too easy to employ over-used words and phrases, however biblical they are, rather than push at one's imaginative boundaries while still staying faithful to revealed truth.

Subject matter

There is an enormous richness of subject matter available to us in the Bible, and we all too easily narrow our range. We have the attributes of God: Father, King, Shepherd, Servant, Teacher, Healer, Redeemer, Deliverer, Lover, Comforter, etc.. We have the great themes of the Bible: creation, holiness, power, grace, unconditional love, listening, purification, repentance, etc.. There is plenty of movement and action to portray: drawing close, 'Come let us bow...', dance, shout, lift the hands, fall face down, send us out, lead us, 'we will follow', etc. There is the cry of the heart: for strength, rescue, the needs of the world, thirst for more of God. There are the issues of God's heart: laments over abortion, child abuse, injustice etc...; themes that encourage obedience, and remind us of His love. We need to touch transcendence, to reach out beyond ourselves, to retain mystery and otherness, while seeking to express something that is real and relevant to life. *"For My thoughts are not your thoughts, Nor are your ways My ways," says the LORD. "For as the heavens are higher than the earth, so are My ways higher than your ways, and My thoughts than your thoughts"* (Isaiah 55:8–9).

We need to capture the mystery of *Christ in you, the hope of glory*, and to know it, together with the reality of God's love and compassion for us. Every aspect of God's revealed character and heart can and should be sung about.

Inspiration...

He has put a new song in my mouth—praise to our God... (Psalm 40:3). *'...God my Maker, who gives songs in the night...'* (Job 35:10). The basis of our inspiration is our relationship with God, and the state of our hearts before Him is therefore of crucial importance. We are looking for songs that flow from the heart, out of our love for Jesus and a response to His love. There seems to be a spiritual element to most music and, as we have noticed already, many people respond more easily to it than to mere words alone. Words with no heart or depth behind them are empty, and can turn out to be no more than a 'resounding gong or clashing symbol'. William Cowper, writer of hymns said, 'I began to compose the verses yesterday morning before daybreak, but fell asleep at the end of the first two lines.... When I awakened, the third and fourth were whispered to my heart in a way I have often experienced.'

Out the abundance of a joyful or hurting heart, the mouth speaks. Brian Doerksen, another wonderful writer of many excellent worship songs, speaking about how he started, mentions that he wrote *Faithful One* out of the agony of trying to do something he could not do. Then, he says, he 'stopped trying to be a worship songwriter' but instead he started to write out of what he was experiencing and who God was making him. Rejecting the idea that songwriting is 'some bizarre mystical thing' but is rather 'just being you', he speaks of seeing his baby daughter look at him, and trying to imagine what her eyes are telling him. In that moving image, he encapsulates something of what 'our spirits cry out to Father God'.

...or hard work?

I have sometimes heard the claim, 'God gave me this song. That's the way He gave it to me. (I know it makes no sense) but I know it's anointed' —which would not, if true, give one much scope for discussion of the content! But worship songs are not canonised, they are not infallible spiritual writing dictated by God; and it is not sacrilegious to shape and mould or even reject a song in favour of an improved one. Not all should be kept; some can be stepping stones to better ones, or one can become two by separating off the chorus, for example. It is good to work at them, as I've mentioned before. Graham Kendrick says it is 10% inspiration and 90% perspiration, and Paul Simon certainly puts most of us to shame when he speaks of the time it takes for him to complete a song to his satisfaction: four to six weeks when he works steadily, but as long as four to six months if not working steadily.

It has rightly been pointed out that the hard work begins when the writer has written the words of his first draft and finds it to be unsatisfactory. Then you begin to edit the work; you employ your own experience and powers of analysis, as a 'craftsman': improving and polishing, until it is as good as you can make it.

Passion is needed as well as hard work. David Ruis a worship leader and writer has remarked that, 'With passion you can fill the stadiums of the world'.

Lyric writing

When writing lyrics, one should try and avoid watered down less than scriptural concepts, such as, 'Come to Jesus and be happy'. Jargon or Christian clichés, sometimes described as the 'language of Zion', should be avoided, particularly if they are likely to be incomprehensible to those outside the household of God (not to mention many inside it as well!) It has been said you should never include a line that you need to explain. I personally have trouble with songs that use the name 'Jehovah'. Introducing a transliterated name for God without sufficient explanation (which cannot usually be done within a song) can in some circumstances be unhelpful, particularly if those we are seeking to introduce to Jesus as their Lord and Saviour are in the congregation. Having said that – and we should, of course, be centred on Jesus – we do need to convey the revealed truth about each person of the Trinity, and we can do this through song without much difficulty, and avoiding obscurity.

Songs should be understandable, accessible; and we need to find creative ways of proclaiming eternal truths freshly. Do not try to cover too much ground in a song, with too many concepts and ideas. Do not be afraid of being simple, without being simplistic; *'It is easy to be simple and bad; being simple and good is very difficult.'* Hal David once said. Avoid phrasing which gets out of hand. Extreme but memorable examples may help us to avoid this trap:

O send down sal. O send down sal. O send down salvation.
O catch the flee. O catch the flee. O catch the fleeing sinner, Lord.
O take the pil. O take the pil. O take the pilgrim home.

Likewise one can fall into the trap of unnecessary rhyming, just for the sake of it:

You died for me, and set me free on Calvary.

I've been born from above
on the wings of a dove
by the Spirit of love.

There are other ways of being far more subtle, like the near rhyming of Shakespeare: wrong/young – fast/guest etc.. The rhythm of the words is just as important as rhyming. Try to avoid putting the emphasis on syllables falling in the wrong place, and clumsy phrasing. It is worth seeing how it works when read; does it read like poetry? The main difference between a poem and a song is that a poem is complete in itself, whereas a song is fulfilled by the melody.

Although one should beware of excessive repetition, word play can sometimes be very effective. A lyrical technique which I find very helpful is to take a word or phrase and repeat it with variation each time. My own attempt at playing with words in a rhythmic manner is the following song about grace:

OUGHT OUGHT

Ought, ought, must, must
Better, better do that
How can I keep these rules today
Try, try, hard, hard, effort, effort, more now
How can I keep these sins at bay
I can't make it, I can't fake it
When I try to be so good
I can never be the perfect saint
Although I know I should

Grace, grace, love and mercy
Show me how to be set free
Jesus gives a brand new start
Grace, grace, love and mercy
Is the way to live as free
Jesus writes these laws upon my heart x2

I'll cry, cry, laugh, laugh, even though I fail, fail
I don't have to make it on my own
I'm saved, saved, free, free
I'll never, never die, die
I've set my sights on a heavenly home
I can make it, no need to fake it
There's change going on within my soul
I receive His grace to live
While bit-by-bit, I'm being made whole

Phil Lawson Johnston

'Horse and carriage'

Words and melody work together like a marriage (or a horse and carriage!); let lyric and tune express the same emotion and feel, rhythmically matching, falling and rising at the same time. Try to marry lyrics with appropriate major and minor chords. A weak chorus should not go with strong verses; if the verses are strong, maybe there is no need for a chorus at all, and a refrain at the end of each verse would be enough. Does the tune work on its own or is it too dependent on the lyrics? Can it be whistled?

The range of a song can be crucial as to whether people will sing it easily. I feel that many songs in the books are written too high, and with the majority of congregations not being made up of highly skilled singers, I find that I am constantly lowering the keys. There are some songs (my own included) which have low verses with high choruses, with the result that it is hard to establish what key to play them in at all. Also, if the tune is too complex, with too many changes and variations, people will tend not to sing. Therefore, simplicity is important, even though it can be frustrating for those who would love something more sophisticated. It boils down to whether a song enables people to worship or not; whether it expresses what they want to say to God in a tune that grabs their heart, or whether it challenges them to go deeper with God.

Those of us writing the songs do not necessarily know how they are going to work until we have tried them. I am sure I am not alone in being surprised at how some songs take off unexpectedly, and others that I have been convinced were the best ever, have made no impression at all!

There is great value in co-writing with someone else. Historically, there have been many successful partnerships. In some cases, one was stronger on lyrics the other on melody. I have had a little experience of co-writing, with a friend, Colin Rank, and then, once, I spent two days with Chris Bowater with the intention of doing some writing. We both came with ideas for songs, and managed to complete them successfully. Co-writing creates something that is more than the combined style of the two writers; it produces something new and fresh. I would love to do more when the opportunity arises.

Plagiarism?

What about borrowing tunes or styles? Whilst copyright rules apply, there is some precedent for using similar tunes or styles to others in order to speak in a language that is relevant for the generations one is trying to reach without being over influenced by the world around us. It has been done throughout church history: Luther, Isaac Watts, Cowper, Booth, all took popular songs of the time and used them as hymn styles, and as we have remarked already, were heavily criticised by the churchmen of their day. Booth replied by asking, 'Why should the devil have all the best tunes?'

It is not just the church hymn writers that have done this. Many pop and rock songs have been based, intentionally or not, on classical or classic melodies.

Taking an existing song as a starting point can help. It has been said that true originality lies not so much in the ability to come up with new ideas, but in the way you rearrange the old ones; and that our musical perceptions are really an amalgam of everything we have ever heard before. Many songwriters are happy to admit that they have gleaned much from a variety of sources as part of the creative process. Certainly, much can be learned from studying other writers, trying to see why a certain song works: is it the structure, the way the lyrics fit, or the memorable 'hook line'?

Melody, harmony and rhythm

I agree with the theory that to produce a song effectively you need each element of melody, harmony and rhythm. Melody should be provided by vocals, harmony by other vocals or instruments, and rhythm from percussion or a rhythmic instrument such as a guitar. Some songs depend more on rhythm and/or harmony to make them work. The simplicity of Taizé or the Iona Community music blossoms when the harmonies are added, and the African style of singing unaccompanied except by percussion has a life and excitement all of its own. Incidentally, during a trip to Zimbabwe I found that, when they sang, they tended to drift sharp (I was trying to find the key they were singing in, and every time I found it they had moved up a semitone!), whereas in Britain we tend to go flat when singing accappella. I have no idea why this should be so, and it has little significance, but I found it interesting!

Some songs sung without any rhythm are dull and bland, yet adding rhythm can transform them. Changing the rhythm of a song that is not working can also give it a completely different feel. However, there are songs that are written primarily for a full band to play, and when you try to play them without the complete backing they do not seem to work at all. I am sure it is a mistake that many of us have made from time to time!

How I write a song

I hope you will allow me some self-indulgence as I want to describe the process that I go through when I set out to write a song, in the hope that it might help others who are seeking to do the same

First of all, I am not sure whether to call myself a 'songwriter' or 'composer'. Sometimes I think of it in restaurant terms: some are like the top establishments, and some are like the local burger chain. Some would class me close to the latter, but I would like to think of myself as somewhere in between: perhaps a comfortable local pub, or even a modest restaurant on my good days. At least I hope my menu has improved over the years! In the early days I often had the melody before the lyrics. I am told that this is the case with many famous songwriters, but more recently I have found the ideas for lyrics come first and then the tune soon after. Most often, it all comes together, and they develop in tandem.

Sometimes a single word or phrase will spark off a train of thought, such as 'grateful' or, 'give me a hearing heart'; or a single word from the Bible, such as 'magnify' (Psalm 34:3). Then, often, the rhythm of one sentence will suggest the rhythm of the tune, so that the two begin to emerge together. Then it might be a Scripture passage set to music: e.g. 'I Pray...' (see Ephesians 3:16f); *May the Lord answer you...* (Psalm 20); *I seek You...* (see Psalm 63); *If My people...* (II Chronicles 7:14); *He will rejoice over you...* (Zephaniah 3:17).

I find that an issue, theme or concept can often inspire as well, perhaps a theme from Scripture: 'wings of eagles'; 'wind'; 'river'; 'water' or 'rain'; 'Let the bride say "Come"'; 'aroma of Christ', etc. In many songs I will link a number of scriptures on a common theme, for example: 'well watered garden' [see page 246], (linking scriptures Isaiah 42:17–18; 55:1; John 7:37; 4:13: Isaiah 58:11; Jeremiah 31:12; Song of Solomon 4:15; Psalm 23; Matthew 11:28; Numbers 21:17). Two issues I have been concerned about have inspired songs: *The child never knew* (child abuse), and *Lament for wasted lives* (abortion). I have mentioned the story behind these in chapter twelve.

Once, I felt so concerned how much the name of Jesus was abused as a swear word and His divinity so under attack, that I wanted to write a song that expressed firmly that 'Jesus is the name we honour; Jesus is our God'.

At other times I have had a personal need, which I have expressed in song, such as *Comfort to my soul, Ever faithful ever true, Home for eternity, I throw myself on Jesus,* and, *You still love me.* Another time, I just wanted to express my desire to sit at Jesus' feet and enjoy His presence, and wrote, *Father we adore You.... You are the Fountain of life.*

Recently, I decided to write a song about striking the balance between truth and love. I felt that there were many Christians around who were so concerned about safeguarding the truth that they were losing sight of the importance of love. Others were so keen to be loving and tolerant that they were letting go of the truth of God's word. Paul encourages us to speak the truth in love, (Ephesians 4:15). Wanting to explore the relationship between the two, I decided to write it in the form of a four-verse hymn. The tune is fairly predictable and typically hymn-like, but it needed to be a vehicle for the lyrics and to be easily picked up. I have quoted it at the start of chapter five.

I would classify many of my songs as 'ministry songs', that is to say, songs I would use for times when people are being prayed for, or when I feel it right to sing a song of affirmation of God's love: *I have loved you*, *Let Jesus love you*. Similarly, some would be classified as intercession songs: *I look for a man*, *We see the tears*, *Keep my heart tender*. I have not often had to write a song 'to order', but when I was compiling a selection for the album *Value Me*, I had no title song, so I had to put my mind to writing to a brief that was narrower than usual. I tried to put myself into the mind of someone who has little or no self-esteem, who cannot easily receive the words 'Jesus, loves you'. It is printed in chapter seven. As I had chosen to attach a song of mine to each of the chapters of this book, I found that there were some missing, so I set myself the task of writing at least three songs specifically for this purpose. One is included at the beginning of this chapter: *A Noble Theme*.

Sometimes an idea for a song will appear from having a quiet time with the Lord, or from a sermon that I have heard or a book I have read. *Keep me as the apple of Your eye* was inspired by a talk and Psalm 17:8. I wrote the first verse of one of my most recent songs, *We were made for worship* before I had got out of bed, inspired again by the chapter of that name, and finished it before I had had breakfast! It usually takes much longer than that, though. At other times I have had inspiration while walking the dog. I often have my clearest thoughts when out on the local meadow, occasionally using a dictating machine to record them. I have found that I have a greater freedom with the words and melody without the limitations of any instrument, and as soon as I get home I pick up my guitar to work out what key I have written it in!

I have tried to break away from my previous normal song structure of 'verse chorus, verse, chorus', etc., and use a refrain instead —a repeated line at the end of each verse. I have also been introducing more 'bridges' to my songs, to add variety and also to bring in the idea of the 'Selah', or the pause for thought, from the Psalms.

I believe, as I have already stated, that the subject matter is the priority, and the melody is there primarily to be a vehicle for the lyrics.

Songs in the Bible

It is said that David wrote 73 psalms of praise, lament, pleading, yearning, repentance; and Solomon 1,005 songs and 3,000 proverbs. (See I Kings 4:32.) Apart from the Bible's hymnbook, the Psalms, a number of other songs are recorded throughout the Bible, and I commend them to you for further personal study. For convenience, some are listed here:

Song of Moses (Exodus 15) — praising God for deliverance.
Song of Miriam (In her eighties!) with tambourine and dance, (Exodus 15:20).
Israel's song (Numbers 21:17).
Song of Moses (Deuteronomy 32:1–43). Preceded by: *Then Moses spoke in the hearing of all the assembly of Israel the words of this song until they were ended...* (Deuteronomy 31:30).
The Song of Deborah and Barak (Judges 5:2–31). Victory again.
David's lament (II Samuel 1:19–27) —over the death of Saul and Jonathan.
David's song (II Samuel 22:2–51) —thanks for deliverance from his enemies.
Song of Songs Solomon's love song.
Isaiah's songs (Chapters 5, 27) —songs of fruitful and unfruitful vineyards; (chapters 12, 26) —songs of praise.
Mary's Magnificat (Luke 1:46–55).
Zechariah's song (Luke 1:68–79).
Revelation songs (4:8,11; 5:9–10,12–13; 7:10,12; 11:15–18; 12:10–12; 15:3–4, the Song of Moses and the Song of the Lamb; 16:5–7; 18:2–10,16–24; 19:1–8). Many of these are shouts or cries rather than specific songs, but could be musical at the same time.
Paul's songs There are also a number of passages in Paul's epistles, which it is thought may possibly be hymns: for example, the doxology in Romans 11:33–36, and the credal passage Philippians 2:6–11.

The song of the heart

When all is said and done, the most technically perfect song will still only be as nothing unless it flows from a passionate heart. It may bring pleasure to the hearers, receive praise from the musical purist and be performed on great platforms, but unless its source is the love of God dwelling in one's heart, it will be as *sounding brass or a clanging cymbal* (I Corinthians 13:1).

It is therefore imperative that those of us who are seeking to express His heart through our songs, keep our own hearts filled with His love through the Spirit, and guard our relationship with Him. He is looking for fruit from His body, the church, which will glorify the Father and draw the world to faith in Him. So, in psalms and hymns and spiritual songs, sing and make melody in your heart to the Lord. This is His favourite song!

15

CAPTURED BY THE WONDER —WORSHIPPING CREATOR GOD

CAPTURED BY THE WONDER

I am captured by the wonder of Your almighty hand
The beauty of creation in every golden strand
Running through the earth, sweeping over seas
Encompassing the firmament above

I am captured by the wonder of colour, sound and smell
The frosted leaves in winter, the heaving ocean swell
See the snow-capped hills, feel the faintest breath
Brushing gently through the branches of the trees

It leads me back to praise again

It's too wonderful, it's too marvellous
It's too vast a thought, all too glorious
To fully comprehend

THE SONG OF THE FATHER'S HEART

I am captured by the wonder of insect, bird and beast
The artistry in nature, creating such a feast
Running through the earth, flying through the air
And gliding through the waters of the deep

I am captured by the wonder of a mind that could conceive
Such everlasting splendour growing from a seed
From the child's first cry to the final song
That will echo throughout all eternity

It causes me to lift my voice and cry

It's too wonderful, it's too marvellous
It's too vast a thought, all too glorious
To fully comprehend

Creation speaks a language we can start to understand
The grandeur and the detail show Your almighty hand

It's Your world, it's Your world, it's Your world

Phil Lawson Johnston Copyright ©2004 Cloud Music

Viewing the grandeur and yet the detail of all that surrounds us, one cannot help but be overawed by the beauty and majesty of God's amazing creation. How can we, with our limited skills, begin to reflect His glory? Compared to Him, what we produce, however pleasing to the senses it may be, will always seem to be inadequate. And yet, when we express ourselves creatively, we are only manifesting something of His own nature, and thus it can be seen as worship. It can be shown in a myriad of ways, many of which are not recognised as works of art. Perhaps the most perfect 'art form' is the creation of a child, or it can simply be expressed in the way we lay a table, arrange flowers, practise hospitality or cast a fly. It stands to reason that creatures who are made in the image of their Creator will reflect His creativity.

However, one can be easily ridiculed for contending that there is a God who created the world. One will be told in no uncertain terms that science has buried that idea once and for all, and that people who believe in a transcendent Creator God are idiots to be pitied. The voices that shout the loudest, and with the most intellectual sounding reasoning, pour scorn on anyone who could be so naïve as to think that evolution does not hold all the answers to the universe's origins. I am no scientist (I failed all my science exams), but the little I have read about the arguments for creationism indicates to me that evolution is indeed only a theory, and that there are so many holes in the supposedly incontrovertible fossil record as to throw sufficient doubt upon it. As an artist I cannot help feeling that there are other possible explanations to the similarity between species. Look at any artist's work and there are bound to be similarities between their various pieces. One can often trace a progression as their style develops, but that does not mean that one piece evolved into the next without any outside influence or intervention, although that is analogous to what evolutionists claim. There are many books that are useful, but I have recently found Lee Strobel's *The Case for a Creator* to be extremely helpful in my understanding of the matter.[1]

Observing the world around me, I have no trouble whatsoever in believing in a Creator God. The detail of the veins on a leaf, the intricate design of the swallowtail butterfly, the beauty, colour and opulence of a sunset, and then the diversity of a completely different sunset the following evening, all speak to me of a grand Designer and Artist. So much in creation has no purpose but to bring pleasure to the beholder. At the same time there is so much that is rarely seen if at all by anyone, such as a flower on a hillside that is never visited. To the human eye there seems to be something like humour in the design of some animals and insects, although each has its reason for living, even if it may be just to be part of the food chain. I believe one of the main purposes in creation is to keep us humans in our place. As we view the wonders of creation, we can scarcely help but realise our own inadequacies and weaknesses, especially when one discovers how fragile we are faced with the power there is in nature. There are no greater respecters of nature than the fishermen who brave the fury of the merciless seas. Such reflections drive us back to wonder at the remarkable fact that we are loved and valued by the Creator of it all; the arrogance of those who stubbornly deny any possibility of a mind that designed all that we see never ceases to amaze me.

WHO AM I?

As I feast my eyes upon the hills
And drink the colours of the sky
I hear the music whistle through the trees
But I feel the wind is passing by

As I stop to consider the stars
O, what glory I see!
It leads me back to the question again
O, who am I?
O, who am I that He should want to die for me?
Why so much pain? why so much misery?
Forsaken on a dirty tree

Who can climb His holy hill?
Who will share His home?
Clean hands and a heart as pure as snow
O, I know He will not deny
O, who is He that He should give so much
To one such as I?
Why so much love from one
Who left His home and majesty?
O man, what are you
That you should deserve one such as He?

When the naming of the stars is done
And man thinks he rules the sky
The giant question mark will still remain
O, who am I?
Who am I?
Who am I?

Extract taken from the song "Who am I?" by Phil Lawson Johnston
Copyright ©1982 Thankyou Music*

My intention here, though, is not really to pursue arguments and engage in debate concerning the existence of a Creator, as there are many who are far more qualified and skilled than I am to carry out that task, and the classical arguments for the existence of God have been defined and refined over many centuries. Suffice it to say, *The heavens declare the glory of God; And the firmament shows His handiwork. Day unto day utters speech, and night unto night reveals knowledge. There is no speech nor language where their voice is not heard* (Psalm 19:1ff). But I would like to explore a little of how we can worship a Creator God through our own creativity, based mainly on my own experience as an artist/craftsman.

There are a number of verses which have helped mould my own thinking, and which have served as timely reminders to keep my focus centred upon God Himself, and not on the art for its own sake. There is always a danger of being so caught up in one's own creativity, and so proud of what one produces, that it can border on idolatry, like that of those who, *...exchanged the truth of God for the lie, and worshipped and served the creature rather than the Creator, who is blessed forever. Amen.* (See Romans 1:25.)

I once engraved a table top for a friend, with a verse and a picture of dancers praising God. I was very pleased with it, and not a little proud of what I had created, and the recipient seemed to be also very happy. I borrowed it back for an exhibition and managed to break it in transit. I was devastated, but God spoke to me clearly through it to show me that I had to guard myself from becoming too proud of my achievements. I have never forgotten the experience, and I have often had to stop myself from falling into the same trap again. That is not to say that it is wrong to be pleased with what one does if one has done it well. After all, it only reflects something of God's own character when He expressed His own satisfaction with the creation: *And God saw that it was good.* (See Genesis 1). The art can become more important for its own sake than the purpose for which it has been given. C.S Lewis illustrates this in *The Great Divorce*, when he describes an artist who starts by seeing the light, and who sets out to portray something of that light so that others might catch glimpses of it. He then drifts into creating the art for the sake of the art, and forgets to continue looking at the light, which then becomes obscured. His 'parable' warns of the danger to every poet, musician or artist, of becoming ever more and more interested in their own work, then their own personalities, and then just their own reputations. Only grace can save them from that deadly end.[2]

I am pleased that the first reference of an individual being filled with the Spirit of God in the Bible is an artist/craftsman, Bezalel. *"See, I have called by name Bezalel.... And I have filled him with the Spirit of God, in wisdom, in understanding, in knowledge, and in all manner of workmanship, to design artistic works... ..and to work in all manner of workmanship.* (See Exodus 31:1ff.) And another who has great ability close to my own craft is Huram, *...a skilful man, endowed with understanding... skilled to work in gold and silver, bronze and iron.... ...and to make any engraving and to accomplish any plan which may be given to him...* (II Chronicles 2:14).

A prayer I like to pray for God to bless my work is Psalm 90:17. *And let the beauty of the LORD our God be upon us, and establish the work of our hands for us; Yes, establish the work of our hands.* [The word rendered here as 'beauty' may also be translated 'favour'.]

St. Paul urges us to do everything for God's glory. *Therefore, whether you eat or drink, or whatever you do, do all to the glory of God* (I Corinthians 10:31).

I have had the privilege of being able to pursue creativity in two different fields: songwriting and engraving. My life has been balanced between these two occupations for over thirty years now, and I know that, compared with so many who have little or no job-satisfaction, I have a remarkably fulfilled life. It does not bring any income guarantees, as I am at the mercy of those who might wish to commission me to engrave something, or publish a song, but the fact that I can choose how to spend each day is a luxury I would never want to take for granted. I find, in some ways, that I have the best of two worlds: when I am engraving, I am, by-and-large, on my own, apart from the times when I am meeting a client or delivering a piece, whereas when I am out singing my songs or leading worship, I am generally surrounded by people.

My glass engraving covers a very wide range of subject matter, some of which is fairly mundane: initials, an inscription and company logo for example, whereas other commissions are more artistic in nature: a wildlife scene, or a collection of interests. However, the design of a couple of initials into a monogram can be as challenging, artistically, as the most complex scene. I have to keep a commercial mind throughout it all, as well as maintaining artistic integrity. I have always sought to place care at the top of my priorities: care for detail, care in execution, care in doing something that is pleasing to the recipient. I have always signed each piece, in minute writing, usually somewhere underneath, accompanied by the date, and either an Ichthus fish sign or, in the early days, *Sole Deo Gloria* (to God only be the glory), or, simply, *Jesus cares*. I have wanted the care that I have tried to practise in my engraving, as well as in my dealing with people, to show in some way the care that Jesus has for each one of us. I have not always succeeded, but it has been my aim and my desire to serve Him in this way. I have not felt it appropriate to use my art as a means of presenting a particularly overt Christian message. I do not believe that every piece of 'Christian' art should be like a tract, (e.g. two puppies and a verse about comfort!) any more than I believe that every Christian should never stop speaking about their faith. I am not sure whether there is even such a thing as a 'Christian artist', only artists who may have a Christian faith. Their lives should speak as loudly, if not louder, than their words or designs. This is not to say that I never portray Christian scenes in my engraving. I have engraved the Last Supper, Jesus stilling the storm, and countless verses for special occasions. I have often engraved unborn children, to try and remind people that a foetus is a human being. These have been used as conversation pieces for exhibitions.

If I have a 'mission statement' at all, it would be as follows: My intention is to create on glass designs that not only are pleasing to the eye and accurate in what they are portraying, but also reflect in some way the care and attention to detail of the Creator whose work we observe in the world around us.

Much of what I engrave is purely decorative in nature, not making any statement other than expressing beauty. I was encouraged to read that Van Gogh painted some of his scenes of orchards in blossom simply because he thought that people would like them. Too much scorn has been directed towards decorative art by so-called art experts who have placed 'real art' on such a pretentious pedestal that those of us who think it is perfectly valid to express beauty for its own sake have sometimes lost confidence in what we do. Although I would be regarded as very old-fashioned, I find that much (not all) of the conceptual art that finds such recognition (and such prices!) lacks integrity and is only created to shock. Figurative art has had a hard press for many years, and been unfairly treated, again at the hand of self-proclaimed art experts. So much is judged on a purely subjective basis anyway.

Whatever an expert might say about what I do, I find that generally I have very pleased customers. When one is praised as a Christian, it can make one feel awkward inside, as one wants God to have the glory for what we do. To Him be all the glory. In all that I do, I aim to be the best that I can be. I want to pursue integrity and avoid compromise. I have always admired Daniel and his friends for refusing to accept the food and drink offered to them by their Babylonian captors. Sometimes it is right to make a stand. I heard the story of a fine artist who was training at an art school and was constantly under pressure to paint erotic subjects. She refused and it nearly led to her being thrown out. She persisted, however, and in the end came out top of her year. To cap it all, and I feel this was God's honouring of her stand, a high profile buyer purchased two of her largest paintings at her final exhibition.

Cultivating truth and keeping motives pure can only be pleasing to God, as Paul taught: *Finally, brethren, whatever things are true, whatever things are noble, whatever things are just, whatever things are pure, whatever things are lovely, whatever things are of good report, if there is any virtue and if there is anything praiseworthy – meditate on these things. The things which you learned and received and heard and saw in me, these do, and the God of peace will be with you* (Philippians 4:8–9).

It comes back to where we started: we are created to worship God; Father, Son and Holy Spirit. We worship Him when we gather together in a congregation; we worship Him on our own as well; and what we do through our creativity, or whatever activity and occupation we are involved in, is not in some entirely separate compartment of life, because it is the *whole* of a Christian's life that is meant to reflect the image of God which marked mankind before it was spoilt in the Fall, and which is being restored in us as we are transformed by Jesus Christ. Having discovered how much our heavenly Father loves and values us, and to what lengths He went to rescue us from the state of sin, our response should be to love Him in return, with all our heart, all our mind and all our strength. We are to give Him our best in personal and public worship, and we are to give Him our best as we live out our diverse callings, honouring Him in every area of our creativity.

Notes

[1] See Lee Strobel, *The Case for a Creator*, 2004, Zondervan.
[2] See C. S Lewis, *The Great Divorce*, Harper Collins.

POSTSCRIPT

There is so much more to say about worship, and I have only scratched the surface. It will take many more books to begin to plumb the depths. What I have attempted to do is take you on not so much a journey, but more a sightseeing tour, observing some of the aspects of worship that I have found in Scripture and from my own experience. I know there are many new 'sights' for me to discover, but I hope that some of the themes we have visited together will lead you to explore further and inspire you to live for Jesus.

There will come a time when we will all be gathered around the throne of God, to gaze at last upon His face and have our whole beings changed to be like Him; when the bride will be ready for her Bridegroom and the marriage feast of the Lamb will be upon us. The kingdom of God will have finally reached its fulfilment, and the whole of creation will be brought under the Lordship of Jesus Christ. What a day that will be, when every tear will be wiped dry, and every disagreement and dispute will fade into insignificance. We will hear heavenly music, which will make our puny efforts at praise seem so mediocre, and the Song of the Father's heart will finally captivate our hearts and souls, and there will be a wonderful eternity to be spent with Him.

LET THE BRIDE SAY, 'COME'

This is the mystery
That Christ has chosen you and me
To be the revelation of His glory
A chosen, royal, holy people
Set apart and loved
A bride preparing for her King

THE SONG OF THE FATHER'S HEART

She's crowned in splendour
And a royal diadem
The King is enthralled by her beauty
Adorned in righteousness
Arrayed in glorious light
The bride in waiting for her King

Let the bride say, 'Come'
Let the bride say, 'Come'
Let the bride of the Lamb say
'Come, Lord Jesus'
Let the bride say, 'Come'
Let the bride say, 'Come'
Let the bride of the Lamb say
'Come, Lord Jesus, come'

Now hear the Bridegroom call
Beloved, come aside
The time of betrothal is at hand
Lift up your eyes and see
The dawning of the day
When as King, I'll return to claim My bride

Phil Lawson Johnston & Chris Bowater
Copyright ©1992 Sovereign Lifestyle Music Ltd

DISCOGRAPHY

CLOUD ALBUMS, Kingsway Music.

Free to Fly
Watered Garden
The Resting Place
Hallowed Ground
The Vine
The Promise
We Will Honour You

SOLO ALBUMS

Comforter, Kingsway.
Father of Compassion, Kingsway.
Value Me, Bible Reading Fellowship.
Home for Eternity, Kingsway.

WORSHIP IN THE ROOM

Worship in the Room No. 1
Your Presence, Cloud Trust.
Worship in the Room No. 2
Your Faithfulness, Cloud Trust.
Worship in the Room No. 3
I Pray, Cloud Trust.
Worship in the Room No. 4
You Value Me (re-release of Value Me), Cloud Trust.

OTHERS

Together for Jesus, Kingsway.
The Glory of Jesus, Message for Our Times.

By the same author:
[Contributor to] *In Spirit and in Truth*, Hodder & Stoughton.
Value Me (with Shelagh Brown), Bible Reading Fellowship.

BOOKS RECOMMENDED FOR FURTHER READING

Becoming Fully Human, Patrick Whitworth, Terra Nova Publications
Celebration of Discipline, Richard J. Foster, Hodder & Stoughton
Facedown, Matt Redman, Survivor
Living Liturgy, John Leach, Kingsway
Passion for Your Name, Tim Hughes, Survivor
Real Worship, Warren W Wiersbe, Baker Books
Recapture the Wonder, Ravi Zacharias, Integrity Publishers
Reflections on the Psalms, C S Lewis, Harper Collins
Salvation's Song, Marcus Green, Survivor
The Dangerous Duty of Delight, John Piper, Multnomah Publishing
To Know You More, Andy Park, Kingsway
Unquenchable Worshipper, Matt Redman, Survivor
Whatever Happened to Worship, A.W. Tozer, Kingsway